WESTERN INDIA IN HISTORICAL TRANSITION

Seventeenth to Early Twentieth Centuries

Western India in Historical Transition

Seventeenth to Early Twentieth Centuries

HIROYUKI KOTANI

MANOHAR
2002

First published 2002

ISBN 81-7304-445-7

Published by
Ajay Kumar Jain for
Manohar Publishers & Distributors
4753/23 Ansari Road, Daryaganj
New Delhi 110002

Printed at
Rajkamal Electric Press
Delhi 110033

Contents

Preface

Indian society became known to the Japanese academic circles mainly through the writings of Western thinkers prominent in the nineteenth and early twentieth centuries, specifically Karl Marx and Max Weber. Beginning with the critical re-examination of Marx's and Weber's thinking on Indian society and history, I also started my study on Indian history. This initial examination included not only a theoretical criticism of Western ideas concerning India inherited by Marx and Weber but also an empirical rethinking of Indian history itself. Following this methodological line, I have continued to be engaged in the study of the socio-cultural history of western India from the seventeenth to early twentieth centuries drawing mostly on medieval Marathi documents and legal documents of the Bombay government.

This present volume is composed of nine papers I previously wrote or read on various occasions and three papers prepared especially for this volume. The original titles of the former group of papers are given in the Bibliography. Though thus being a collection of independent papers, every effort has been made to ensure that this volume is as comprehensive and consistent as possible by extensively revising the earlier papers and adding the new ones. The Introduction is also intended to contribute to delineating the salient socio-cultural changes that have taken place in western India before and after the commencement of British colonial rule. Further, a fairly exhaustive Index has been prepared to have it serve in parallel as a glossary of technical terms in the original languages as well as of those rendered into English under colonial administration.

In my endeavour, I am greatly indebted to the late Dr. Hiroshi Fukazawa who was so very generous in allowing me free use of medieval Marathi documents he had painstakingly collected during his stay in Pune. As a measure of my gratitude to him, I have appended the 'Introduction' written by me for his posthumous anthology, *The Medieval Deccan: Peasants, Social Systems and States, Sixteenth to Eighteenth Centuries*, to this volume.

I am grateful to the members of two study groups, *Fukashokuminsei Kenkyukai* (Untouchability Study Group) funded by Mitsubishi Foundation (1989-1990) and *Institutions, Networks and Forces of Changes in Contemporary South Asia* financed by the Japanese Ministry of Education, Science, Sports and Culture Grant-in-Aid for Scientific Research on Priority Areas Programme (A) for the years 1998-2000. The discussions in these study groups have unquestionably revitalized my interest in Indian history and society, and the financial aid accorded me through them have enabled to bring my study on Indian history to a conclusion. Finally, I am pleased to thank Mr. Patrick Fulmer who has helped me in refining the English text and Ms. Sae Nakasone who has always stood ready to assist me in computerizing the data, preparing the camera-ready copy of this volume, and many other tasks required for publication of this volume.

14 February 2001 HIROYUKI KOTANI

Abbreviations

1. For reference to medieval Marathi documents, the following abbreviations with Roman numerals denoting the volume number and Arabic numerals indicating the document number are used:

A.S.S.: Bhārat Itihās Saṃśodhak Maṇḍal, ed., *Aitihāsik Saṃkīrṇa Sāhitya*, 13 vols., Pune, 1934-67.

Jedhe: *Kārī va Āmbvade-Jedhe Deśmukh*, Srī Rāmadāsīcīṃ Aitihāsik Kāgadpatreṃ, Rāmadās āṇi Rāmadāsī Granthamālā, Bhāg Tīsavā, Dhule, 1930.

M.I.S.: V.K. Rajvade, ed., *Marāṭhyāṃcyā Itihāsācīṃ Sādhaneṃ*, 22 vols., Poona and Bombay, 1898-1919.

Oturkar: R.V. Oturkar, ed., *Peśve Kālīn Sāmājik va Ārthik Patra-vyavahār*, Pune, 1950.

S.C.S.: Bhārat Itihās Saṃśodhak Maṇḍal, ed., *Śiva Caritra Sāhitya*, 13 vols., Pune, 1926-65.

S.G.R.A.O.: G.C. Vad, ed., *Selections from the Government Records in the Alienation Office Poona*:

1 *Kaifiats, Yadis, &c*, 1908.
2 *Decisions from the Shahu and Peshwa Daftar*, 1909.
3 *Sanads and Letters*, 1913.
4 *Treaties, Agreements and Sanads*, 1914.

S.P.D.: G.S. Sardesai, ed., *Selections from the Peshwa Daftar*, 45 vols., Bombay, 1930-34.

S.S.R.P.D.: G.C. Vad, ed., *Selections from the Satara Rajas' and the Peshwas' Diaries*, 9 vols., Poona and Bombay, 1905-11.

2. R.E.I.H. stands for *Selection of Papers from the Records at the East-India House, relating to the Revenue, Police, Civil and Criminal Justice under the Company's Government in India*, 4 vols., London, 1820-26.

3. For reference to judicial decisions handed down by the Bombay Sadr Divani Adalat, the predecessor of the Bombay High Court, the following

abbreviations with Arabic numerals after them denoting the page whence the case starts are used:

1 B.S.D.A: *Reports of Civil Causes adjudged by the Court of Sudur Udalut, for the Presidency of Bombay, between the Years A.D. 1800 and A.D. 1824; divided into Two Parts.* Vol. I, compiled by H. Borradaile.
2 B.S.D.A.: Ibid., Vol. II.
3 B.S.D.A.: *Reports of Selected Cases decided by the Sudder Dewanee Adawlut, Bombay (1820-40)*, 1843.
4 B.S.D.A.: *Reports of Civil Cases determined in the Court of the Sudder Dewanee Adawlut of Bombay, 1840 to 1848*, compiled by A.F. Bellasis, 1850.
5 B.S.D.A.: *Selected Decisions of the Court of the Sudder Dewanee Adawlut of Bombay*, compiled by James Morris, 1852.
6 B.S.D.A.: Ibid., Part II (1848-50), 1852.
7 B.S.D.A.: Ibid., Part III, 1853.
8 B.S.D.A.: *Cases disposed of by the Sudder Dewanee Adawlut of Bombay*, compiled by James Morris, Vol. I, 1854.
9 B.S.D.A.: Ibid., Vol. II, 1855.
10 B.S.D.A.: Ibid., Vol. III, 1856.
11 B.S.D.A.: Ibid., Vol. IV, 1857.
12 B.S.D.A.: Ibid., Vol. V, 1858.
13 B.S.D.A.: Ibid., Vol. VI, 1859.
14 B.S.D.A.: *Selected Decisions of the Sudder Dewanee Adawlut of Bombay*, compiled by E. Harrington, Vol. VII, 1860.
15 B.S.D.A.: Ibid., Vol. VIII, 1861.
16 B.S.D.A.: Ibid., Vol. IX, 1862.

4. For reference to judicial decisions handed down by the Bombay, Calcutta and Madras High Courts, the following abbreviations with Arabic numerals before them denoting the volume number and Arabic numerals after them indicating the page whence the case starts are used:

C.: *Indian Law Reports, Calcutta Series.* (A.D. 1875 onwards)
B.H.C.R.: *Reports of Cases decided in the High Court of Bombay.* (1862-75)
B.: *Indian Law Reports, Bombay Series.* (1875 onwards)
Bom.L.R.: *Bombay Law Reporter.*
M.: *Indian Law Reports, Madras Series.* (1875 onwards)

W.R.: *The Weekly Reporter*, Calcutta.

5. For reference to the debates in the Bombay Legislative Council, the following abbreviations are used:

P.C.G.B.: *Proceedings of the Council of the Governor of Bombay.* (A.D. 1862 to 1908)
P.L.C.G.B.: *Proceeding of the Legislative Council of the Governor of Bombay.* (1909 to 1920)
B.L.C.D.: *Bombay Legislative Council Debates.* (1921 to 1939)

The Western Deccan

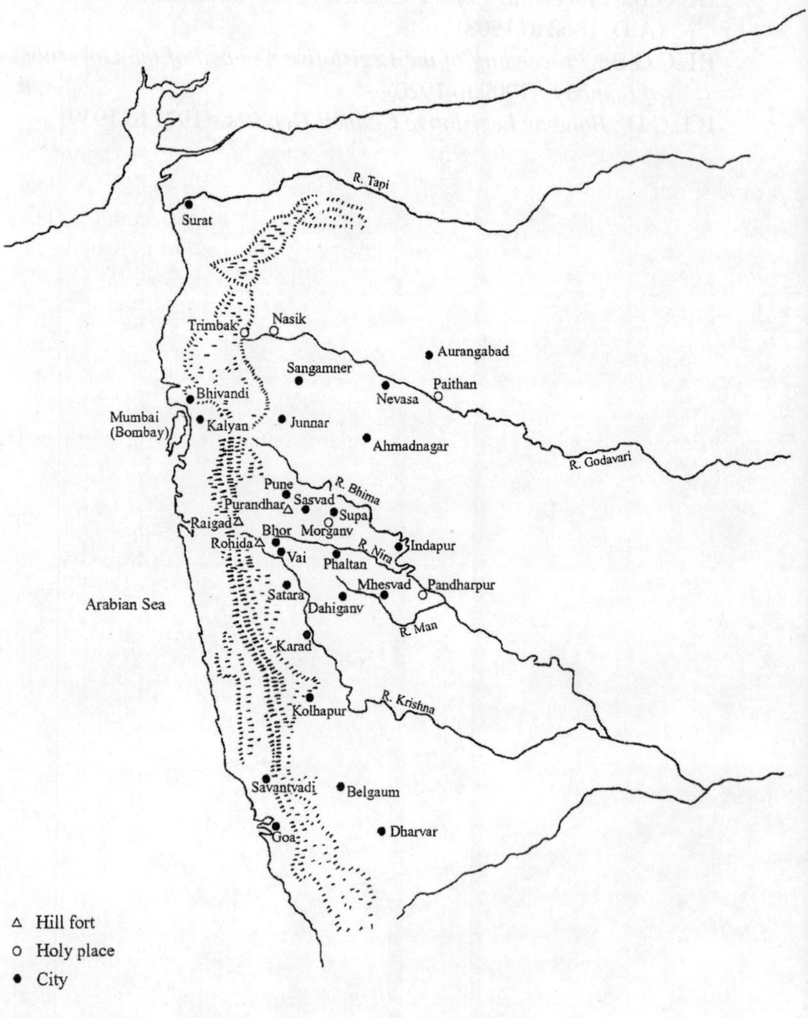

Introduction

The salient features of Indian society and culture in the pre-colonial period and the socio-cultural changes that took place under British colonial rule are the central themes of this volume. With this in mind, I have selected western India, more precisely the western Deccan, Konkan and south Gujarat, as the specific region of my historical studies. The studies of the late Dr. H. Fukazawa capably proved that the medieval Marathi documents relating to western India, exceptionally rich in quality as well as quantity, throw considerable light on socio-cultural conditions of the people living in this region during the seventeenth to early nineteenth centuries. More specifically implied here is the western Indian society and culture just before the commencement of British colonial rule. Further, comparing the historical findings concerning later medieval western India thus drawn from these Marathi documents to the socio-cultural conditions prevailing under British colonial rule enables us to understand the exact nature and extent of the socio-cultural changes that took place in western India during the course of the nineteenth and early twentieth centuries.

The Vatan System and its Disintegration under British Colonial Rule

The Vatan System: The Division of Labour and Exploitation

The system of dividing labour in the local society in later medieval western India can be conceptualized as the Vatan system. The term '*vatan*' (from the Arabic-Persian term '*vaṭan*' meaning native country, dwelling or residence, *vṛtti* in Sanskritic languages) denoted the patrimonial right of being hereditarily engaged in a certain office or work in communities (village community, district=*parganā* community and caste community) with prescribed emoluments or perquisites accruing from it. The full-fledged members of the local society hereditarily possessed their respective *vatans*, such that they were called the *vatandār*. The

Vatan system was comprised of two layers or dimensions, that is to say, the district (*parganā*) level and the village level. The district (*parganā*) level *vatandārs* included the Deshmukh (head of the district community), Deshpande (accountant of the district community), the head (*mhetar*) of a caste community which formed its primary collective within the boundary of a district, and several others. The Patil (village headman) and Kulkarni (village accountant) were representative *vatandārs* of the village community, while the *vatandār* Kunbi (peasants) constituted the main body of the *vatandārs* of the village who were also known as the *mirāsdār* (from the Persian term '*mīrāthdār*'), *thalkarī* or *thalvāika* (both from the Sanskrit term '*sthala*'). The *bārā balute* or *bārā balutedār* (twelve sorts of *balute* holders, *balute* meaning perquisites) of the village, often interpreted as village servants, served the village community as an aggregate. The *bārā balute* (*bārā balutedār*) generally included the Sutar (carpenter), Lohar (ironsmith), Kumbhar (potter), Parit (washerman), Nhavi (barber), Joshi (village priest), Gurav (temple keeper) and some untouchable castes such as the Mahar, Mang and Chambhar (see Table 5 of Chapter 1). The relationships among these various *vatandārs* constituted the basic structure of the division of labour in the local society in later medieval western India.

In the villages of later medieval western India, however, there existed also a body of people known collectively as the *upārī* (outsiders). The *upārī* were peasants or artisans who were employed by the village community without being bestowed any *vatan* of the village. The *upārī* peasants as village tenants cultivated the lands which lapsed to possession of the village community by reason of dying out or wandering away of the original owners (*vatandār* Kunbis). The *upārī* artisans such as the *upārī* Sutar and *upārī* Lohar were recruited by the village community when the families of the *vatandār* Sutar and *vatandār* Lohar of the village were extinguished for a certain reason. Thus, the *upārī* peasants and *upārī* artisans played the role of filling in the vacancy brought about in the Vatan system under such circumstances as already mentioned. As such, the *upārī* were indispensable for the village community to complement the unstableness of the Vatan system.

Though the Vatan system primarily constituted the system of the division of labour in the local society, it included at the same time the exploitative relationship between the local community leaders and community members. The local community leaders, specifically Deshmukhs, accumulated various rights to take perquisites from local community members, mainly *vatandār* Kunbis, in addition to their being granted the rights of *jāgīr* or *inām* by the state. These rights to the land as well as on the people living on it gave rise in the course of time to the exploitative relationship between Deshmukhs and community members. One of the focal points of discussion in Chapter 1 thus concerns the historical characterization or conceptualization of this exploitative relationship incorporated in the Vatan system.

The controversy as to whether or not the concept of feudalism or feudal social formation is applicable to medieval Indian societies has been raging since the 1970s. This issue continues to depend on how feudalism is defined in terms of the social formation. In this regard, Chapter 1 proposes to expand the Euro-centric concept of feudalism to facilitate its applicability to non-European medieval societies, and thus to make it possible to site non-European medieval societies within the framework of universal history. Basing on this expanded concept of feudalism, the exploitative relationship incorporated in the Vatan system can then be characterized as the feudal social relationship, though neither such local magnates as the Deshmukh were commonly designated as the landlord nor *vatandār* Kunbis as the serf.

Discrimination against the Untouchable in the Vatan System

Included without exception in the Vatan system were a certain number of untouchables such as Mahars, Mangs and Chambhars. They were respectively called the *vatandār* Mahar, *vatandār* Mang and *vatandār* Chambhar of the village community. Chapter 1 as well as Chapter 6 aim to shed light on the ambivalent nature of their existence in later medieval western India.

Notable jobs assigned to these untouchables by the village community were the skinning of dead cattle, tanning of the rawhide thus skinned and making of such leather goods as ropes for tying draught bullocks, buckets for drawing water from the wells and footwear. Since the agriculture in medieval western India was closely linked with cattle breeding and thus the number of cattle was enormous, this work relating to cattle skins was indispensable for the peasants and village community itself. As such, these individuals were important members of the *bārā balute* or *bārā balutedār* of the village.

The other villagers discriminated against them as people, physical contact (*sparśa*) as well as social contact (association, *saṃsarga*) with whom was deemed to constitute *doṣa* (sin) for the contactee. In the case of classical law books such as the *Manusmṛti*, physical contact with Chandala (*Caṇḍāla*) was considered to bring pollution to the contactee (cf. *Manusmṛti* edited by G. Jha V-84). This difference in dealing with physical contact with the untouchable between medieval western India and ancient India is one of the focal points of discussion of Chapter 10.

The discriminated in the Vatan system such as the *vatandār* Mahar simultaneously played the very important role in the village ritual of *śānti* conducted to pacify the anger of the *devī* which was expressed in such extraordinary natural phenomena as earthquakes and epidemics like cholera. They attained a state of high spirituality on these occasions. Thus, the so-called untouchable in later medieval western India served in an indispensable ritual role in the village community.

Some portion of Mahars and Mangs who had not been incorporated in the village community possessed the *vatan* of *nāik* (head of guards) of hill forts or *ṭhāṇas* (soldier station in main town). As such, they constituted a part of the power apparatus of the state. These Mahars and Mangs living outside the village community continued to retain the nexus with their brethren in villages, acting in concert whenever a dispute affecting them all arose.

This composite nature of the untouchable in later medieval western India gave their existence a sort of ambivalence.

Landed Property in the Vatan System

Undoubtedly a certain sort of landed property of the peasantry existed in medieval India though traditional Western thinking continued to deny it (Kotani 1979). The problem for historians then is the dificulty in clarifying the exact nature of the landed property of the peasantry prevailing in medieval India. Keeping this in mind, Chapter 2 deals with the specific characteristics of the landed property in later medieval western India. What provides a clue to the solution of this problem is the Marathi documents called *vatan patra* (or *mirās patra*) which were issued to attest to the grant or transfer of *vatan* (*mirās*) to some person. A large number of *vatan patras* translated into English in the early part of the nineteenth century are also available. The findings drawn from these documents denote that the landed property of the peasantry in later medieval western India, that is to say, the *vatan* land of the *vatandār* Kunbi was not absolute in its nature in the sense of the modern landed property in Europe. Rather the former involved a much wider social implication than the latter which was expressed in the fact that the purchaser of the *vatan* land could enjoy all of the rights and privileges as a full-fledged member of the village community. In other words, the landed property of the peasantry was communal in nature.

Dyadic Relationships at Work in the Vatan System

Whether or not the concept of the Jajmani system is applicable to the village communities in medieval India has remained a controversial problem. The concept of the Jajmani system by which the division of labour in the village was understood to be composed of a large number of dyadic and individual relationships between *jajmāns* and their *kamīns* or *kāmkarnevālās* stands in opposition to the more traditional thinking of seeing the communal and holistic division of labour in medieval Indian villages. The latter understanding finds its typical expression in Karl Marx's *Das Kapital* which referred to 'one dozen village servants' of the Indian village community (Buch 1 Kapitel 12, 4). The relationship between the Jajmani system and the communal division of labour in the village community in later medieval western India constitutes the main theme of the discussion in Chapter 3.

The late Dr. Fukazawa found that the *bārā balute* (*bārā balutedār*) of the villages in later medieval western India were the village servants of a similar nature as those described in *Das Kapital.* This means that the Jajmani type of division of labour was not prevalent in later medieval western India. At the same time, however, he found that the only exception to this existed in the relationship between the village Joshi as the *upādhyā* (*gharopādhyā*) and villagers (*yajmānas*) which was the dyadic relationship between two families held hereditarily from generation to generation. According to him, this relationship between the *upādhyā* (Joshi) and his *yajmānas* might have constituted the prototype of the Jajmani system (Fukazawa 1991: 199-240).

Discussed in Chapter 3 is that many other dyadic relationships in addition to that between the *upādhyā* and his *yajmānas* are discernible between the villagers and various village servants such as the *vatandār* Parit, *vatandār* Mahar and *vatandār* Mang. These dyadic relationships incorporated in the system of the communal and holistic division of labour under the Vatan system would have become prominent when the Vatan system began to break up under British colonial rule.

Disintegration of the Vatan System under British Colonial Rule

The Vatan system had been gradually disintegrating under the administration of the Bombay government. The status of the *vatandār* Kunbi (peasants) as opposed to the *upārī* peasants (village tenants) disappeared first as a result of the introduction of the Raiyatwari settlement. The Raiyatwari settlement deprived the landed property of the *vatandār*

Kunbi sustained by the Vatan system of its communal or privileged nature (see Chapter 2). Thus, the term *vatan* which was translated as the 'hereditary office' in the Elphinstone Code (A.D. 1827) that laid the foundation of the Bombay administration did not include the *vatan* of the former *vatandār* Kunbi.

The other *vatans* such as those of the Deshmukh, Deshpande, Patil, Kulkarni and *bārā balute* were preserved under the early administration of the Bombay government. In the 1850s and 1860s, however, most of the *vatan* of the Deshmukh and Deshpande were abolished through the administrative procedure called 'commutation'. Further, the Bombay Hereditary Offices Act of 1874 excluded the *vatans* other than those of the Patil, Kulkarni, Mahar and some others from the legal category of the hereditary office (hereditary public office) leaving them to remain, so to speak, as private posts (*vatans*) in the village community. Again in the last decade of the nineteenth and early decades of the twentieth centuries, the office of the Kulkarni as the hereditary village accountant was replaced by the stipendiary office of the *talati* who was to be appointed by the government through the administrative procedure known as 'resumption'. This resulted in the *vatan* of Kulkarni also being abolished by the 1910s.

In spite of this continuum of change in the Bombay administration, the Mahar *vatan* had been tenaciously maintained as the most important hereditary office throughout the nineteenth and the first half of the twentieth centuries. In 1928, B.R. Ambedkar introduced into the Bombay Legislative Council a bill meant to improve the working conditions of the *vatandār* Mahar and to abolish further the Mahar *vatan*. In the course of discussion of his bill, a Bombay government high official tacitly admitted the fact that a considerable portion of the tasks done by the *vatandār* Mahar for the government was unpaid labour. This implies that the abolishment of the Mahar *vatan* through its replacement by a stipendiary office must have financially burdened the Bombay government heavily, which was the sole reason for the government's opposition to the Ambedkar bill. Thus, the abolishment of the Mahar *vatan* was postponed until India gained independence. (As to the Mahar *vatan* and the process towards its abolishment, see Chapter 7.)

The most controversial 'private' *vatan* excluded from the legal category of the hereditary office by the Bombay Hereditary Offices Act of 1874 was the village Joshi *vatan*. The village Joshi as the *upādhyā* (*gharopādhyā*), who generally served as the Kulkarni of his village as well, maintained the hereditary dyadic relationship with his *yajmānas*.

As such, he could claim fees, as a matter of right, from his *yajmānas* whenever any ritual was conducted in the latter's homes, whether he actually officiated at it or not. This privileged right of the village Joshi began to be contested in the 1870s, specifically by the members of the Satya Shodhak Samaj established in 1873 by Jotirao Phule in Pune. As a result of their strenuous struggle through decades in the courts of law and the Bombay Legislative Council, this privileged right of the village Joshi as the *upādhyā* (*gharopādhyā*) was finally done away with in 1926 by the Invalidation of Hindu Ceremonial Emoluments Act. (The abolishment of the Joshi *vatan* is considered in Chapter 8.)

Accordingly, the Vatan system had been gradually breaking up under British colonial rule in its public sector (the hereditary offices) as well as its private sector (unofficialized *vatans* such as that of the village Joshi) though unofficial relationships between the *vatandārs* and other villagers might have been maintained even after the abolishment of public *vatans*.

The Caste System and its Transformation under British Colonial Rule

The Caste System as the 'Social Status System'

The relationship between the status system to be established and maintained by the state (designated here as the 'state status system') and the graded social ordering of the society to be sustained by the society itself (designated here as the 'social status system') has remained one of the most difficult points of theoretical discussion in the historical studies. In the case of Indian history, the focal point of controversy has been the caste system. The important contribution of the late Dr. Fukazawa to historical understanding of the caste system consists in his findings that the readmission of the excommunicated to his caste required the sanction of the government (in this case, the Peshva government of the Maratha kingdom), and that the government intervened at all times to settle disputes arising over the caste practises or the caste ranking between various castes (Fukazawa 1991: 91-113). Thus, he succeeded in proving that the caste system was, in one aspect, the 'state status system'. In spite of this, the essential nature of the caste system, however, should be understood to consist in the aspect as the 'social status system' since the caste system lacked the characteristic of being legalized after being rearranged by the state and subsequently of being forcibly imposed onto the society by the state as the 'state status system'. In other words, the medieval Indian states merely depended on the caste system as the graded ordering of the society itself for maintaining societal order and stability without developing their own devices for putting the society in order. In this sense, the caste system substituted for the 'state status system' though it was often backed by the state power apparatus, as a result of which the caste system took also on an appearance of the 'state status system'.

Based on this historical understanding of the caste system, Chapter 4 attempts to further the historical study of the caste system by introducing the categorization of the rural caste and urban caste which differed from each other in their essential natures and functions. The respective unit or extent of the primary collectivity of the rural caste and urban caste was the district and the town. Both of these, however, have continued to constitute the secondary network of the caste stretching across the extent of a district in the former case and of a town in the latter case to connect similar primary collectives of neighbouring districts and towns respectively. These secondary networks of the castes began to be expanded and strengthened from the last decades of the nineteenth century to give a renewed, specifically political, function to the castes.

The 'Caste Autonomy' Policy of the Bombay Government

The well-known 'caste autonomy' policy of the Bombay government was formulated by the Elphinstone Code which provided that the 'caste questions' not involving any legal cause of action did not come under the jurisdiction of the civil courts of law. Put another way, caste was recognized as a sort of body corporate which could make its own rules and exclude the members who violated them from it. Chapter 5 aims firstly to trace the historical process of the formulation of the caste autonomy policy from the beginning of the nineteenth century to 1827 when Mountstuart Elphinstone, the then Governor of the Bombay Presidency, promulgated in all 27 regulations collectively known as the Elphinstone Code. The second aim of Chapter 5 is to measure the actual extent of the caste autonomy allowed to the castes in the Bombay Presidency in comparison with the cases in the Bengal and Madras Presidencies.

The caste autonomy policy rendered ever increasing strength to the castes as the social organization though the caste system itself began to gradually diminish its role as the maintainer of societal order under the modernized legal administration of the British. This again has contributed to the expansion and consolidation of the secondary network of various castes from the last decades of the nineteenth century. British colonial rule had thus been making Indian society more and more caste-oriented or caste-bound though not caste system-oriented.

The Pivotal Ideology in Pre-colonial and Colonial India

The Predominating Ideology in Pre-colonial India

Several sets of dichotomies have being claimed to be functioning in the Indian states and societies in history. One of the most well known is the pureness-impureness opposition which put the Brahman at the uppermost position of pureness in the caste system and the untouchable at the lowest. Thus, societal order and stability is assumed to have been maintained by the stratifying or gradating function of the ideology of pureness-impureness. The other well-known one is the auspiciousness-inauspiciousness opposition which recognizes the auspiciousness embodied in kingship or the king's person as the pivotal ideology at work in pre-colonial India in maintaining the social as well as the natural order.

The focal point of difference between these two sets of dichotomous ideas consists in the fact that the former places emphasis on the self-regulating faculty of the Indian society with the Brahman as its ideological regulator, while the latter gives weight to the function of the king or the state headed by the king in maintaining social order. Thus, the problem is again, in essence, how the relationship between the society and the state in Indian history should be considered.

Chapters 9 and 10 focus on this problem with special reference to later medieval western India. There are two main findings of these chapters. First, the state ritual of *śānti* conducted by the Brahman for maintaining auspiciousness and avoiding inauspiciousness had practically nothing to do with the village rite of *śānti* which was performed by the *vatandār* Mahar and *vatandār* Mang as the main actors for appeasing the anger of the *devī*. This means the state ideology or kingship's ideology of auspiciousness-inauspiciousness did not penetrate all the way down to the local society. Second, the purification ceremony (*prāyaścitta*) conducted by the Dharmadhikari of sacred places for removing the sin from the sinner played the crucial role in maintaining societal order by making it mandatory for the sinner who was excommunicated from his caste to undergo *prāyaścitta* for readmission. In the local society, the Dharmadhikari prescribed and actually performed the purification ceremony of *prāyaścitta* quite independently of the state since they were *vatandārs* sustained by the Vatan system. This means that the ideology of sin (*doṣa*) and purification (*prāyaścitta*) rather than the idea of ritual pureness-impureness functioned as the pivotal ideology in keeping social order in the local society.

Thus, Chapters 9 and 10 put more weight on the self-regulating capability of the society in medieval India than the medieval Indian state's role in maintaining societal order.

Historical Changes in Ideology in Colonial India

Important changes seem to have taken place in the ideology during the course of the nineteenth and early twentieth centuries under British colonial rule. The most interesting terms in Marathi indicative of these changes are those of *sovaḷā-ovaḷā*. *Sovaḷā* and *ovaḷā*, being derived from the Sanskrit terms of '*sa-maṅgala*' and '*a-maṅgala*' respectively, originally referred to auspiciousness and inauspiciouness. They began to change their meaning, however, into pureness-impureness probably in the nineteenth century to become more and more popular among Marathi-speaking people in the twentieth century. This change in the meaning of *sovaḷā-ovaḷā* seems to reflect the important aspect of the ideological changes brought about under British colonial rule as it may show that the idea of pureness-impureness began to emerge as the predominating ideology only in the nineteenth century (see Chapter 9). The actual process of this change is, however, yet to be scrutinized.

Development of Hindu ideology or the collective consiousness of being Hindu is, without doubt, one of the most crucial themes of the historical study on modern India. Chapter 11 attempts to trace the development of Hindu identity in the early phase of British colonial rule. Two sets of the dichotomous idea had been handed down to the British. One was the Hindu-Musalman dichotomy in the Persian context and the other the Gentoo-Moor dichotomy of Portuguese origin. In the first half of the nineteenth century, however, the Gentoo-Moor dichotomy fell into disuse leaving the slightly changed dichotomy of Hindu-Mahometan to remain the sole framework of the colonial perception of Indian society. Thus, all Indian people who did not think of themselves as Mahometan (Muslim) were forced to profess themselves as Hindu once this conceptual framework of Indian society actually began to work as the political system under British colonial rule. This means British colonial rule played the crucial role in preparing the ground on which Hindu ideology was to develop.

As contrasted with Chapter 11, Chapter 12 addresses the question as to how the people in the Indian subcontinent attempted to accommodate the British as a newcomer within the pre-existing framework of distinguishing themselves from 'others' with special reference to late seventeenth-to-early twentieth century Maharashtra. In the pre-colonial age, they held several self-identities inclusive of the ethno-regional identity as the people of Maharashtra being distinct from the outlanders, religio-cultural identity as opposed to the Muslim, and the political identity of *Svarājya-Moglāī*. They attempted to incorporate the British within this pre-existing framework or the collective consciousness of 'ourselves-others' under British colonial rule. The British, however, constituted an entity that outreached this pre-existing framework as a result of which the framework itself had to be transformed or modified. This transformation or modification in their self-identity or the collective consciousness had a close relationship with the development of the idea of Hindutva that gave rise to the so-called communal problems appearing later in the twentieth century.

Explanatory Remarks

Romanization

Proper nouns of common use such as the names of persons, castes, villages, towns and districts are transcribed in the customary or expediential forms with the initial upper case letters but without any diacritical marks. The other techinical terms of Indian languages including those of Arabic-Persian origins are printed in italic lower case letters with diacritical marks. In the chapters on modern Indian history (Chapters 5, 7, 8 and 11) , however, diacritical marks are generally omitted.

Quotations

While quoting from English documents, the original texts are preserved throughout making no alteration or correction, and without inserting [*sic*] to the questionable portions thereof. The terms or sentences in the square brackets [ ] inserted in the quotations are added by the author to the original texts for the sake of explanation while the terms or sentences in the parenthesis ( ) are original.

I

Social Relationships and Property Rights

1

The Vatan System in the Seventeenth-Eighteenth Century Deccan: Towards a New Concept of Indian Feudalism

Introduction: The Concept of Feudalism

Here, I want to discuss the universality and peculiarity of Indian feudalism by analysing the historical sources of the seventeenth-eighteenth century western Deccan. A controversy has been raging as to whether the concept of feudalism is applicable to the history of Indian society (see e.g. Mukhia 1979; Sharma 1983; Jha 1987; Kulke 1995: Introduction; Mukhia 1999; Jha 2000). This problem depends on how one defines feudalism.

The general concept of feudalism as a social formation can be summarized as follows:

1. Direct producers are basically peasants who hold land sufficient to maintain their families, but the amount of land does not exceed that which can be cultivated by family labour forces without the help of subordinate labourers like slaves. Their title to the land they cultivate is that of occupation under the proprietorship of the landlord class, such that they can not be evicted so long as they pay rent to their landlord. In the case of a developed feudal society, peasants' title to the land they cultivate attains the nature of *de facto* proprietorship under *de jure* proprietorship of the landlord class.

2. The exploiting class stands above the direct producers. These exploiters are collectively called the landlord class because they claim proprietorship right over the land that peasants cultivate.

3. The landlord-peasant relationship, in consequence, is the most basic feature of feudal social formation. The general framework of

understanding this relationship is that the landlord class, even though the legitimate owners of land, cannot claim rent from their peasants by normal economic methods because peasants are independent in the production process from their landlord (i.e. they own basically all of the means of production). Thus, landlords must have recourse to what is commonly called extra-economic compulsion, which comprises armed retinue and judicial rights of the landlord over the peasants.

This concept of feudalism is a well-known and universally accepted one, being derived mainly from historical facts in medieval Europe. Of course, the concept itself is not a historical fact, but it is an abstraction from historical facts. As this concept of feudalism embodies the peculiarity of European history, it is not proper to use it as the criterion or norm with which to decide whether a society is feudal or not.

Rather we should try to analyse, initially, the basic social relationships peculiar to a society. Several questions are prominent here: Who are the direct producers? What sort of relationship do they have with land or nature? Who are the exploiting class? What sort of rights do they have over surplus products? What is the fundamental framework with which to understand the relationship between the direct producers and the exploiting class? These are the issues to be resolved before a society may be labelled feudal. Only through analysing the peculiarities of various medieval societies can we build a solid base on which to try to develop a universal concept of feudalism free from European prejudice.

This chapter thus has two aims. First, I want to discuss the peculiarities of social relationships in medieval Indian society by taking up the seventeenth-eighteenth century Deccan as the special subject of my analysis because a multitude of historical material in the Marathi language has been published and it is now possible to delineate the social structure in the later medieval Deccan. Second, after clarifying the peculiarities of the social relationships in Indian medieval society, I will try to place them within the general framework of feudalism, and, in the process, modify the Euro-centric concept of feudalism.

Land Arrangement in Village and Peasant Land-holdings

Land Arrangement in Village

It remains rather difficult to demonstrate the actual conditions of the land-holdings and land management of peasants in medieval India due to a lack

Table 1: *Inām* land given to Moreshvar Temple

Village	*Thala*	*Cāvara*	*Rukā*	Cultivator
Morganv	Thopatya	1	7	
Mayevadi	Vagtenbhi	1/2	6	Malharji Jagthap
Nayganv	Paritdhune	1/2	6	Nagoji Borkar
Pandhare		1	1	Goyaji Dhangar

of adequate historical source materials. But through the *inām-patra* (land grant deed), it is possible to gain some concept of peasants' land-holdings and land management in the later medieval Deccan.

In the *inām-patra*, it is often seen that the same lands were indicated by two different types of denominations. One unit or type of denomination is *bighā* or *cāvara* (1 *cāvara* = 120 *bighā*) which denotes without doubt land area (square measure), and the other is *rukā* (*kās rukā*) or *ṭakā* (*kās ṭakā*, 1 *ṭakā* = 48 *rukā*), the meaning of which is somewhat ambiguous. Table 1 gives the contents of the *inām-patras* given to the Moreshvar Temple in the village Morganv, Karhepathar District, Pune Province, during 1647-54 (S.C.S. III 532, 534, 544).

In Table 1, we find four pieces of land indicated by the two types of denominations. In these four cases, one *cāvara* corresponds to 7, 12, 12 and 1 *rukā* respectively. This means that there is no correlativity between the two types of denominations and that, consequently, *rukā* indicated something other than land area (square measure). If so, what did *rukā* indicate?

In later medieval Deccan, village land was divided into about a dozen *thalas* (from the Sanskrit word '*sthala*' meaning place), and a specific number of *rukā* was attached to each *thala*. We will take the village Morganv as an example. This village consisted of 11 *thalas* and had, in all, 295 *rukā* (see Table 2. Ṣ.C.S. III 564).

The *thala* itself consisted of several peasant land-holdings, to each of which a specific number of *rukā* was attached. As an example, the composition of Pachpatya *thala* of the village Morganv is shown in Table 3 (S.C.S. III 574).

This type of denomination of land in *rukā* had a close relationship with the tax system of medieval Deccanese governments under which taxes were levied on villages as a whole. In villages, the gross sum of taxes was allotted to each peasant according to the number of *rukā* he

Table 2: *Thala* of the village Morganv (1698)

Name of *thala*	*Rukā* in all	*Rukā* of *khālisa* land	*Rukā* of *inām* land
Tavir	35	28.5	6.5
Pacham	36	36	0
Chyahal	32	25	7
Kad	32	28.5	3.5
Kolta	39	39	0
Pachpatya	48	44.5	3.5
Thopata	15	8	7
Khomna	19	12	7
Manya	15	6	9
Pusala	12	0	12
Kavji Bopaji	12	5	7
Total	295	232.5	62.5

Table 3: Pachpatya *thala* (1776)

Peasant land-holding	*Rukā*	Land piece	Land area in *bighā*	Land class	Land area in *bighā*
I	23	1	230	First class	180 *bighā*
				Second class	40 *bighā*
				Rocky land and third class	10 *bighā*
II	6	2	145.25	Second class	50 *bighā*
				Third class	95.25 *bighā*
III	3.5	3	23.75	First class 1.5 *rukā*	57.5 *bighā*
	(*inām*)	4	33.75	Second class 2 *rukā*	
IV	3.5	5	64.5	First class	35 *bighā*
	(*inām*)			Second class	20 *bighā*
				Third class	9.5 *bighā*
V	12	6	194.75	First class 120 *bighā*	230.25 *bighā*
	(*inām*)			Second class 74.75 *bighā*	
		7	35.5	Uncultivated and hilly land	

held. So, the number of *rukā* shows the tax for which each peasant was assumed to be responsible as a ratio of all taxes levied on the village. For example, the peasant land-holding I of Table 3 owed theoretically 23/295 of all taxes levied on the village Morganv as a whole. But the actual process of allocation of taxes to each peasant was somewhat more complicated. In a source material pertaining to the village Nehatni, Pune Province (1671. S.C.S. VII 54) we can find the actual process of allocation given in some detail:

This village consisted, in all, of 625 *rukā*:

Khālisa lands (from which taxes were paid to the state)		
Jīrātī (unwatered land)	286	*rukā*
Bāgāitī (watered land)	30	
Kuraṇa (meadow land)	12	
Pāṇḍharī (residence area)	4	
	332	*rukā*
Inām lands	293	*rukā*
Total	625	*rukā*

On this village the following taxes were levied:

Ain nakt (cash tax)	191.75	*hon*
Bābā nakt (tax in kind but commuted to cash)	306.75	
Tabakhū (tobacco tax)	8.00	
Total	506.50	*hon*

In this year (1671) 46 *hon* being deducted from this sum, actual taxes levied were 460.5 *hon*. On the other hand, the total number of *rukā* of this village was 625, but after deductions from this number of tax-free land of Mahar (11 *rukā*), *kuraṇa* (meadow, 12 *rukā*) and tax-free land of Sheikh Sala (15 *rukā*), the number of tax-bearing *rukā* was 587. Thus all taxes levied on this village as a whole were divided into 587 portions. The consequence was as follows:

Ain nakt ... 1.5 *hon* to each *sajgāṇī* (6 *rukā*)
Bābā nakt ... 2.75 *hon* to each *sajgāṇī*

Accordingly, if one peasant had land denominated as 6 *rukā* in this village, he was responsible for the payment of *Ain nakt* 1.5 *hon* and *Bābā nakt* 2.75 *hon*, in all 4.25 *hon*.

Table 4: *Inām* land with the name of cultivator

Year	*Rukā*	Land area (*cāvara*)	Cultivator	Source
1. 1592-93	12		Ahmad Patil	M.I.S. XV-366
2. 1622		1	Tan Patil	S.C.S. XII-120
3. 1622-23		1	Babaji Mulanah	M.I.S. XV-394
4. 1627-28		2	Nag Patil	M.I.S. XX-206
5. 1641		3	Lakhman Dhangar	S.C.S. III-660
6. 1644-45		1	Sukabda Satvaji	M.I.S. XX-208
7. 1649		1	Dharoji Khaera	S.C.S. II-152
8. 1649-50		1 1/4	Tukoji Karpya	M.I.S. XX-209
9. 1655	24		Padmaji Honap	S.C.S. II-130

He might not pay this sum to the village community directly because each *thala* had joint responsibility for the sum of taxes allotted to the *thala* according to the number of *rukā* attached to it. Therefore peasants seemed to pay, initially, their share of taxes to the *thala* to which they belonged and if some members of the *thala* happened to fail to pay, other members of the *thala* were jointly responsible for the arrears.

In this way, villagers had joint responsibility for the payment of taxes on a twofold level, that is to say, on the level of *thala* and finally on that of the village at large.

Land-holdings and Land Management of Peasants

The question arises as to why the taxes which each peasant had to bear were regulated by the number of *rukā* and not by the acreage of each peasant land-holding. The reason should be sought in the peculiarity of agricultural conditions in the later medieval Deccan. Tables 1, 3 and 4 will be employed to try to derive some concept about the actual conditions of agriculture and peasant land-holdings.

When the state decided to give an *inām* to someone, it ordered local officials to proceed to the village concerned and to 'decide the boundaries of land to be granted and then name the cultivator (*prajā*)' (S.C.S. II 115). In Tables 1 and 4 we find some cultivators so named by local officials. Thus, the real meaning of a grant of *inām* land was that the cultivator, whose taxes were assumed to correspond to the intended sum of the grant, was selected by state officials, making him responsible to pay to the *inām* holder taxes which he had previously paid to the state.

If this proposition were to be accepted, each of the *inām* lands in Tables 1, 3 and 4 corresponded to one peasant land-holding and, consequently, peasant land-holdings I and II of Table 3 also constituted separate peasant land-holdings. When we see Tables 1, 3 and 4 afresh here, we find that they reveal a rather astonishing fact. Specifically, the land-holdings of cultivators (peasants) were very large and quite roughly denominated. One *cāvara* being equivalent to nearly 30 hectares, the land-holdings of cultivators in Tables 1, 3 and 4 were 15 hectares at the smallest and 90 hectares at the largest. There are many more source materials which show that peasant land-hodings in the later medieval Deccan were very large (S.C.S. I 81, V 802; S.S.R.P.D. III 397, and others). Moreover, these large peasant land-holdings were not scattered over a wide area in many small parcels, but formed one compact lot of land. In the case of the peasant land-holding I of Table 3, land measurement was given as follows (S.C.S. III 575)[1]:

North	15.75	West	15.5
South	18.5	East	11.5
	34.25		27
divided into halves	17.125		13.5

17.125 × 13.5 ≒ 230 *bighā*

This measurement shows that the land was one compact lot of land, the shape of which might be like the following (left), and that the acreage of this land was calculated by deeming it as a rectangular piece of land as illustrated below (right).

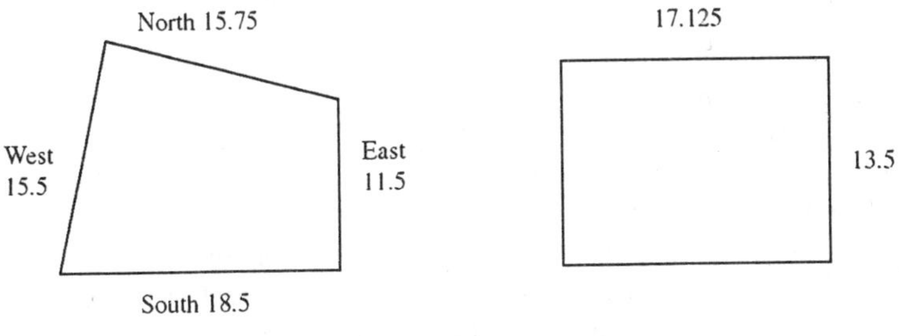

Again, in the case of the peasant land-holding II of Table 3, land measurement was shown as follows (S.C.S. III 575):

North	10	East	18.5
South	5.3	West	21
Middle	6.75		
	22.05		39.5
divided into three parts	7.35	divided into halves	19.75

$$7.35 \times 19.75 = 145.25 \text{ } \textit{bighā}$$

This measurement seems to indicate that the shape of this peasant land-holding was like the dented pentagon drawn below (left), but it was transfigured, on paper, to the following rectangular form (right) so as to facilitate the calculation.[2]

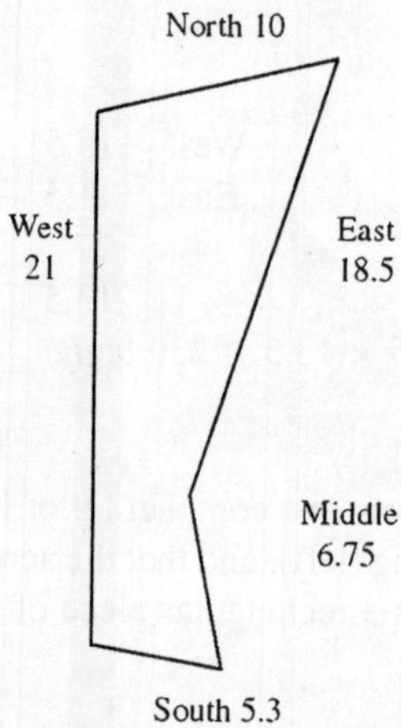

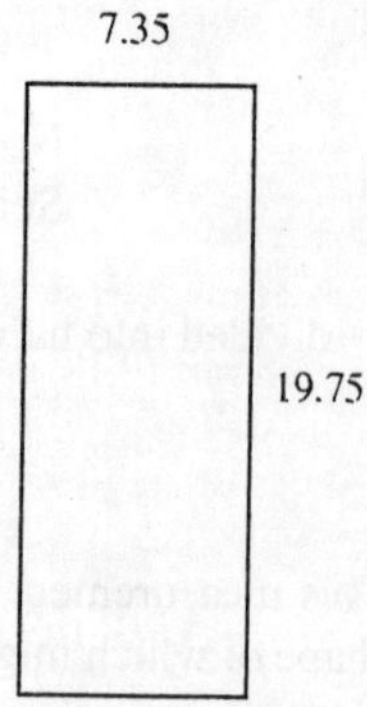

This type of rough calculation of the acreage of land could have meaning only in a locality where land was so abundant in proportion to the population that the amount of land held by peasants was very large and not parcelled into small lots. Thus, we can understand that peasant land-holdings in the later medieval Deccan were lumped together into large compact lots of land.

The question may then be asked as to how peasants managed these large lots of land from 15 to 90 hectares. In this respect, one problem is the nature of the family in medieval India. In many sociological studies, it has been indicated that the basic form of the family among Indian people has been the joint family (extended family). But there are practically no historical sources which show that the family in Indian history was a joint family. It seems rather more proper to think that the basic family form in medieval India was a nuclear family, that is to say, parents with some children. According to a paper on *jizya* of Nevasa District (S.C.S. IV 694. 1684-85), for example, there were 144 villages in this *parganā*, but 74 villages being exempted due to desolation, *jizya* was only levied from 70 villages. In these 70 villages, there were, in all, 564 families, and with children, elderly men, the physically handicapped and paupers being deducted, there remained 563 adult and healthy males other than paupers in 525 families. This means that each family, in general, had only one adult and healthy male member, and that thus the basic form of the family was not the joint family.[3]

Thus, in the medieval Deccan, a very large amount of land was managed by nuclear family peasants. From this fact, we can infer that agriculture in the medieval Deccan was not intensive but was extensive. In this regard, it is quite suggestive that we see in *inām patras* items of income like *tūpa* (*ghī* = clarified butter) and *kaḍbā* (a bundle of hay) along with cash and grain. For example, in the list of items of income from the *inām* land given in the village Pasarni, Vai District, we see 4 *maṇ* 19 *śer* of *tūpa* and 176 bundles of hay along with 13.75 *hon* of cash and 17 *maṇ* 22 *śer* of grain (M.I.S. XX 151). From these sources we can infer with some certainty that in the medieval Deccan agriculture was closely combined with cattle breeding and a considerable portion of the land held by peasants was used as *kuraṇa* (meadow land) or grazing land for cattle. Thus, in any peasant land-holding only a small portion of the total area might have been used for cultivation and the cultivated portion shifted from one section of the holding to another from year to year.

Under these circumstances, it is practically meaningless to measure minutely the acreage of land which each peasant held for collecting taxes according to the acreage of his land. Given this condition, the amount of labour force which each peasant family can command, regardless of the acreage of his land-holding, plays the decisive role. This means that, in connection with deciding how the taxes levied on a village as a whole should be divided, it is more proper to allocate the taxes according to the amount of labour force employed than to the acreage of land held by each peasant. Thus, a unit that shows the tax-bearing capacity of each peasant (which might correspond to the amount of labour force a given family could field) was devised which was *rukā*. *Rukā* therefore had the function of ensuring a kind of fairness in the allocation of taxes among the members of a village community. It was this mechanism of allocation within the village community that made it possible for the village to survive the heavy pressure of taxes imposed by the state.[4]

Community Structure of Local Society

Plural and Stratified Structure of Communities

The general image of Asiatic society, which has been nourished in the social sciences of modern Europe including Marxism, is that there are numerous village communities at the bottom of society which are completely isolated from each other, and over these village communities the state reigns as the sole binder of otherwise scattered units of society. Indian society has been understood within this framework because it has been regarded as the archetypical Asiatic society.[5]

But this image of Indian society is quite removed from reality. In the later medieval Deccan, the community structure was not unitary like that of the village community but was plural and stratified. Moreover, class relations were contained in these communities themselves.

VILLAGE COMMUNITY

No doubt, there was a village functioning as the base of the community structure. In the later medieval Deccan, the membership of a regular member of the village community was denoted as *vatan.* A peasant as a regular member of a village was thus known as *vatandār* Kunbi, while a temporary tenant introduced from outside a village was denoted as *upārī* (outsider peasant).[6] In the village, there was one set of service providers collectively known as *bārā balute* (12 *balute* artisans), which generally included the Sutar (carpenter), Lohar (blacksmith), Kumbhar (potter), Nhavi (barber), Parit (washerman), Joshi (astrologer), Mahar (untouchable), Chambhar (skinner, untouchable) and Mang (untouchable), and in some cases Gurav (temple keeper), Sonar (goldsmith) and some others. They were denoted as *vatandār*, like *vatandār* Sutar, when they were regarded as the regular members of the village. In such cases when a Sutar was employed temporarily by the village, he was denoted as *upārī* Sutar (outsider carpenter). *Bārā balute* were maintained by the village as a whole and were given an annual payment of grains or cash and/or an allotment of a small portion of village land often free from tax or any other charge.[7]

The primary division of labour inside the village was between *vatandār* Kunbis and *bārā balute.* Evident in many source materials is the phrase *sāṭhī prajā va bārā balute* (60 peasants and 12 sorts of artisans), which refers to the entire membership of a village (e.g. S.C.S. I 22, VIII 70). This phrase demonstrates that in the later medieval Deccan, the ideal ratio of the division of labour between peasants and artisans was regarded as 60 peasants with 12 sorts of artisans though the social reality was often different from this ideal as shown in the above-mentioned *jizya* record of Nevasa District.

In the village, there existed several other *vatandārs* besides *vatandār* Kunbis and *bārā balute*. In the first place, there were village leaders like Patil (village headman), Kulkarni (accountant) and Chaugula. They had *vatan* of their own like *Pāṭīlkī vatan* and *Kulkarṇīpaṇa vatan*. Then there were some commodity producers and sellers who were not maintained by the village as a whole such as Teli (oilman), Tamboli (seller of *pānsupārī*), Mali (gardener) and Koshti (weaver). These commodity producers and sellers were admitted into a village by being given the *vatan* of each trade. In the case of the Teli, for example, only the member of the Teli *jāti* (caste) who was given *Telī vatan* by a village could open an oil shop in the village. This means that even members of the Teli *jāti* could not do their work in a village without being given *Telī vatan* from the village. Through this arrangement the village community could control the development of the commodity economy inside the village. The division of labour between peasants and these commodity producers and sellers formed the secondary division of labour inside the village.

Thus, the framework of the division of labour inside the village consisted of various *vatandārs*, with a body of *upārīs* existing outside a set of *vatandārs*. This village community system primarily formed by the *vatandārs* often became deficient because of changes in the life cycle of *vatandārs* or due to devastation from famine and war. It was the role of *upārīs* to fill the deficiency thus brought about and maintain and bolster the village system.

PARGAṆĀ COMMUNITY

The Indian village community has often been regarded as an isolated and independent unit of society. But it might have been quite difficult for the village community to survive had it been isolated. The village community in medieval India was, in reality, a rather unstable institution. To make up for this instability, scores of village communities grouped together and formed an upper level of community structure. This upper level of community structure corresponded to the extent of *pargaṇā* (district). The '*pargaṇā* community' usually consisted of 20 to 100 villages. Leaders of this community were Deshmukh and Deshpande, and they had their own *vatan* like *Deśmukhī vatan*. When any dispute such as a boundary dispute between two villages occurred in a '*pargaṇā* community', Deshmukh called and presided over a meeting of the '*parganā* community' for reaching a decision or compromise. Even law suits submitted to the state were often entrusted to a meeting of '*parganā* community' (*parganā* meeting). Especially, the inheritance, purchase and transfer of *vatan* had to be confirmed by the *parganā* meeting. Its decision and confirmation by the *parganā* meeting was recorded in *mahzar* which was written by Deshpande and signed by the participants.[8]

JĀTI COMMUNITY

While the village community and '*parganā* community' formed a vertically stratified structure, the '*jāti* community' featured a horizontal and trans-village structure. Each *jāti* (caste group) formed a primary collective within a *parganā* which is called the '*jāti* community' here. In every *parganā*, there were heads of '*jāti* communities' like Sutar *mhetar* (head of carpenter caste). These heads exercised control over the members of his '*jāti* community'. They had their own *vatan*, like *Sutār mhetarkī vatan*, by which they could take small perquisites from the members of their *jāti*. When any problem arose which disturbed their *jāti*, e.g. in relation with the state, the *mhetar* as the representative of the *jāti* negotiated with the state. In 1649-50, the official of the state (in fact, the *jāgīrdār*) ordered the Chambhar *jāti* of Supa District to pay tax in cash instead of tax in kind, namely, in shoes made of skin which themselves used to be levied. The *mhetar* of Chambhar *jāti* appealed to the *jāgīrdār* to be allowed to pay tax in kind as before, and obtained an order which approved the appeal and ordered the members of Chambhar *jāti* of Supa District to act under the guidance of this *mhetar* (M.I.S. XV 12).

The '*jāti* community' thus formed the primary group within the limit of *parganā* firstly and then formed the secondary network with the same '*jāti* community' of the neighbouring *parganās*. For example, when a dispute occurred with respect to the customary rule of marriage between the Simpi (tailor) of Sasvad District and Pune District, the members of the two '*jāti* communities' as well as neighbouring '*jāti* communities' held a meeting (*jāti pañca*) and settled the problem (S.P.D. XX 230).[9]

Among '*jāti* communities,' however, there were some *jātis* which had a different structure from these *parganā*-wise *jātis*. The so-called untouchable *jāti* like the Mahar and Mang, and the *ādivāsī* (tribes) like the Koli, Ramoshi and Bhil were assumed to be the original inhabitants of the Deccan, small portions of which had been absorbed in the lowest stratum of the newly developed agricultural village as scavengers or village watchmen (thus usually as the untouchables). But much greater portions of them continued to dwell in the hills outside the village and they enjoyed close relations with their brethren within the villages. Accordingly, these '*jāti* communities' retained a sort of tribal structure as well which went beyond the limit of *parganā*. This tribe-like structure gave these *jātis* a mobile and militant character because of which some heads of these *jātis* obtained *nāik* (head of guards of hill forts) *vatan*.

Thus, the community structure of the local society in the medieval Deccan was plural and stratified as a complex of a vertically organized community structure (village community–*parganā* community) and a horizontally organized community structure (*jāti* community–tribes). At the same time, a '*parganā* community' was linked with other '*parganā* communities' nearby. Similarly, a '*jāti* community' shared relationship with the same '*jāti* communities' of the neighbouring *parganās*. Only within these complicated networks of community structures could the village community reproduce itself with some stability. In this sense, the village community in medieval India was neither isolated nor self-sustaining as imagined in the European mode of thought.

Vatan System as the Basis of the Social Formation

As stated before, the community structure of the local society was plural and stratified, but the principle that regulated the community structure at the bottom was *vatan*. Thus, it is appropriate to call the entire structure of the local society in the later medieval Deccan the Vatan system.

The Vatan system primarily indicated a division of labour (system of parts or roles). The most fundamental form of the Vatan system was the division of labour between the *vatandār* Kunbi and *bārā balute*. However, when a body of 'free commodity producers' began to come into existence as a result of the development of productivity and division of labour within the local society, the Vatan system came to include a division of labour based on the exchange of commodities. Thus, a secondary *vatan* like *Telī vatan* was formed. An *abhaya patra* (deed of assurance) given to a Tamboli from the Patil of the village Garade, Pune Province (1783) clearly shows the role of secondary *vatans*. The relevant passage reads as follows:

> You proceeded before me and stated. 'If you give me the *Tāmbolī vatan* of this village, I will reside in this village, open shop and enjoy the *vatan*.' Therefore, the *Tāmbolī vatan* of this village was given to you, and *vatan* land was allotted to you ... you pay two rupees yearly to the state as the tax and live happily.
>
> (Oturkar no. 71)

These holders of secondary *vatan* were not maintained by the village as a whole like *bālā balute*. They sold their commodities in the village and lived on their earnings. But they could not carry on their business in the village without being given *vatan* from the village.

Primarily, the relation between community leaders (Deshmukh, Deshpande, Patil and Kulkarni) and peasants as well as the relation between *jāti* leader (*mhetar*) and *jāti* members also exhibited a division of labour (relation of office). But these *vatans*, especially that of Deshmukh and Patil, had a tendency to be separated from their office and become private property. As a result of this tendency, *vatan* became objects that could be divided, sold and transferred freely in the course of the sixteenth century at the latest.

In the document written at the time of division of the *Deśmukhī vatan* of Jedhe Deshmukh (Bhor, Pune Province) among five brothers (1659-60), the following items of perquisite were enumerated (Jedhe 15):

1. Shawls [*pāsoḍī*] commuted to cash payment of 505 *ṭakā*.
2. *Sist sālābād*, commuted to cash payment of 219.75 *ṭakā*.
3. Curds, commuted to cash payment of 13.75 *ṭakā*.
4. Goats [*bakare*] for Dasara, commuted to cash payment of 42 *ṭakā*.
5. Bedsteads from the Sutar, commuted to cash payment of 45.75 *ṭakā*.
6. *Rābnūka* [labour] from the Mahar, commuted to cash payment of 18.75 *ṭakā*.
7. *Sotra* from the Gurav, commuted to cash payment of 2.75 *ṭakā*.

These perquisites seem to have primarily been the tribute offered to the headman of the '*parganā* community' (Deshmukh) from the members of the community. These items of tribute must have been paid formerly either in kind or by rendering labour service. But in the seventeenth century almost all of them came to be commuted to cash payment. Thus, tribute to the head of a community began to change its nature and gradually came to assume the character of a cash perquisite. In this process of change, these *vatans* like *Deśmukhī* and *Pāṭīlkī* began to be sold and purchased frequently and were accumulated in the hands of one and the same person.[10]

Along with this process, new *vatans* that had nothing to do with the division of labour within the local society were newly created by the state and given to the state officials or local leaders. *Sardeśmukhī* and *Sarpāṭīlkī* were some of these new *vatans*. These *vatans*, having

Table 5: Vatan system

Parganā I Deshmukh Deshpande *Mhetar* of a *jāti*	II Sardeshmukh Sardeshpande Sarpatil Sarkulkarni
Village I Patil Kulkarni Chaugula *Vatandār* Kunbi *Bārā balute*	II Teli Tamboli, etc.
Market town II *Śeṭa* (head of market) *Mahājana* (accountant of market)	Fort II *Sarnāik* *Nāik*

I = Primary *vatan* II = Secondary *vatan*

no part to play in the division of labour in the local society, were purely the private property of the grantees. As long as they were *vatans*, however, the perquisite accompanying the *vatan* was levied directly from the members of the local society in addition to the taxes due to the state. Thus, the Vatan system, which had primarily only accommodated the relationships of the division of labour, was enlarged to contain all relationships of exploitation within the local society. (Table 5 summarizes the structure of the Vatan system.)

What then might have been the reason that the Vatan system came to incorporate the relationships of exploitation? The reason seems to be as follows. With the development of productivity, the 'social surplus' began to be accumulated within the local society, though this 'social surplus' could not take the form of landed property in the medieval Deccan. In a society where land had a value in itself and one could appropriate the labour of other people by holding the title to a piece of land, social development might be expressed in the change or development of the form of landed property. But, as stated before, in the medieval Deccan, land was considerably abundant in proportion to the population. In this type of society, a social system based on the principle of landed property was difficult to develop, so an increase of the 'social surplus' did not enhance the value of land itself. Thus, the 'social surplus' created by the development of productivity within the local society tended to be transformed into the perquisites of community leaders who were in the position to control the distribution of social wealth in the local society. In other words, the increased 'social surplus' tended to enrich the *vatans* of community leaders. These *vatans* thus turned into a kind of private property. In this process, community leaders like Deshmukh and Patil began to be transformed into the ruling and exploiting class within the local society.

Class Relations in Local Society

Formation of 'Local Lord' Class

In 1674, Shivaji was crowned at Raigad and took the title of *Chatrapati* of the Maratha kingdom. The moving force behind the formation of the Maratha kingdom was the 'local lord' class consisting mostly of Deshmukh families in the so-called *deśa* districts of the Deccan. With the transformation of the *vatan* form of social organization, Deshmukh had been gradually emerging as the ruling class of the local society. And, at the same time, they began to play a vital role in the state machinery at the local level. Deshmukhs received various emoluments from the state as rewards for their civil and military services. The principal forms of their emoluments were: (1) *jāgīr* (or *mokāsā*, *saranjām*)—the right to take the amount corresponding to the taxes of the state from the designated *parganā*. (*Jāgīr*, being annexed to the office, was withdrawn after the individual left office.); (2) *inām* was a hereditary right to levy taxes from the designated *parganā* or village; (3) *Sardeśmukhī* was generally a tenth of the taxes of the state that was collected separately from and in addition to the taxes due the state. The territory of the Maratha 'local lord' class was an accumulation of various titles or rights over various lands. For example, the territory of Mane Deshmukh who had the *Deśmukhī* of Mhesvad and Dahiganv Districts on the river Man, a branch of the river Bhima, itself a branch of the Krishna River, took the complicated form shown in Table 6 (S.C.S. V 845, 847).

We can see from Table 6 that Mane Deshmukh accumulated the rights of *Deśmukhī* and *Sardeśmukhī* along with the *inām* in Mhesvad and Dahiganv Districts. Thus, Mane Deshmukh held almost complete landlord rights over these two districts. However, the right over these two districts was not expressed as a landownership right but still as the accumulation of two *vatans* and *inām*. This was due to the peculiarity of society in the medieval Deccan where land-holding itself was not the decisive factor. Mane Deshmukh had one or two of the three rights over

Table 6: Territory of Mane Deshmukh

Name of *parganā*	I *Deśmukhī*	II *Sardeśmukhī*	III *Inām*	*Jāgīr*
Mhesvad	○	○	○	
Dahiganv	○	○	○	
Kaladhon		○	○	
Ankaluj		○		○
Kaseganv		○		○
Brahmapuri		○		○
Sangole		○		○
Bhalavni		○		○
Najire		○		○
Ubartapa		○		○
Pangaritapa		○		○
Bhalki				○
Chicholi				○
Nilge				○
Adpadi		○		
Mangalavede		○		
Elapur		○		

the other districts. In these districts, the right of the Manes coexisted with the rights of other people. Accordingly, in many of these districts, the Deshmukh, Sardeshmukh and *ināmdār* (or *jāgīrdār*) collected their emoluments separately from peasants. This state of affairs must have been heavily burdensome for the peasants.

Since Maratha 'local lords' came mostly from Deshmukh families, their territory was not very extensive and military men in their service rarely exceeded a thousand. Let us take Jedhe Deshmkh as an example to examine the structure of the military force of Maratha 'local lords'.[11]

The ancestors of Jedhe Deshmukh family were Patils of the village Nere, Junnar Province in the northern Deccan, but, for some reason or other, they came to Utoroli, a hilly district near Pune in the early part of the sixteenth century. Here, they began to serve under the Deshmukh of this district. When there was no heir to the Deshmukh family, Jedhe went to Bidar, the capital of Barid Shahi dynasty and obtained the *Deśmukhī vatan* of this district. But Khopade, the son-in-law of the former Deshmukh, ambushed and killed him on his return. An orphan of Jedhe was fostered by a Deshmukh of the neighbouring district. When grown up, sincc he contended repeatedly with Khopade, a *parganā*

Table 7: *Bārā mulve* of Jedhe Deshmukh

Name of *bārā mulve*	Number of *ṭakā*
Gholap	2
Petkar	1.5
Kodalkar	3
Mahala	2.25
Godavla	1.5
Jedhe Velangkar	3
Asamdar	2
Badbakar	1.5
Khocharya	1.5
Sanas	1.5
Tupe	1.5
Vanjoji Dekana	1.5
Indroji Jedhe	2.25
Chudana	1.5
Sonji Karkari	2
	28.5

(S.C.S. II 337)

meeting was held and the *Deśmukhī vatan* of this district was divided into two parts. Bhor was given to Jedhe and Utoroli to Khopade. In this process, a group of retainers called *bārā mulve* (12 original retainers) supported the Jedhes. Jedhe had promised that he would give *bārā mulve* one half of the emoluments of *Deśmukhī* after winning it. Considerable hardship would have been caused the peasants, however, had he and *bārā mulve* each levied their emoluments separately from peasants. So this arrangement was given up after obtaining the *Deśmukhī vatan* of Bhor, and instead, the village Kari, one of four *inām* villages of Jedhe, was given to *bārā mulve*, after which they decided to reside in this village.

In 1618, the village Kari consisted of 40 *ṭakā* in all. These *ṭakā* were allocated among *bārā mulve* as shown in Table 7. The remaining 11.5 *ṭakā* were allocated among the Deshmukh, Sutar, Lohar, Chambhar, Kumbhar, Parit, Sonar, Gurav, Joshi, Mahar and some others. This arrangement was almost the same even in 1652-53 (Jedhe 19). The military force which Jedhe commanded through these retainers amounted to nearly seven hundred men (M.I.S. XVI I).

In the 1690s when Jedhe joined the army of Rajaram, the second son of Shivaji, his military force was incorporated into the military system of the Maratha kingdom. In 1707-8, the head family of Jedhe held the title of *senā pañcsahastrī* (commander of 5000 soldiers) and was given an annual payment of 700 *hon* (Jedhe 30). According to a document written in 1716-17, the Maratha government made annual payments even to some *bārā mulve* (Jedhe 39).

Thus, military forces of the Maratha kingdom were based on the military forces of Maratha 'local lords'.

Relations between 'Local Lords' and Peasants

As stated before, many Deshmukhs had become influential 'local lords' by the end of the sixteenth century at the latest. But this does not mean that they had lost their function as the head of the '*parganā* community'. As long as they ruled the land and men in the name of Deshmukh, they were required to discharge the duties of Deshmukh to the end. As an example, in 1629, the Deshmukh of Nevasa District submitted a petition to the ruling state, running as follows:

> The army of the Mughals came to our villages and damaged *śivār* [village land] and gave the remaining grass to their cattle. They cut down unripe crops and took them away. Thus, the villagers are in a helpless condition. What is more, Bhonsle, *jāgīrdār* of this district, took away the villagers' cattle and seized even the smallest amount of money. As a result, the villagers have despaired and deserted the village. The village is desolated. For this reason, I beg revision of the amount of the tax levied on this village.
>
> (S.C.S. IV 691)

In 1692, the Deshmukh and Deshpande of Indapur District petitioned for a reduction of the tax of this district because there was no rain and crops had failed in its previous year (S.C.S. III 648). Even in 1769, the Deshmukh and Deshpande of Nanemaval District presented a petition to the state for a reduction in the tax because of devastation from war and drought (S.P.D. XXXIX 123).

Abhaya patra shows clearly the function of Deshmukh as the head of the '*parganā* community'. In the year 1691 when Jedhe Deshmukh joined the Maratha army, the following *abhaya patra* was issued:

> In the 18th year from the coronation of *Chatrapati* Shivaji, this *abhaya patra* was given by Rajaram to the Deshmukh, Sarjarav Jedhe, Deshpande, Patil, Kulkarni, Chaugula, the other *vatandārs*, *śeṭa* and *mahājana* of *parganā* Rohida. You pro-

ceeded to Chanji [Jinji], seat of King Rajaram, and stated: '*Vatandārs* and the peasants of this district pledge allegiance to your Majesty. So, please issue an order to the effect that the *vatan* of all *vatandārs* of this district continue as it did under the Nizam Shahi and Adil Shahi dynasties, and give us the *abhaya patra*.' Therefore, pleased by your pledging allegiance to the king, the district concerned was entrusted to Ramachandra Amatya and Shankaraji Pant Sachiv. They will make decisions on *vatan* after taking your statements into consideration, and will issue *vatan patras*. Their *patras* have the same effects as those of the king. According to their *vatan patras*, the king will continue your *vatans*.

(M.I.S. XV 349)

In this document, it can be seen that the Deshmukh as the head of the '*pargaṇā* community' submitted the petition to the state to continue all *vatans* in the district when the '*pargaṇā* community' elected to come under the control of the Maratha kingdom. In another *abhaya patra* of 1628, *vatans* of the Deshmukh, Deshpande, Patil, Kulkarni, *bārā balute* and Mahar were mentioned as being continued by the state (S.C.S. XI 64). This means that what was ensured by *abhaya patra* was the Vatan system itself. *Abhaya patra* constituted an assurance that no change be brought into the social relations of the local society.

Another occasion when the function of Deshmukh as the head of the '*pargaṇā* community' came into view was, as stated earlier, *pargaṇā* meeting. When any trouble occurred in the *pargaṇā*, the Deshmukh called a *pargaṇā* meeting and presided over it. In the case of a prolonged dispute pertaining to the *Pāṭīlkī vatan* of the village Pasarni, Vai District, at least four *pargaṇā* meetings were convened. They proceeded as follows (S.C.S. VIII 70):

THE CAUSE OF THE DISPUTE

The *Pāṭīlkī vatan* of this village was the hereditary patrimony of Kondji. Since this village was overcome by famine and desolated, however, Kondji could not pay the contracted sum of the taxes to the state. Thus, he fled from the village. (The taxes were levied on the village as a whole, and the Patil was responsible for the payment of the whole amount of the taxes.) The *havāldār* (Collector) of the *pargaṇā* called him back, and gave him a notice that his *Pāṭīlkī vatan* would be confiscated and conferred on another person if he could not pay the taxes. Since he still could not pay, he was imprisoned. The *havāldār* summoned Rikame and

Yevare and said that two-thirds of the *Pāṭīlkī vatan* would be conferred on them if they paid the taxes. They answered that they would pay it if a *mahzar* to this effect was issued.

Mahzar I

Thus, the *havāldār* ordered the Deshmukh of the said *parganā* to convene a *parganā* meeting and issue a *mahzar* to ensure that two-thirds of the *Pāṭīlkī vatan* of the said village was given to them. Accordingly, a *mahzar* was issued and the *Pāṭīlkī vatan* was divided into three parts among Rikame, Yevare and Kondji.

Thala Patra I

After five or six years, the dispute broke out again. Kondji sued the Sadr (judge) to fix the *thala* (literally, the place) where the case was to be decided, and to send both parties there. Accordingly, an order to this effect being issued by the Sadr, both parties went to the Deshmukh of this *parganā* to ask him to name the *thala*. The Deshmukh named the village Taleganv as the *thala*. They then went to the village Taleganv, and a meeting was held there. At this meeting, the *Mahzar* I that Rikame and Yevare possessed was declared invalid because no sign of *sāṭhī prajā va bārā balute* of this village was put on it. Consequently, Kondji's right to the *Pāṭīlkī vatan* was confirmed and the *Thala patra* I to this effect was issued. Kondji presented it to the Deshmukh and Sadr with the result that Rikame and Yevare were ousted from the village.

Thala Patra II

Since Rikame and Yevare continued the dispute, however, the village Chimanganv was named as the *thala* again, and another meeting was held there. At this meeting also, the *mahzar* that Rikame and Yevare possessed was determined to be invalid because it was enforced to be written by the official in charge of tax collection. And the *Thala patra* II was issued to the effect that they should abide by the decision of the meeting of the village Taleganv.

Mahzar II

Considering all of these processes, the meeting of this *parganā* (1667) decided that Kondji was right. Accordingly a *mahzar* to this effect was issued for Kondji. Participants in this *parganā* meeting were the *havāldār*, *majmudār*, 9 other *parganā* officials, 6 *śetas*, and 43 Patils of the neighbouring villages with the Deshmukh of this *pargaṇā* as the president (*sabhā nāik*).

Thus, Deshmukhs continued to fulfil their function as the head of the '*pargaṇā* community' even after they had turned into ruling 'local lords'. Additionally the relationship between Deshmukh and peasants was not expressed as one of a landlord-serf but continued to be expressed as a relationship between *vatandārs*, i.e. a relationship expressing the division of labour within a *pargaṇā* community.

Conclusion: A Reconsideration of the Concept of Feudalism

From the foregoing analysis of the social structure in the seventeenth-eighteenth century Deccan, the following points can be concluded:

1. The direct producers were the peasants who owned all the means of production including the land. In general, they were not part of a joint family (or extended family) but constituted a nuclear family which did not depend on subordinate labour like that of slaves.

2. The main exploiting class of the local society was the community leaders, especially Deshmukh who had turned into the rural ruling class by the end of the sixteenth century at the latest. But they were not denominated as landlords or feudal lords. The title which gave them the authority to rule the land and people was *Deśmukhī vatan* even after their transformation into the rural ruling class. This state of affairs was due to the fact that in the medieval Deccan where land was abundant in proportion to the population and agriculture was closely interwoven with cattle breeding, landownership could not be the decisive factor in appropriating surplus labour of the direct producer.

3. Thus, the class relationship between the rural ruling class and peasants was not expressed as one of a landlord–serf, that is to say, it was not a relationship of landownership as in medieval Europe.

4. The rural ruling class could not monopolize judicial rights over the peasants because, so long as their title to rule the peasants was based on *Deśmukhī vatan*, their behaviour was restricted within the framework of the local society, namely the Vatan system, to which they belonged.

The question then arises as to whether or not we can call such a society feudal. My answer is in the affirmative. If feudal society is defined as a society in which the basic 'relationship between men and men' is expressed as one of landownership, then medieval Deccanese society cannot be called feudal. However, the decisive point is the nature of the 'relationship between men and men' in connection with the appropriation of surplus labour and not the judicial explanation of that relationship through landownership. Even the same 'relationship between men and men' can take forms other than the relationship of landownership in a society where land is not the decisive factor due to the conditions of nature and agriculture.

Granted that a feudal society not based on the principle of the landownership relationship is possible, the concept of feudalism is required to be expanded to include various societies where the basic 'relationship between men and men' is that between the peasants (who possess all the means of production themselves and whose main labour force is family labour without subordinate labour like that of slaves) and the exploiting class (whose denomination can be various). It is within the context of this expanded concept of feudalism that society in the later medieval Deccan can be called feudal.

Notes

1 The unit of length and width of the land used in this land measurement is *dorī* which is equivalent to 20 *kāṭhī*. *Kāṭhī* is a measuring rod of 'five *hāta* (hand) and five *mūṭha* (fist)', nearly equal to 2.5 m. Thus, one *dorī* is about 50 m. One *bighā*, being a square *dorī* (≒ 50 m × 50 m), is about 2500 sq. m, nearly equal to 0.6 acre. *Dorī* as a measuring tool might have been made of 20 pieces of *kāṭhī* connected toghether by *dorī* (rope).

The units of an area (square measure) are as follows:

1 *pāṇḍa* = 20 square *kāṭhī*
1 *bighā* = 20 *pāṇḍa* = 400 square *kāṭhī*
1 *cāvara* = 120 *bighā*

2 The method of land measurement in the medieval Deccan as shown in this document was well known to the British administrators of the Bombay government. Robertson recorded in his report how a piece of land had been measured as follows:

Width		Length	
	34		126
	31		141.5
	31		267.5
	25		
	121		
Average	30.25	Average	133.75

30.25 × 133.75 = 4046 (*square kāṭhī*) = 10 *bighā* 2.5 *pāṇḍa*

Thus, this land of hexagonal shape was measured by transfiguring it into a quadrilateral with sides of average width and length (Report of Captain Robertson, Collector of Poona to Commissioner, dated 1 May 1820. R.E.I.H. : IV 208).

3 As to *jizya* records pertaining to the medieval Deccan, cf. Kulkarni 1996: 176-208. See further, Chapter 3, note 1 of this volume. The joint family seems to be a rather new phenomenon which has been mainly brought about by 'modernization' or urbanization processes under colonial rule because it is generally found in densely populated urban areas and not in rural areas.

4 The motive of the state in measuring land was to ascertain the maximum tax-bearing capacity of each village. Land was measured, though roughly, and classified into three classes, namely the first (*āval*), second (*dum*) and third (*sīm*), to each of which a specific amount of tax per *bighā* was fixed. By multiplying the numbers of *bighā* of each land class in a village by respective amount of tax per *bighā*, the state could ascertain the maximum amount of taxes (known as *kamāl jamā*) leviable on the village. This maximum amount of taxes was usually reduced according to the condition of the crops, and levied on the village as a whole. That is, the state had no intention of controlling each individual peasant by means of land measurement. The village community, on the other hand, allocated this lump sum of taxes among its members not according to the acreage of land held by each peasant so ascertained by land measurement but according to the specific number of *rukā* each peasant held.

5 See H. Kotani, *Marx and Asia: A Critical Examination of the Concept of Asiatic Mode of Production* (in Japanese), Tokyo, 1979.

6 H. Fukazawa, 'The Land-system and the Peasantry', in Fukazawa 1991: 174-90.

7 H. Fukazawa, 'Rural Servants in the Maharashtrian Village; Demiurgic or Jajmani System?', in Fukazawa 1991: 219-25.

8 As to *mahzar*, see Gune 1953.

9 As to the details of this dispute, see Chapter 4 of this volume.

10 As to accumulation of *Deśmukhī* and *Pāṭīlkī vatans*, see Perlin 1978: 208-13.

11 As to Jedhe Deshmukh, see Wink 1986: 172-78.

2

Land Rights of Peasants in the Vatan System and British Concept of Landed Property

Introduction

Land rights in pre-colonial India have been a controversial subject of historical studies in India as well as abroad. Peasants' right to the land they cultivated, intermediary land rights of local dignitaries such as *zamindars* and *taluqdars* and the state's claim over the land under their sovereignty have been focal points of historical discussion pertaining to Indian history since the 1960s.[1]

Under British colonial rule the so-called land systems or land tenures in India became the focal administrative issue since the land revenue, whether it should be held as land tax or land rent, constituted the most reliable financial base for British colonial administration. As a result of this, many documents on the land systems of India, parliamentary minutes, administrative reports and independent books, appeared in the nineteenth century which also have been stimulating historians' continuous interest in this research field.

This chapter aims to characterize the salient feature of the peasant's land right in pre-colonial India with special reference to the medieval Deccan under the Maratha kingdom, and further with a perspective on its transformation under British colonial rule. As indicated in Chapter 1, the principal social system in the later medieval Deccan can be conceptualized as the Vatan system in which all sorts of the proprietary right enjoyable by the community members were prescribed by the *vatan* possessed by each member. Thus, the peasant's land right as well was incorporated within this Vatan system and the process of transformation of this right also closely correlated with the changes made in the Vatan system under British colonial rule.

Peasant's Land Rights in the Pre-colonial Deccan

As this topic of peasant's land rights in the pre-colonial Deccan has been dealt with somewhat minutely in Chapter 1 drawing on medieval Marathi documents, a brief review will suffice here.

Bighā and Rukā: Two Types of Land Denomination

It is often observed in medieval Marathi documents dating from the seventeenth to the eighteenth century that the same land is designated by two different types of denomination, that is, *bighā* and *rukā*. As an example, I will take up a letter issued by the Peshva govenment in 1770-71, confirming a *kharīdkhat* (land-sale deed). The seller of the land, a *thalkarī mirāsdār* (full-fledged member of a village community, more commonly known as *vatandār* Kunbi) by the name of Malji bin Jebaji Nhave, possessed a 3-*rukā* land in the Tanapuri *thala* (the division of village lands called Tanapuri). He had dug a well in this land and created a garden land of 7 *bighās* in it. As he got deeply in debt, he sold this 7-*bighā* land together with the well and trees on it to a tenant residing in a different village, Vyankatrao Kashi Durve by name, for Rs. 250 (S.S.R.P.D. VII 433).

This document clearly shows that *mirāsdārs* (*vatandār* Kunbis) had the proprietary right over the lands they cultivated, as H. Fukazawa formerly indicated (1991: 158-61). The implication of this document, however, seems much wider and deeper than merely proving the existence of the proprietary land rights of *mirāsdārs*. The term bearing this wider implication must be that of *rukā* as it is doubtless that *bighā* is a unit of area (square measure) in its simplest meaning. In this case, the garden area sold was a 7-*bighā* land, that is, it was nearly equal to 4 acres. This garden plot was, however, situated in a land lot designated as 3 *rukās* within the Tanapuri *thala*. What then might one ask does this land unit of *rukā* mean?

Rukā and Taxation System of the Maratha Kingdom

The term *rukā* bore a close relationship with the taxation system of the Maratha kingdom under which taxes were levied on the village as a whole. In the terminology of British land administration, this type of taxation was known as the 'village rent'.

Moving ahead to the key point, the number of *rukā* attached to the land of each peasant (*mirāsdār*) indicated the proportionate part of the 'village rent' for which each peasant was responsible. In the case of the village Nehatni, Pune Province (1671), as an example, the total number of the tax-bearing *rukā* of this village was 587, while the total amount of taxes levied on this village as a whole was 460.5 *hons*. This meant that a land plot denominated, for example, as 6 *rukās* in this village should have generated a tax amount of 4.25 *hons*. In other words, a peasant (*mirāsdār*) holding a land plot denominated as 6 *rukās* had to contribute 4.25 *hons* as his allocation for the village (S.C.S. VII 54). In this sense, the *rukā*-type land denomination expressed a mutual relationship with respect to the allotment of taxes among the peasants (*mirāsdārs*) of the same village. The term *rukā* thus closely correlated with the communal structure of the village as a collective or cooperative body.

Returning to the aforementioned example of the 'land-sale deed' of the 7-*bighā* land, the purchaser obtained the land as *vatanī mirās* land. This implies that the purchaser was admitted into the village as a *mirāsdār* (*vatandār* Kunbi), that is, as a full-fledged member of the village community as opposed to an *upārī* who was a temporarily residing tenant, though this point is not sufficiently clear from the wording of this document. This is the case with the following *vatan patra* as well.

In 1752, the Deshmukh and Deshpande of Sasvad District as well as the Patil of Sasvad gave the *vatan patra* (certificate of *vatan*) of the following purport to Baburao and Tukoji, two sons of Bhikaji Sinde presently residing (*hālī vastī*) in this town:

> You came to us and stated as follows: 'We have been living in this town for a long time and you have given a *vāḍā* [residence land] to live on in this town. Now please give us a *mirās* land to cultivate [*śeta thala mirāsī*].' Taking your representation into consideration, we will give you a land of 2.5 *khaṇḍī* situated in the Ambe *thala*, after demarcating the boundaries.... Pay the currently fixed land-tax and cultivate the land. Live happily enjoying the *mirās*. We have given this *mirās* for generations in your posterity.
>
> (A.S.S. V 72)

This document (*vatan patra*) denotes that the hereditary proprietary right in the *mirās* land of 2.5 *khaṇḍī* (*Khaṇḍī* is also a sort of *rukā*-type denomination of land.) was bestowed on the two *upārīs* presently residing in Sasvad. The implication here is that the two *upārīs* were admitted as *mirāsdārs* (*vatandār* Kunbis), that is to say, as full-fledged members of the community by the township of Sasvad. Though it is not clear why the township of Sasvad accepted them as *mirāsdārs* seemingly without any payment, it may be that the township of Sasvad expected the two former *upārīs* to contribute to the town for some part of taxes levied on the town as a whole.

Vatan patra was also known as *mirās patra*, many examples of which were translated from the original Marathi into English in the early part of the nineteenth century under British colonial rule. These *mirās patras* throw considerable light on questions that remain somewhat vague with respect to the aforecited *kharīdkhat* and *vatan patra*.

British Administrators' understanding of *Mirās Patra*

Finding of Private Landed Property

After conquering most of the western Deccan in 1818, British (East India Company) colonial administrators took a keen interest in the system of land tenure in the so-called Conquered Territories. They strenuously endeavoured to find who was the proprietor of land from whom they were to collect land tax. In this task, important questions that cropped up were: Was the peasant the proprietor of the land he cultivated? Or was the village body the sole proprietor of all lands that were situated within the boundary of the village? Or was there any other intermediary proprietor of land? British administrators made every effort to answer these questions, because if they could find the proprietor of the land in question, they could then levy land tax on him.

Mountstuart Elphinstone, the then Deccan Commissioner (later the Governor of Bombay from 1819 to 1827), wrote in his well-known report dated 25 October 1819 which was published later under the title of *Report on the Territories Conquered from the Paishwa* (Bombay 1872), as follows:

> As I was particularly directed to attend to the tenures of land, I have called on the Collectors to furnish the requisite information.... The deed of sale enclosed in Captain Robertson's letter of March 9th, throws a clear light on the manner in which the Meerasee tenure was regarded by the people and by the government. The result of those reports and of my own inquiries is, that *a large portion of the Ryots [ra'īyat] are the proprietors of their estates* [italics original], subject to the payment of fixed land-tax to Government; that their property is hereditary and salable; that they are never dispossessed while they

> pay their tax, and even then they have for a long period (at least thirty years) the right of reclaiming their estate on paying the dues of the government. Their tax is fixed; but the late Maratha Government loaded it with other impositions, which reduced that advantage to a mere name. So far however was this from destroying the value of their estates, that although the Government took advantage of their attachment to make them pay considerably more than Oopree, and though all the Meeraseedars were in ordinary cases obliged to make up for failures in the payment of each of their body, yet their lands were salable, and generally at ten years' purchase....
>
> An opinion prevails throughout Maratha country, that under the old Hindoo government all the land was held by Meerasees, and that the Ooprees were introduced as the old proprietors sunk under the tyranny of the Mohamedans. This opinion is supported by the fact, that the greater part of the field now cultivated by Ooprees are recorded in the village books as belonging to absent proprietors and affords ... a strong presumption that the revenue system under the Hindoos (if they had a uniform system) was founded on private property in the soil.[2]

Elphinstone thus found that 'a large portion of the Ryots are the proprietors of their estates'. In evidence, he referred to the 'deed of sale' enclosed in Captain Robertson's letter of 9 March, which I could not find in the government records. Fortunately, however, Robertson's letter to William Chaplin, the successor of Elphinstone as the Deccan Commissioner, dated 10 October 1821 also enclosed many documents of this same sort (English translation of Marathi originals). Of them, documents known as *meeras puttee* (*mirās patra* or *vatan patra*) throw considerable light on the nature of peasant's land rights in the pre-colonial Deccan. The following is the letter of confirmation of *meeras puttee* issued by the Deshmukh and Deshpande of *prānt* Pune:

> A writing (aj nuvusth) by the Daismook and Daispandie of the pranth of Poona to Papoojee bin Goendjee Dawry and Mulharjee bin Essajee Bhoir and Bhowanjee and Mancoojee, and Madjee Essajee Bhoir, of the village of Maun, turruf Havaily, of the pranth aforesaid, Sin 1209 (A.D. 1799) is given to you as follows, that[:]
>
> You have come to Poona and stated that you have been for a long period Sookawasthee inhabitants [free or contented resident tenants at will] of the aforesaid village, but that you had no wuttun to aid it, and

> the village had got deeply into debt from the famine, and for Circar's [government's] rents in the famine and from other causes, and that you had represented to the village your willingness, possessing no wuttun to aid it in its pecuniary embarrassment, if it would confer on you fields and houses in meeras and paulnook in the same way as the other Meeraseedars enjoy theirs, and that thereupon the villagers having taken your request into consideration, had given you, on the payment of Rupees 150, six rookas of the ghutcool field called kullum durra, in all eight rookas, from which was deducted as a remission half a rooka, leaving 7.5 rookas, and for which you obtained a meeras puttee, in which was also specified the land for houses in the village, and also three items of paulnook, and which meeras puttee is written by the Koolkurnee, and that you having entered on the possession and enjoyment of the aforesaid rights, now wish them confirmed by us.[3]

This letter of confirmation of *meeras puttee* (*mirās patra*) issued by the Deshmukh and Deshpande refers to the *meeras puttee* certifying that the 6-*rukā* land was given by the village Maun to five persons together with the lands for houses and three items of 'paulnook'. It is thus very clear that this *meeras puttee* provides a much broader and deeper meaning or implication than the mere transfer of a land plot from a village to a man. Colonial administrators such as Elphinstone, however, could not understand this wider implication, only seeing in it the existence of private landed property of peasants.

This *meeras puttee* indicates that the village body of Maun conferred a portion of the 'ghutcool' (*gatkula*) land of the village together with house lands and social privileges ('paulnook', *pāḷṇūk*) of three items to five 'Sookawasthee' tenants presently residing in the same village. *Gatkula* land means the *mirās* land (land possessed by a *mirāsdār* as his hereditary property) which passed over to the village body by reason of the dying out or wandering away of a *mirāsdār* family for some reason or other. Sookawasthee (*sukhavastī*, meaning the happily living) was a tenant of a village community as a whole who had a residence in it but had no *mirās* land or the *mirāsī* right of the village. Thus, what this *meeras puttee* conferred on the five *sukhavastī* tenants in return for the payment of Rs. 150 as a pecuniary aid for the village during periods of difficulty was, in substance, the right as *mirāsdārs* (full-fledged members of the village community) with lands to cultivate as well as to live on them together with the same social privileges which other *mirāsdārs* of this village enjoyed. It is thus this nature of *meeras puttee* or *vatan patra* which bore a much wider social implication than the mere transfer of a land plot.

This letter of confirmation of *meeras puttee* and many other documents of similar nature show, without doubt, that there existed private landed property of the peasant in the pre-colonial Deccan. It was therefore by no mistake that the British colonial administrators became aware of the prevalence of peasant's landed property. They summarily stopped at this point, however, and could not fully recognize the much broader and more important implication of what was termed the land sale in the pre-colonial Deccan.[4]

Two Aspects of Land-holding
Proprietary Rights and Social Relations

Proprietary Rights: Private Aspect of Land-holding

Properties like landed property generally have two aspects. One is the private aspect and the other is the social aspect. These two aspects of properties are separated in modern societies. In modern jurisprudence, the proprietary right is assumed to be the right to 'use and abuse' some thing. This refers to the private aspect of property which is the proprietor's absolute right to enjoy and dispose of some thing. In other words, the private aspect of property denotes the relationship between a man and some thing. On the other hand, the social aspect of property embodies the relationship between one man and other men which accrues from the fact that the man comes to possess some thing. This social aspect of property is, in modern jurisprudence, called a contract and separated from the proprietary right. In pre-modern societies, however, these two aspects of property were not separated from each other. In fact, property like land-holding in pre-modern societies had these two aspects united in itself.

As we have seen previously, there were two different types of land denominations in the pre-colonial Deccan. Of these two, the *bighā*-type land denomination primarily referred to the private aspect of land-holding, that is to say, to the relationship between the proprietor and the land. On the other hand, the *rukā*-type land denomination primarily referred to the social aspect of land-holding, that is, to the social relations into which the holder of the land entered.

Social Relations: Social Aspect of Land-holding

In the above-cited English translation of the letter confirming *meeras puttee*, we have seen that the purchasers of the 6-*rukā gatkula* land of the village were admitted into the village body as *mirāsdārs* and given house lands as well as three items of social privilege (*pāḷṇūk*). In another *meeras puttee* pertaining to the village Errowna (1785), the 'Sumvust Dehijin' (*samast dahījan*, meaning the whole villagers) of the village sold the 6-*rukā* land plot to the Kulkarni of Ahmadnagar to raise money for erecting a Maruti temple. The last phrase of this *meeras puttee* states that 'the purchaser has been admitted into the village body as a meeras bhow (*mirās bhāū*)', [5] which means a member of the 'brotherhood of *mirāsdārs*' of a village.

While the concrete substance of the three aspects of social privilege (*pāḷṇūk*) referred to in the above-cited English translation of the letter confirming *meeras putte* is not clear, in another *meeras puttee* pertaining to 'kutsery (*kacerī*) of Kandwa Bzoerg', the 'Sumvust Dehijin' of the village gave the purchaser of the 6-*rukā* land plot of the village 'the dignity like the other Meerassadars, of his wife being invited to holiday and marriage feasts in the families of Meerassadars'.[6] This proves that the *pāḷṇūk* given to the purchaser of the 6-*rukā* land plot included the right to enjoy social association with other members of the village community such as the invitation to a marriage feast as a full-fledged member of the community.

Thus, *meeras puttee* or *vatan patra* in the pre-colonial Deccan, which British administrators like M. Elphinstone understood merely as a 'deed of sale', contained, in fact, a much richer social meaning than the simple buying and selling of land. What was conferred on the man who obtained *meeras puttee* or *vatan patra* was, in substance, the membership right of a village (town) community. Land rights conferred by *meeras puttee* or *vatan patra* was based on this membership right and, in this sense, incorporated within the framework of the communal structure of the village conceptualized as the Vatan system. The purchaser of land denominated by a certain number of *rukā*, could enjoy their right in land only as a member of the village (town) community, as the *mirās* right was sustained by the Vatan system itself. In other words, there existed no landed property of peasants independent from the social relationships which jointly constituted the Vatan system.

Thus, the proprietary land right enjoyed by peasants in the later medieval Deccan differed in essence from those in modern societies.

Introduction of Raiyatwari Settlement

On the assumption that the peasant's proprietary right in land, as discovered by the early colonial administrators such as Elphinstone, was identical with the modern landed property in England, the Raiyatwari Settlement was introduced in the Bombay Presidency in the first half of the nineteenth century.

G. Wingate and H.E. Goldsmid, the founders of the Raiyatwari Settlement in the Bombay Presidency, explained its fundamental principle in their so-called 'Joint Report' written in 1840 as follows:

> As proprietary rights are fully recognized under our settlement, and the Board's objections, if applicable to Sir T. Munro's system, are equally so to ours, we deem it incumbent to state our reasons for believing the Board to have arrived at a mistaken conclusion upon this important point. It appears to us that a proprietary right in land can only be destroyed by the imposition of an assessment so heavy as to absorb the whole of the rent, for as long as the assessment falls in any degree, short of the rent, the portion remaining will give a value to the land, and enable its possessor to let or sell it, which of necessity constitutes him a proprietor. Whether or not Sir T. Munro disregarded the rights of the real proprietors, and recorded the land simply in the names of the actual occupants, who thus became responsible for the payment of the assessment, we do not think it necessary to inquire, but we unhesitatingly record that our settlement recognizes all existing proprietary rights, and that the proprietor has the fullest liberty to assign his land to under tenants upon whatever terms he chooses, and which right is everywhere exercised.[7]

Thus, they proclaimed that the principle of the Bombay system of land-tax administration was not to absorb the 'whole rent' which means the 'economic rent' in the terminology of the political economy.[8] Equipping themselves with this theory, they embarked on the reorganization of the land-tax system early in the 1840s, after the land-tax administration of R.K. Pringle, their predecessor, had devastated the country.[9]

The land-tax rates of Pringle were based on the principle that the land tax of all classes of land should constitute 55 per cent of the rent, that is to say, the net produce [= gross produce - (cost price + average profit)]. In this case therefore the more fertile was a land the bigger would the profit of the cultivator (= net produce - land tax) become.

As opposed to this, Wingate made it his principle that all classes of land should produce the same amount of profit for the cultivators irrespective of the land's fertility, granted the same amount of capital be invested on the lands. In this case, the more fertile the land was the heavier the land tax was to become along with the proportional gradation of the land's fertility.

Thus, both Pringle and Wingate based their land-tax rates on the rent theory of the political economy. The economic conditions prevailing in India at that time, however, were so different from those in England that the land-tax rates of both Pringle and Wingate were destined to disagree with the Indian social reality and in fact amounted almost to rack-renting. This becomes clear only when their land-tax rates are compared to those of Goldsmid based on the expediential principle that the land tax of all classes of land should be settled in accordance with the customary rates obtaining in pre-colonial western India. The land-tax rates of Goldsmid thus reached were almost half of those of Pringle and Wingate.[10]

Conclusion

The land rights of peasants in the pre-colonial Deccan designated as *mirāsī* or *vatanī mirās* was incorporated within the framework of the Vatan system which comprised various communal relationships among the *mirāsdārs* (*vatandār* Kunbis) and *bārā balute* of a village. This land right was therefore not 'absolute' by nature as in the case of the modern property right, while it incorporated a broader implication than the modern landed property. The proprietor of the *mirāsī* or *vatanī mirās* land also had the right to possess a house land in the *vāḍā* (residence area of a village) and could enjoy social privileges such as invitation to a marriage feast of a fellow *mirāsdār* (*vatandār* Kunbi) or participation in village festivities. At the same time, the proprietor of the *mirāsī* or *vatanī mirās* land had to take joint responsibility of the village community specifically in reference to taxes levied on the village as a whole. Thus, this land right of *mirāsī* or *vatanī mirās* constituted its possessors full-fledged members of the village community with its accompanying rights and duties. On introduction of the Raiyatwari Settlement, British administrators in the Bombay Presidency did not take into consideration this peculiar nature of the land rights enjoyed by *mirāsdārs* (*vatandār* Kunbis), only seeing in it the private landed property in the modern sense. It is therefore a matter of course that the Raiyatwari Settlement functioned towards changing the nature of the land rights of peasants and thus disintegrating the communal structure of the villages based on the Vatan system. This was done by separating the land rights of the peasants from communal relationships among *mirāsdārs* (*vatandār* Kunbis) and *bārā balute* which had been sustaining the very land rights of peasants in the medieval Deccan.

Notes

1 The monumental work in this field of historical research is, without doubt, I. Habib's *Agrarian System of the Mughal India 1556-1707*, Bombay, 1963.

2 Report of the Honourable Mountstuart Elphinstone to the Governor-General, dated 25 October 1819, in R.E.I.H., Vol. IV, pp. 159-60.

3 H.D. Robertson, Esq. to William Chaplin, Esq. dated 10 October 1821, in R.E.I.H., Vol. IV, pp. 538-39, para. 44.

4 'The respectability of a Meerassdar' itself was recognized to a certain degree by administrators of the Bombay Presidency, though it did not influence the land policy of the Bombay government. See Guha 1987: 120-21.

5 This *meeras puttee* runs as follows:

> A *meeras puttee* is erected in Sicky 1707 Sumverstser (A.D. 1785) ... in favour of Gunnesh Konhere, Koolkurnee of Ahmednugger kusba ... by the Mocuddum and Seerusth Dashyjan of the village of Errowna, turruf Havaily, of the aforesaid pranth ... to the following effect, viz. In the aforesaid village it having been unanimously agreed to erect a temple to Shree Marotee, and also unanimously resolved to raise the funds requisite for doing so, by granting land in meeras on paying a sum of money, and you having accepted the offer, we made an agreement for your receiving six rookas of land on the payment of Rupees 301. Now, ... you are hereby constituted the owner in meeras of six rooka of the sourthern part of Kokerpathee thul, which altogether consists of twenty-four rookas of land. The description and bounds of the portion thus assigned to you are as follows: [Here roads and boundaries of other fields are described.] You are also hereby entitled to occupy the under-described ghutcool land within the village, in length fifty haths and in breadth twenty-five. [Here enter the bounds.] The above described six rookas of land of the Kokerpathee estate (thul), and vacant spot in the village for building upon, are accordingly hereby assigned to you in meeras, which you and your descendants shall enjoy unmolested, it being incumbent on you, however, to pay the sarra due to the Dewan [government], and the Khurrede Gulla, and

jewar ava, and other dues (wugheiry, purely pawn), whatever they may be, according to the custom of the village.... We have admitted you to be a meeras bhow: neither do we or any other person possess any right of interference in the above described lands ... [R.E.I.H., Vol. IV, pp. 534-35, para. 38].

6 Ibid., para. 46.

7 Report made to the Revenue Commissioner, under date the 27th October, 1840, by Mr. Goldsmid and Captain Wingate, as to the applicability to the Deccan of the plan of settlement followed in the North-Western Provinces, and furnishing information as to the Revenue System obtaining in the Deccan, and the operations carried on by the Revenue Survey Department, *Official Correspondence on the System of Revenue Survey and Assessment best adapted and more or less completely carried into effect in the Collectrates of Poona, Sholapoor, Ahmednuggur, Belgaon, and Dharwar, in the Bombay Presidency with an Appendix*, Bombay, 1850, Appendix p. 2.

8 The following extracts from Wingate's letter dated 23 December 1848 prove that the 'rent' in their report means the 'economic rent' of the political economy:

> 13. The most effective means at our command for preventing the land becoming the inheritance of a pauper, or at least poverty-stricken, peasantry, is to afford the greatest possible facilities for its conveyance from one party to another, so that when a cultivator becomes impoverished, and, by his inability to cultivate his land properly, deprives the community of the wealth it is capable of producing, that the land may get into the hands of some one better able to turn it to advantage....
>
> 16. I am inclined to think the process for ejectment just described would prove a very effective expedient for realizing the revenue, and when it failed in this, it would yet have the obvious advantage of getting land out of the hands of a person unequal to the discharge of the responsibility connected with its occupancy, and wherever there happened to be a demand for land, secure, by the sale of the title to the highest bidder, that it should fall into the possession of a person of means. By thus bringing land into the market, traders, pensioners, and other parties having capital, would probably be induced to lay it out in the purchase of land, to the great benefit of agriculture and the community at large [*Official Correspondence on the System of Revenue Survey and Assessment...*, pp. 67-68].

9 As to the causes of failure of Pringle's settlement, see Hatekar 1996.

10 See Tables D and E in Kumar 1968: 118, 120 for comparison of the land-tax rates of Pringle, Wingate and Goldsmid.

3

Dyadic Relationships at Work within the Vatan System with Special Reference to the Jajmani System

Introduction

As indicated in Chapter 1, the system of the division of labour in the local society in the later medieval Deccan can be conceptualized as the Vatan system. The Vatan system comprised two dimensions or layers, that is to say, the district (*parganā*) level and the village level. Of these two, the village-level division of labour constituted the basic dimension, wherein existed one set of service providers collectively called *bārā balute* or *bārā balutedārs* (12 sorts of *balutedārs* or *balute*-holders), with *balute* meaning remuneration or perquisites given to them by the village community. The *bārā balute* usually included: (1) artisan castes such as the Sutar (carpenter), Lohar (ironsmith) and Kumbhar (potter); (2) service castes like the Nhavi (barber) and Parit (washerman); (3) religious personnel comprising the Joshi (priest), Gurav (temple-keeper) and Maulana (Muslim mentor); and (4) some untouchable castes like the Mahar, Mang and Chambhar (Fukazawa 1991: 209ff.).

Each *balutedār* had respective *vatans* such as *Sutārkī*, *Jośīpaṇa* and *Mahārkī*, such that *balutedārs* were also called *vatandārs* (*vatan*-holders). *Balutedārs* were indispensable members of a village community, with their *vatans* being bestowed on them by the village community, while they belonged to their respective castes at the same time. Thus, for example, anyone who was not a member of the Sutar caste could not be the *vatandār* (*balutedār*) Sutar of a village, but conversely, no Sutar could be the *vatandār* Sutar of a village without possessing the *Sutārkī vatan* of the village by inheritance or other means. This denotes that the system of the division of labour in a village in the later medieval Deccan was formed by the combination of two different types of communities, that is, the village communities (so to speak, regional communities) and the caste communities (that is, network-type communities).

This division of labour in a village between the *balutedārs* (*vatandārs*) and the *vatandār* Kunbis (peasants who were the full-fledged members of a village community) still remains a difficult subject for historians, with many details yet to be scrutinized. The first example of this difficulty is whether the average size of the villages in the later medieval Deccan was large enough to accommodate all of the members of *bārā balute*.[1] The second was what the actual relationship was between an individual *balutedār* and peasants (*vatandār* Kunbis) within the fabric of the communal or aggregate relationships between the *balutedārs* and the village community as a whole. This chapter specifically aims at addressing the second of these problems with special reference to the so-called Jajmani system in the historical perspective of structural changes in the system of the division of labour which were brought about during the nineteenth century under British colonial rule.

The Concept of the Jajmani System in the Historical Context

One of controversial topics of the historical study concerning India has been whether or not the Jajmani-type relationship between peasants and service providers existed in medieval societies in India. The major trend of sociological studies on the Jajmani system tacitly regards the Jajmani-type relationship as a relic of the systems of division of labour in pre-capitalist societies such as Indian village communities. These studies thus necessarily presuppose that the Jajmani-type division of labour existed in medieval societies of India. Simon Commander, as an example, asserted that the Jajmani-type relationship, as such, had been giving way to a more individual or commercial system of dividing labour even in the 1930s when W.H. Wiser first found the Jajmani-type division of labour in a village in northern India and thus put forward the concept of the Jajmani system (Commander 1983).

Opposing this prevailing view, Peter Mayer claimed that the Jajmani system is of recent origins, probably being formed in the last quarter of the nineteenth century. One of the grounds on which he based his contention is the fact that *mirāsdārs* and *balutedārs* (*vatandārs*) in south India and the Deccan in the eighteenth and early nineteenth centuries were nothing other than 'servants of an entire village' which is assumed to be incompatible with the Jajmani-type relationship. In his proof of this, he quoted several passages from H. Fukazawa's article, 'Rural Servants in the Maharashtrian Village: Demiurgic or Jajmani System?' (Mayer 1993: 365-66).

The conclusion of Fukazawa's article is that the *bārā balute* were 'village servants' serving the entire body of the village and being renumerated by the village as an aggregate in the form of service lands and/or agricultural products with payment in cash in some cases. He further asserted that the communal or holistic relationship between peasants and 'village servants' (*bārā balute*) was transformed into a bundle of individual relationships between a particular peasant and a particular service provider during the course of the nineteenth century as a result of the gradual breaking up of the holistic system of the division of labour in village communities under British colonial rule (Fukazawa 1991: 199-244). Peter Mayer drew upon this conclusion of H. Fukazawa to prove the non-existence of the Jajmani-type relationship in medieval societies in India and thus the recent origins of the Jajmani system.

Fukazawa, however, pointed out an important aspect pertaining to the village Joshi which Mayer completely neglected. The two medieval Marathi documents translated into English by Fukazawa clearly show that there existed an individual or dyadic relationship between the Joshi-Kulkarni of a village and a peasant family (first document), and between a Brahman family and some villagers (second document). In the second document, the villagers who required the private services of the Brahman priest were designated as his *yajmānas* (Fukazawa 1991: 235-37; Kulkarni 1996: 172-73). Though the village Joshi was a sort of 'village servant' who conducted the village rituals, he held individual and dyadic relationships as family priest (*gharopādhyā*) with other villagers as well which might have constituted the 'prototype of the so-called jajmani system' (Fukazawa 1991: 237). This implies that one such alternative phrasing of a question as follows is very problematic: Whether this constitutes the Jajmani system or the holistic ('demiurgic' in Fukazawa's terminology) system of the division of labour. These two systems of the division of labour actually coexisted in medieval Indian villages as discussed by Fukazawa and will be further proved below.

Dyadic Relationships within the Vatan System

Thus, there are two remaining problems to be investigated. For one, it must be true that the *bārā balute* (*balutedārs*) served an entire village body and were renumerated by a village as a whole. One must ask, however, what the individual relationships were between an individual *balutedār* and villagers, in addition to the holistic relationship between the *balutedārs* and the village community. For another, it must be unquestionable that the holistic or communal relationship between peasants and the *bārā balute* was transformed into a more individual or commercial relationship during the course of the nineteenth century through gradual breaking up of the holistic system of the division of labour in the villages. The question here then, however, is what the concrete process of this transformation was.

Concerning the first problem, that is, the dyadic relationships between an individual *balutedār* and each peasant in a village, some documents in Marathi are of interest. As an example, in the certificate (*dākhalepatra*) given to the Parit (washermen) of Cheul District, their duties and perquisites are enumerated as follows:

1. When the Parit spread *pāighadyā* [the cloths at a wedding that are spread from the place at which the bridegroom's party alight to the house of the bride], they shall take four *lahārīs* [1 *lahārī* = 3 *ānas*] with a meal.
2. When the Parit overlay *maṇḍapa* [an open hall erected temporarily for a marriage ceremony] with cloth, they shall take four *lahārīs* with a meal.
3. When the Parit give a robe and turban [cleansed by them] to the bridegroom at the marriage of the Shudra castes, they shall take two *lahārīs*.
4. When the Parit sing a song on the occasion of a marriage of the Shudra castes, they shall take one *lahārī* with a meal.
5. When the Parit wash the clothes of the bride and bridegroom, they shall take one *lahārī* from the bride and two *lahārīs* from the bridegroom.
6. On the occasion of Dasara, the *zamīndār* shall give a turban [cleansed by the Parit] to the following persons: Deshmukh, Deshpande,....
7. When the Parit wave a burning lamp around the head of an idol on the occasion of Dasara and Navaratra, they shall take one *sajgāṇī* [two *pāis*].

(S.C.S. X 4)

This document denotes that the Parit had various dyadic and individual relationships of services-perquisites with peasants on differing occasions. The Parit as a member of *bārā balute* must have been rewarded for his service to the village by the village as a body. However, he could get perquisites from individual peasants when he provided specific services to them. This indicates that there existed dyadic and individual relationships between each *balutedār* and each peasant operating within the framework of the holistic system of dividing labour in a village.

These dyadic and individual relationships between each *balutedār* and each peasant are discernible as well in the case of untouchable castes. In a lawsuit decided in the Bombay Sadr Divani Adalat (the predecessor of the Bombay High Court existed up to 1862)[2] in 1849, the following points were confirmed by the court and both parties to the suit as well:

> ... that by ancient usage, whenever a bullock died in the village, the Mahars took off the skin, and made it over to the owner of the animal, receiving renumeration in grain for their trouble, at the rate of five seers for a large bullock, and four seers for a small one;....
>
> It appears that the special appellants [*vatandār* Mahars] in this case do not object to the right of the wutundars [peasants] to receive back the skins of such of their dead bullocks as were used for draught: they urge that the disposal by the owners of the carcasses of other animals not used for draught is illegal, and contrary to usage;... the defendants [peasants] do not appear to have prevented the plaintiffs [*vatandār* Mahars] from carrying away the skins of other animals.
>
> (6 B.S.D.A. 68)

Two important points should be emphasized in this decision. First, it was the custom of the country that the *vatandār* (*balutedār*) Mahars of a village could take the skins of dead animals other than draught bullocks as their perquisites. One Marathi document of the year 1776 confirms that the *vatandār* Mahar of a village could take the skins of dead animals of villagers even including *vatandār* Mangs other than draught bullocks (S.S.R.P.D. VI 816). (See Chapter 6 for the English translation of this document.) The second point which is relevant to the problem of dyadic and individual relationships between each *balutedār* and peasants is that the *vatandār* Mahar received renumeration in the form of a certain amount of grain for their service of skinning dead bullocks and delivering the skins to the owners. This means that there were dyadic and individual relationships of services-remuneration between the *bārā balute* and the peasants in the case of the *vatandār* Mahar as well. Thus, dyadic and individual relationships operating within the framework of the Vatan system are discernible not only with the village Joshi (*gharopādhyā*) as proved by H. Fukazawa but also with other members of *bārā balute* like the *vatandār* Mahar.[3]

These dyadic and individual relationships between the *bārā balute* and peasants at work within the framework of the holistic system of dividing labour in a village (the Vatan system) might have become prominent when the holistic system of dividing labour in the village communities collapsed. However, the problem here revolves around the concrete process of the collapse or disintegration of the holistic system of the village communities under British colonial rule (the second problem posed earlier).

Important source material throwing light on this second question and again on the first one is another legal decision held by the Bombay Sadr Divani Adalat. This document was formerly utilized by W.H. Wiser for the purpose of proving that the Jajmani system had been further strengthened by civil law under British colonial rule, though it seems to be a misinterpretation of the document as will be shown below (Wiser 1988: xxvi-xxvii). The following quotation is the written legal decision handed down by the court which pertains to *balute haqqs* of the *vatandār* Lohar of a village in Dharwar District. (Wiser extracted the underlined portion below from this document in his work.)

Hunnappa, Lohar, Plaintiff, Appellant,
versus
Hunmunna, Sepoy, Defendant, Respondent.
Rupees 20-0-0

This action was filed by the Plaintiff, in the Court of the Moonsiff of Roan, to recover from the Defendant his bulloottee hucks, for the year 1838, in the village of Hosour, within the Dharwar Zillah. The Plaintiff stated that, by the ancient custom of the country, he, as the hereditary village ironsmith of Hosour, was entitled to 11 phalies of jowaree and 1.5 ruts of kurbee from the Defendant. Plaintiff therefore laid his claim at ten times the value of these articles, and filed this suit to recover the same and to establish his right to the said hucks.

The Defendant though summoned did not attend to reply.

The Moonsiff of Roan (Gondoo Temajee) held that the Plaintiff, as the hereditary ironsmith of his village, for which he paid a tax to Government, was entitled, by the custom of the country, to receive from the Defendant, a fellow villager, his bulloottee hucks, whether the Defendant employed Plaintiff as an ironsmith or not. The Moonsiff therefore gave judgment in the Plaintiff's favor.

On appeal the Zillah Judge (J.A. Shaw) was of opinion, that it did not appear the Plaintiff was obliged to work for the Ryots [*ra'īyat*], and therefore he considered it rested with the Ryots whether they employed the Plaintiff as an ironsmith, and paid him his hucks or not; for these reasons the Judge reversed the Decree of the Moonsiff. Costs on the Plaintiff.

The Plaintiff then prayed the admission of a special appeal in the Sudder Dewanee Adawlut, which was allowed, on the grounds that the decision passed by the Judge appeared contrary to the custom of the country and subverted the Bulloottee system.

The Sitting Judge (G. Giberne) held that the Zillah Judge has taken an erroneous view of the subject, and that his decision tended to upset a custom universally acknowledged, and endangered the constitution and foundation of all village communities established from time immemorial. The Sitting Judge was satisfied with the evidence taken before the Moonsiff, and considered the Bullootteedars were entitled to their hucks from every villager, according to the rules of the village communities; and that if the villagers declined to employ their services, to which they were entitled, they must pay the Bulloottee hucks. Under this view, the Sitting Judge referred the case to a full Court for final judgment.

The full Court (present S. Marriot, G. Giberne, and D. Greenhill) concurred in the opinion of the Sitting Judge, and therefore reversed the Decree of the Zillah Judge, and affirmed that of the Moonsiff. Costs on Defendant.

(4 B.S.D.A. 8)[4]

This document provides clues for clarifying the actual relationship existing between peasants and the *bārā balute* (*balutedārs*) as well as the concrete process of the breaking up of the holistic system of the division of labour in the villages.

Firstly, the court held that Hunnappa, 'the hereditary village ironsmith' (*vatandār* Lohar) of the village Hosour was entitled to receive his 'bulloottee hucks' (*balute haqqs*) comprising a certain amount of jowaree and kurbee, from 'a fellow villager', Hunmunna. Indicated here is that *balute haqqs* were collected individually and directly from each villager, such that there existed the dyadic and individual relationships between the villagers and individual *balutedārs* within the holistic framework of the Vatan system as demonstrated earlier. Conversely, these dyadic and several relationships between peasants and the *bārā balute* were bound together to constitute the holistic or communal division of labour in the village communities.

Secondly, the court also held that the *vatandār* Lohar was entitled to receive his *balute haqqs* from an individual peasant, even though the peasant did not ask or declined his services as an ironsmith. In other words, the *vatandār* Lohar could claim his *balute haqqs* as a matter of right regardless of whether he provided his services. The court generally admitted this right of *vatandārs* (*balutedārs*) on the ground that it constituted the 'foundation of all village communities established from time immemorial'. The meaning here is that the dyadic and individual relationship between villagers and a *balutedār* was not a relationship that was somewhat analogous to either Jajmani-type relationship as was indicated by Wiser or to a contract between two independent parties. In other words, the individuality or severalty of this dyadic relationship was merely a part of the holistic communal division of labour in village communities.

It follows from the foregoing discussion that the concrete process of the breaking up of the holistic system of dividing labour in the village communities was the abolition or disavowal of the *balutedārs*' communal right to receive *balute haqqs* as a matter of right from villagers whether they served the villagers or not. This right of *balutedārs* constituted the focal point of legal issues under British colonial rule since it was at variance with the concept of the freedom of contract.

Of this right of *balutedārs*, the most severely contested in the Bombay Sadr Divani Adalat and Bombay High Court was that of the village Joshi (*vatandār* Joshi) as *gharopādhyā* to officiate at ceremonies in villagers' homes (his *yajmānas*' homes) and receive *haqqs* from them. The leading case in this regard had been Special Appeal No. 3674 of 1857 in which it was decided that the *vatandār* Joshi of a village was entitled to receive his *haqqs* from villagers who celebrated a marriage, even though they did not request the *vatandār* Joshi's services, employing other Brahmans to officiate at the ceremony (11 B.S.D.A. 111). This decision was in line with the above-mentioned decision of the Bombay Sadr Divani Adalat pertaining to the *vatandār* Lohar.

This line of judicial judgement began to change in the 1880s, however, under the influence of the concept of the contract as well as from the political pressure of the Satya Shodhak Samaj, the organ of the

Non-Brahman movement in Maharashtra, established by Jotirao Phule in 1873.

In 1888, a dispute between the *vatandār* Joshi of the village Otur and villagers who were activists of the Satya Shodhak Samaj occurred over the hereditary right of the *vatandār* Joshi. The focal point at issue was whether the *vatandār* Joshi could claim *haqqs* despite circumstances that he was not employed to officiate at a marriage ceremony. Satya Shodhaks claimed that they were not bound to give *haqqs* to the *vatandār* Joshi on the grounds that they followed the Satya Shodhak-style marriage ceremony without performing any Hindu-style rituals. The Bombay High Court admitted their claim and decided that so long as no Hindu-style rituals were performed, the villagers were not obliged to pay *haqqs* to the *vatandār* Joshi (14 B. 167). This new line of decision was confirmed by another decision handed down by the Bombay High Court in 1918 (42 B. 613). Finally in 1925, the *vatandār* Joshi's right to receive *haqqs* as a matter of right from villagers who did not employ his services was legally abolished by the Invalidation of Hindu Ceremonial Emoluments Act enacted by the Bombay government.[5]

This same change is discernible in the case of the *vatandār* Mahar. As mentioned before, the skins of dead cattle other than draught bullocks had been perquisites of the *vatandār* Mahar in the medieval Deccan and in the early phase of British colonial rule as well. In the latter half of the nineteenth century, however, this line of judicial judgement began to change towards regarding the skins of all dead cattle as belonging to the owner of the cattle while alive. The Bombay High Court pointed out in this regard in the decision decreed in 1870 as follows:

> ... it has been repeatedly decided in this court, in suits for proceeds of the carcasses of dead cattle between the Mahars and the ryot owners of the cattle, that the person who owned the cattle while alive has also a right to the property in the dead carcasses of such cattle, and may dispose of it to anybody he pleases.
>
> [8 B.H.C.R. (A.C.J.) 28][6]

This legal and judicial procedure of abolishing the *vatandār* Joshi's and *vatandār* Mahar's communal rights based on the Vatan system proceeded side by side with the non-legal course of the lapse of the similar right of the *bārā balute* in general. Such a disavowal of the communal principle of village communities as this would have given birth to more individual or commercial relationships between peasants and service providers, which in turn would have transformed the organization of village communities based on the Vatan system itself.

Conclusion

The concrete process of the breaking up of the holistic division of labour in the village communities can be concluded as follows. The communally encapsulated dyadic and individual relationships operating between individual *balutedārs* and villagers within the Vatan system began to be dismantled and became prominent in the latter half of the nineteenth century under British colonial rule. The focal point at issue in this process was the *balutedārs*' right to receive the fees (*balute haqqs*) from the villagers even though they did not provide services to them. With the abolition of this hereditary right of *balutedārs*, more direct or contractual relations between service providers and peasants began to emerge though hereditary and personal relationships between them continued to be retained to a certain degree. However, the question of whether or not this transformed dyadic relationship can be characterized as a Jajmani-type relationship remains open for further studies (cf. Orenstein 1965).

Notes

1 It is difficult to find in medieval Marathi documents demographic records that indicate the population composition of villages in the medieval Deccan. The only source material which would be available in this regard are documents pertaining to the collection of *jizya* though they rarely appear in the authentic compilations of medieval Marathi documents.

In 1679, Aurangzeb decided to impose the *jizya* on non-Muslims and actually levied it in the northern part of the Deccan placed under his direct rule (Wink 1986: 78-79, n. 78). Among the documents preserved by the Deshpande family of Nevasa District, there is one document which can be called the *jizya* account of this district for the fiscal year 1684-85. This document provides us with some useful information concerning the population composition of villages of this district as shown in Table 1 below (S.C.S. IV 694).

The *jizya* being levied only on healthy adult males except for paupers, the following can be deduced from the figures in Table 1: (1) The average number of families per village was 8, (2) the average number of males per family was 1.7, (3) the assumed average number of females per family was 1.7, and (4) the assumed total number of persons per family was 3.4.

Table 1: Population Composition of Nevasa District

Total number of villages	144
Villages taxed	70
Total number of families in taxed villages	564
Total number of males in taxed villages	957
Non-taxable males in taxed villages	394*

*29 Elderly, 159 Children, 16 Blind, 162 Paupers, 10 Lepers, 11 Lame, 7 Arm-handicapped

This means that the number of families in one village was very small, and that the family form in villages of the medieval Deccan was a type of nuclear family with an average membership of only 3 or 4 though these finding might be partly due to the devastation caused by the war of invasion of Aurangzeb. Other documents pertaining to the *jizya*, especially unpublished *jizya* records of Indapur District found by A.R. Kulkarni in the Pune Archives, seem to present the similar picture (Kulkarni 1996: 176-208).

2 The Bombay Sadr Divani Adalat was amalgamated with the Bombay Sadr Faujdari Adalat and Supreme Court of Bombay to establish the Bombay High Court in accordance with the High Courts Act of 1861.

3 See also Chapters 7 and 8 of this volume for further details of the dyadic relationships between the *vatandār* Mahar and villagers, and between the village Joshi and villagers respectively.

4 Cases of this sort very rarely appear in the compilations of decisions handed down by the Bombay Sadr Divani Adalat. Another rare example is the case pertaining to a dispute over 'buloote wutun' of the village 'sootar' combined with the office of 'poojaree' in the year 1856 (10 B.S.D.A. 436).

5 For further details of this process of abolition of Joshi *vatan*, see Chapter 8 of this volume. This abolition process would seem to contradict the idea that the gifts (*dān*) given by the *jajmans* (*yajmānas*) to the priest transfer the evil (*pāp*) and poison (*viṣ*) from the former to the latter (Raheja 1988a: 31-33). The village Joshis of the Deccan from the seventeenth to twentieth centuries used to demand perquisites (*haqqs*) as a matter of right from their *yajmānas* with no fear of being imbued with any evil or poison accruing from the gifts.

6 For additional details of this process of abolition of the Mahar *vatan*, refer to Chapter 7 of this volume.

4

Structure of the Caste in Seventeenth-to-Nineteenth Century Western India: The Rural Caste in the Deccan and the Urban Caste in Coastal Gujarat

Introduction

Traditionally, the caste system has been more of a preferred topic for sociologists and anthropologists than for historians. Historical studies of the caste system have been conducted under disadvantageous circumstances due to the dearth of historical source materials, especially of the period immediately following the fall of Harshavardhana's empire, that is to say, the generally assumed period of the formation of the caste system. Recent polemics in sociological and anthropological studies of the caste system are stimulating historians' renewed interest in this field of research, however, since the focal point of these studies is the relationship of the caste system to kingship, which is a topic requiring, by nature, a historical perspective.

Recent studies of kingship in sociology and anthropology emphasize the central role of kingship in maintaining social order through its ritual function of maintaining auspiciouness. This emphasis on the role of kingship, and the ideology of auspiciouness-inauspiciousness embodied in the king's person, is a sort of antithesis to what has been called Brahman-centric understanding of the caste system often associated with L. Dumont by which the pureness-impureness ranking of castes headed by the Brahman is recognized as playing a pivotal role in maintaining societal order. Thus, recent sociological and anthropological studies of kingship in relation to the caste system have succeeded in posing new questions about the caste system though further historical documentation remains an urgent necessity to prevent speculative discussion on kingship.[1]

This chapter aims to throw new light on the structure of the caste in seventeenth-to-nineteenth century western India as an indispensable prerequisite for the study of the caste system in connection with kingship, which constitutes the topic of Chapter 9 of this volume. The focal point of discussion in this chapter will be the categorization of the rural caste and the urban caste. Regarding the rural caste in the Deccan, medieval Marathi documents, exceptionally rich in quality as well as quantity, have been freely utilized while they reveal practically nothing about the urban caste. On the other hand, judicial documents recorded under the early British adminstration, specifically decisions handed down by the Bombay Sadr Divani Adalat (the predecessor of the Bombay High Court)[2] provide quite useful information on the urban caste of coastal Gujarat.

Structure of the Rural Caste in the Deccan

The Rural Caste as the Primary Collective at the District Level

MARRIAGE AND COMMENSALITY

The marital relation (*lagnavyavahāra*) and commensal relation (*anna-vyavahāra*) constituted the ties uniting the collective commonly known as the caste (*jāti*). As such, however, the collectivity of the rural caste was twofold. Its primary unit of collectivity was the district (*pargaṇā*) which consisted of scores of villages. Put another way, the rural caste as the primary collective was welded together district (*pargaṇā*)-wise. This primary unit of collectivity was usually denominated as *gota* in medieval Marathi documents as the expression of the 'Mali *gota* of Sevaganv District' in the following case indicates. This unit of the district (*pargaṇā*) was, however, not a mere administrative unit of a state like the Maratha kingdom. It was in origin the unit of the local society or locality, which had been formed long before the establishment of the Maratha kingdom, with a sort of communal structure employing the Deshmukh and Deshpande as its leaders. The Maratha kingdom merely adopted this pre-existent unit of the local society as its administrative unit. Thus, quite naturally the rural caste as the primary collective was bound together district-wise. The caste collectivity, however, stretched across this primary collective at the district level and formed a secondary network connecting many primary collectives of the same caste in neighbouring districts. That is to say, the primary collective of a district joined with similar primary collectives of neighbouring districts through various ties with ever diminishing closeness as the network extended further out. Accordingly, this twofold structure of the rural caste should always be born in mind when discussing the caste and caste system.

Thus marital relations, one of the mainstays of caste collectivity, included marriages within the boundary of the primary collective at the district level as well as marriages beyond the boundary of a district. It seems, however, that marriages within the boundary of a district were more common than marriages beyond it since in the latter case a number of exceptional circumstances were often involved.

In one case under the Maratha rule in 1765, the caste-membership of a Mali (caste of gardeners) by the name of Bhavan, who had come to Sasvad District from Sevaganv District and continued to live there for some 20 to 25 years, came under suspicion on the ground that his mother might not have been of the Mali caste but of another caste. Nine headmen (*mhetars*) of the Mali of Sasvad District, therefore, informed the government (Peshva government) of this suspicion, in which response the government sent a soldier with an order to investigate. Both parties concerned proceeded to Sevaganv carrying the government order in the company of the soldier. They procured a certificate of the Mali *gota* of Sevaganv District in which, however, nothing whatever about the caste relation of Bhavan's mother was written. Since Bhavan's father was certified as being a Mali, but the caste of his mother thus remained undecided, the caste members of the Mali of Sasvad District suspended their commensal relation with him and his wife's family. Knowing this, the government intervened and suggested the solution that Bhavan be made to hold a caste commensal meeting (*gota jevaṇa*) as a prerequisite for his readmission into the caste to which both parties agreed. Thus, the government commanded the official in charge to order him to hold a commensal meeting in accordance with his means of livelihood. At the same time, the government order was issued to the caste members of the Mali of Sasvad District for the purpose of having them reaccept Bhavan into their caste (Oturkar no. 173).

It was a general practise that a marriage be conducted within the same caste, of the same district, where there was no doubt about the caste-membership of each member. In the above-cited case, however, the caste of Bhavan's mother was under suspicion on the ground that no one knew her personally as Bhavan had come from Sevaganv to settle in Sasvad District. The caste members suspended holding the commensal relation with him, as long as doubt about his caste remained, since the commensal relation with a person other than of one's own caste was prohibited. Thus, the commensality, the other mainstay of the collectivity of the caste, had the twofold function of inwardly consolidating the collectivity of the caste and outwardly distinguishing 'others' from the members of one's own caste.

According to the rule of commensality, it was a sin (*doṣa*) to take a meal with persons of other castes. Ranoji Jadhav of Nasik, as one example, ran mad and began to take his meals with persons of other castes, as a result of which he and his son, Gangaji, were excommunicated by their caste. They went to another village and lived there for two years until Ranoji died while still in his madness. Gangaji repented of their *doṣa* (sin) and thought that if the purification ceremony (*prāyaścitta*) could be performed on the bones of his father, as well as on himself, and if the funeral of his father could be conducted on the banks of the Godavari River, he would be released from the exclusion from the matrimonial and commensal relations of his caste. With this in mind, Gangaji presented himself before the Dharmadhikari of Nasik and asked him to perform *prāyaścitta* for his readmission to the caste (A.S.S. I 194. 1795).[3]

In another case, a Kasar (caste of braziers), Hiraman by name, was excommunicated by reason that he kept a *kuṇbīṇa* (female slave) and had a commensal relation (*annavyavahāra*) with her. The brother of Hiraman, who was also excommunicated on the grounds that his brother's sin was transmitted to him as well, presented the *doṣa-patra* (the statement of sin) to the Dharmadhikari of Nasik and asked him to perform *prāyaścitta* on him in order to be readmitted to the caste (A.S.S. I 190. 1791).[4]

These cases show that the rules regulating the marital and commensal relations were very rigid and that the violation of these rules was regarded as a sin that needed to be purified or removed by the purification ceremony collectively known as *prāyaścitta.* The rigidity of marital and commensal rules, however, did not exclude the possibility of a marriage between different castes, specifically the second marriage of a man with a woman of a lower caste as well as the giving-taking of food between different castes.

An interesting case in this regard was a dispute arising at the end of the eighteenth century between two castes, the Pancham (Vani) and the Charantijangam belonging to the Lingayat sect. This dispute occurred over the practice of marriage and the giving-taking of food. In it, Panchams claimed as follows:

> It is the traditional practice that we Panchams do not accept food in the home of other Lingayat castes than our own. People of other Lingayat castes, on the contrary, take a meal in the home of Panchams. Notwithstanding this practice, Charantijangams now claim that we Panchams also should take a meal in the home of all of the Lingayat castes as they do.

Against this claim by the Panchams, Charantijangams refuted that they would take a meal in the home of all of the Lingayat castes, and that people of all of the Lingayat castes, other than the Pancham, would take a meal with each other. The *pañcāīta* (panchayat) of Lingayat castes was, thus, convened to inquire into the matter and reached the following conclusion:

> It is the practice that in the home of Panchams people of other Lingayat castes may take a meal, sitting in a remoter place [from the dining place of the family], while Panchams may not accept food in the home of other Lingayat castes, and that Panchams may also accept women of other Lingayat castes as a *soyarī* (wife of second marriage). Judging from this practice, the Pancham is acknowledged as the highest caste in the Lingayat sect.
>
> (S.S.R.P.D. V 242. 1799-1800)

This document reveals the following two points with regard to marriage and commensality: Firstly, a man of a higher caste could take a woman of a lower caste as a *soyarī*. This could be understood against the background of the classical concept of *anuloma* (hair in a natural direction) marriage. In classical law books of India, marriage between a man of higher *varṇa* and a woman of lower *varṇa* (*anuloma* marriage) was tolerated, while the reverse case (*pratiloma* marriage) was strictly condemned. This classical concept of *anuloma-pratiloma* seems to have survived in the medieval Deccan in the altered form of *soyarī*. In this practice, the first wife should have been a woman of the same caste, but other wives could be women of lower castes. In this practice connected with *soyarī*, therefore, was reflected the highness-lowness relation among various castes in a given locality.[5] Secondly, social relationships finding expression in the giving-taking of food as well indicated the social ranking of castes. The general rule of the giving-taking of food was that food prepared by a member of a higher caste could be taken by members of lower castes, while members of a higher caste could not take food prepared by a member of a lower caste. This practice of the giving-taking of food prevailed in the medieval Deccan.[6]

The social relationships concerning marriage and commensality thus served two functions. First, the matrimonial and commensal relationships constituted the strong ties which bound the caste together and distinguished 'others' from the caste members. Second, the social relationships among various castes with regard to the second marriage and the giving-taking of food functioned as indicators of the social highness-lowness relation between two castes. An ensemble of these highness-lowness relationships between two castes formed a complete set of social rankings of all castes, which constituted what was called caste hierarchy in a given locality.

CASTE MEETING AT THE DISTRICT LEVEL

The rural caste as the primary collective at the district level, designated as *gota*, assembled itself in a caste meeting called *pañcāita* (panchayat) any time trouble arose within the caste.

In one case, a Teli (caste of oilmen) who participated in the battle of Panipat in 1761, went missing after the complete defeat of the Marathas at the hands of the Afghans. Thinking he was killed in the battle, the father-in-law remarried his daughter to another Teli taking Rs. 30 as the bride price. Some time after, however, the former husband returned home to find his wife remarried. He decided to divorce her by reason that she was regarded as having been polluted by her being remarried with another man while the former husband was still alive. Thus, the caste meeting of the Teli of Sasvad District was convened to certify the former husband's divorce and drew up the certificate of divorce (*sāṇḍkhat*), which was signed by the caste headmen (*mhetars*) and caste members of the Teli of Sasvad District, along with the *śeṭa* (head of a market) and *mahājana* (accountant of a market) of the *kasbe* Sasvad (Oturkar no. 129).

Troubles concerning marital or blood relationships often occurred in the medieval Deccan. To serve as an example, among Guravs (caste of temple-keepers) of Sasvad District, a dispute concerning the problem of whether or not two brothers were 'brothers of bones' (*hāḍbhāū*) arose. ('Brothers of bones' refers to brothers of the same parentage or brothers having a true blood relationship.) To settle this problem, the caste meeting of the Gurav of Sasvad District was convened (Oturkar no. 151).

Adultery was regarded as a sin (*doṣa*) that should be purified or removed by the purification ceremony collectively called *prāyaścitta*. In one such case, the caste meeting of the Mali of Sasvad District gave the following certificate (*gotapata-patra*) to a Sayaji Mali in 1748.

> Your daughter committed adultery [*bad amal*] with a man of the Tamboli such that she should have been punished. She however committed suicide, as a result of which you were excommunicated from the caste [as the sin of the suicide victim being deemed to be transmitted]. You then went to the Hozur [Peshva] and brought an order of the Peshva to the *gota* that ordered us to release you from the sin and make you fit for the commensality [*paṅktipāvana*]. The letter of the Deshmukh, Mokadam and Deshpande as well was sent to our *gota*. Thus all members of our *gota* assembled together in the *kasbe* Sasvad and sat with you in the caste commensal meeting held at your home for two days. You are now purified from your sin and are now fit for the commensality. Any one who opposes this will be seen as a criminal of the state as well as a wrongdoer against the *gota*.
>
> (Oturkar no. 167)

This type of certificate was denominated as *gotapata-patra* or *gota-patra*. *Gotapata* or *gotāī* means a series of ceremonies that were to be performed on the occasion of the readmission of an excommunicated member of a caste. In this case, the *gota* of the Mali of Sasvad District held the commensal meeting with the excommunicated at his home, and at his expense, to purify his sin. After the commensal meeting was over, the certificate of purification was issued by the Mali *gota* of Sasvad District, bearing also signatures of many caste headmen (*mhetars*) of the Mali of Pune, Supe, Sirval and other districts to lend authenticity to this certificate. The interesting point of this case is that the excommunicated was regarded as purified merely by holding the caste commensal meeting at his home without requiring the formal purification ceremony of *prāyaścitta* to be performed by the Dharmadhikari as shown in cases mentioned previously.

Thus, the caste meeting at the district level functioned within the caste as a type of mechanism for regulating social relationships and finding a solution in the event of trouble.

CASTE HEADMEN OF THE RURAL CASTE

The rural caste as the primary collective at the district level had one or several headmen called *mhetar* who played the dual role of outwardly representing the caste and maintaining order within the caste as some of the above-cited cases have already indicated.

In one case, the headman of the Chambhar (untouchable caste of skinners) of Supe District presented himself to the office of Shahaji, the father of Shivaji, who then held this district as *jāgīr*. The headman stated that the Chambhars of this district used to pay tax in kind using shoes instead of cash, but that at present the officials had been forcing them to pay in cash, as a result of which they were in a deplorable condition. The headman of the Chambhar thus appealed to Shahaji for a reversion to the tax in kind with which Shahaji complied and issued an order to the officials of Supe District purporting that they should not take even one *rukā* as tax. Along with this, he further ordered the officials to make all members of the Chambhar of this district, including Baramati Sub-district, obey the headman, Mal, even by force if necessary (M.I.S. XX 12).

The caste headman, thus, represented the caste in relation with the state or *jāgīrdār* by playing the role of protecting the interests of the caste members in return for which the headman could demand obedience from the caste members. The state or *jāgīrdār* also ordered the caste members to obey the caste headman, as the state or *jāgīrdār* required the authority of the caste headman who remained responsible for collecting the tax from the caste members, and then sending it to the district office.

The state bestowed gifts on the caste headman in return for his service of the collection of tax. In Sirval District, as an example, two brother headmen of the Kumbhar quarrelled with each other over gifts from the state which consisted of *taśrīf* (investment of a robe of honour) and *pāna* (betel leaves). In this dispute one party agreed to undergo the trial by ordeal called *ravā divya* (an ordeal of taking up a small piece of iron from boiling oil. S.C.S. I 34-36). A dispute among the Kumbhar headmen of Pune District broke out likewise over the right to receive gifts from the state. In this case, *vaḍīlpaṇa* (seniority) among the headmen was the point of issue as the headman who possessed *vaḍīlpaṇa* could receive gifts from the state including *viḍā*, *pāna*, *lugḍe* (a garment) and the right to wear *ṭiḷā* on the forehead (S.C.S. I 27. 1642).

The caste headman could receive perquisites from the caste members as well. In one case, the caste headman of the Atar (caste of Muslim perfumers) of Pune District appealed to the Peshva government for intervention in his trouble. As the caste headman of the Atar, he claimed, he had the right to receive *śelā* (shawl) and *pāna* on the occasion of marriage or ceremony of circumcision in the home of Atars, but that Buvaji of Pune made trouble for him by refusing to give perquisites. The government acknowledged the headman's claim and issued a deed of decision of the alleged purport (S.S.R.P.D. I 300. 1745-46).

The rural caste as the primary collective at the district level thus included the caste headman who represented the caste and kept it under control as well. In reward for these roles, the caste headman could receive gifts from the state and perquisites from the caste members.

Secondary Network of the Rural Caste

MARITAL RELATION BEYOND A DISTRICT

As mentioned before, the collectivity of the rural caste stretched beyond the primary collective at the district level to form a sort of caste network linking together the similar caste collectives of the neighbouring districts. This secondary network of the rural caste rather more concerned marital relations than of commensality. Marital relations beyond a district, however, often involved exceptional circumstances of one sort or other. It was therefore not uncommon for a marriage of this sort to result in a dispute.

In one such case, a dispute occurred among Koshtis (caste of weavers) of Pune District over the problem of whether or not children born by *baṭīkas* (femal slaves) could be accepted in the caste. The headman of the Koshti of Pune District appealed to the Peshva government for arbitration. He stated that Satvaji of Pune who was born by a *baṭīka* (*baṭkīcā vaṃśa*) had managed to undergo the ceremony of *gotāī* (the ceremony for admission to a caste) in Sangamner District by convincing three Koshtis of Pune to support him and he had actually succeeded in marrying a Koshti woman of Sangamner District, but that there was no practice of accepting into the caste children born by a *baṭīka* among the Koshtis. The caste headman of the Koshti thus petitioned the government to inquire into the matter and make a decision. The government accordingly summoned Satvaji and his three Koshti supporters for investigation. Satvaji claimed that Koshtis used to accept children born by a *baṭīka* and further stated that Koshtis of the villages Valhe and Nimbu would testify to this. The Koshtis of these two villages, however, denied his claim. Satvaji and three others then stated that they would obey the decision of the Koshti of several other districts. The government accordingly summoned caste headmen of Wai, Karad, Baramati and other districts, and respectively asked them whether or not they had been accepting into their caste children born by a *baṭīka* to which all of the headmen answered negatively. Upon hearing this, the government recognized the claim of the headman of Pune District and decided that as Satvaji was born *kaḍū* (bitter), he should not have a marital relation with a *caṅgalā* (good) Koshti (S.S.R.P.D. VII 763. 1768-69).[7]

In this case, Satvaji of Pune, who could not have been accepted in the Koshti *gota* of Pune District by reason of his birth by a *baṭīka*, managed to be accepted by the Koshti *gota* of Sangamner District and actually succeeded in marrying a Koshti woman there. Satvaji must have negotiated to conceal his birth by a *baṭīka* in Sangamner District where no one knew him personally. Marital relations beyond a district often involved such exceptional circumstances as this though there must have been cases unincumbered by such circumstances which hardly appear in a recorded document.

One important point in this case is that the procedure for reaching the decision concerning marriage beyond the boundary of a district itself seems to show that marriage within a district was the general practice. The very fact that the caste headmen of respective districts were respectively questioned as to whether or not the *gota* had a practice of accepting children born by *baṭīkas* suggests that marital relations within the boundary of a district was the rule, for if marriage beyond a district had been prevalent, a more common practice regarding marriage would have developed throughout the various districts.

Another essentially similar case occurred in the Gavli (caste of herdsmen) as well. A woman of the Gavli of Cheul District widowed by her husband's death began to cohabit with Harji, a Gavli of Kalyan District, without performing *muhūrtta* (ceremony of second marriage). A son, Chimaji, was subsequently born to them. Harji on his deathbed asked his formal (first) wife to appeal to the Gavli *gota* of Kalyan District to accept Chimaji into the caste. She accordingly appealed to the Gavli *gota* for the admission of Chimaji with which was complied. Some time thereafter, Chimaji's marriage was arranged to a Gavli girl of Pune District. At that time, the formal wife of Harji petitioned the government to summon the Gavli of Pune District and order them to acknowledge Chimaji as a member of the Gavli *gota* of Pune District. The government thus summoned the Gavli of Pune District and asked whether or not they would accept Chimaji to which they answered affirmatively. Upon this, the government issued an order to the Gavli *gota* of Pune District to accept Chimaji into the caste. At the same time a government order to the Gavli *gotas* of Mahaḍ, Pen and other districts was issued purporting to prohibit them from causing trouble regarding this (S.S.R.P.D. VII 750. 1762-63).

This case of marriage beyond a district as well involved exceptional circumstances of this boy's being born to parents who were not legally married. Furthermore, the fact that there existed no common practice among the various Gavli *gotas* with regard to the admission of such children as this is clear from the very procedure of individually inquiring of caste headmen of various districts.

THE EXTENDED CASTE MEETING BEYOND A DISTRICT

In the case of disputes involving caste members of several districts, the extended caste meeting beyond a district was convened in which representatives (*mhetars* and others) of the caste of many districts participated. The following dispute between the Simpi (caste of tailors) *gota* of Sasvad District and that of Pune District serves as a good example.

Gangaji Simpi of Sasvad District was excommunicated from the caste by reason of violating the marital rule of the caste. Gangaji then went to Pune and managed to be accepted into the Simpi *gota* of Pune District. The Simpi *gota* of Pune District, subsequently, wrote a letter to the Simpi *gota* of Sasvad District purporting that, as they had accepted Gangaji in the caste, the Simpi *gota* of Sasvad District should also behave in the same manner. To this the Simpi *gota* of Sasvad District responded that they did not know of the acceptance of Gangaji by the Simpi *gota* of Pune District, as there was a distance of 8 to 10 *kos* between Pune and Sasvad, and that Gangaji could not be accepted by the Simpi *gota* of other districts since he had not undergone the purification ceremony (*prāyaścitta*) at a sacred place, which was the prerequisite for the readmission of the excommunicated into the caste. The Simpi *gota* of Sasvad District thus suggested that the Simpi *gota* of Pune District would need to obtain the consent of the Simpi *gotas* of other districts for the readmission of Gangaji. The Simpi *gota* of Pune District, however, refused to comply, saying this issue had nothing to do with the purification ceremony at a sacred place or with gaining the consent of the Simpi *gotas* of other districts.

Some time thereafter, some Simpis of Pune District taking Gangaji with them, visited the home of Santaji Simpi of Sasvad to attend a marriage ceremony in his family. This caused great trouble between Santaji and the Simpis from Pune with the result that the Simpis from Pune refused to take a meal in the home of Santaji. At this juncture the government intervened ordering both parties to maintain the commensal relation as it was before. The Simpis of Sasvad District, however, refused to have a commensal relation with Gangaji while the Simpis from Pune

District rejected having commensality with Santaji. In the meantime, the invitation to a marriage ceremony of the family of Phirangoji of Pune was received by several Simpis of Sasvad District. All members of the Simpi *gota* of Sasvad District then assembled together and decided not to attend the marriage ceremony. Three Simpis of Sasvad were, however, obliged to attend it, as Phirangoji insisted on their attendance. After the ceremony was over, Phirangoji forcibly took the three Simpis from Sasvad to the marriage feast though they declined on the pretext of not being hungry. The Simpis of Pune District made Gangaji serve food to Gopalji, one of the three Simpis from Sasvad. Feeling offended, Gopalji left the commensal seat in rejection of this forced action. The Simpis of Pune District were enraged at this and beat Gopalji. Three Simpis from Sasvad, having been outnumbered, could not resist their behaviour. On their return home, the Simpi *gota* of Sasvad District was convened and decided that they should not take a meal in the home of the Simpis of Pune District and not to offer food to the Simpis of Pune District in their own homes as well (Oturkar no. 183).

This dispute was brought up in the meeting of the Simpi caste (*jāti pañca*) for a final decision. The Simpi *gota* of Pune District was decreed as being in the wrong and was levied Rs. 15,000 as a fine (*daṇḍa*), while the Simpi *gota* of Sasvad District was made to pay Rs. 10,000 to the government as a token of gratitude (S.P.D. XXII 230. 1773).

This *pañcāīta* of the Simpi caste could not constitute the caste meeting of a particular district as this case reached across the boundary of a district. It thus had to have been an extended caste meeting in which representatives of the Simpi *gotas* of many districts took part, though the exact composition and scale of this extended caste meeting is not known from the documents above.

Thus, the caste meeting which reached beyond a particular district was convened when any dispute involving several districts occurred. The extended caste meeting beyond a district did not, it seems, have a regulated form as was the case with the caste meeting held at the district level. The composition and scale of the extended caste meeting beyond a district is therefore assumed to depend on various circumstances such as the nature of the issue or the gravity of the situation.

To sum up briefly here, it can be said that the rural caste as the primary collective in the medieval Deccan, which was bound together within a district (*parganā*), formed the basic unit of collectivity of the caste, while the secondary network of the rural caste encompassing similar primary collectives in neighbouring districts constituted the secondary level of the collectivity of the caste. This twofold structure of the collectivity of the rural caste in the medieval Deccan brought about the necessity of holding caste meetings at two levels, that is, the caste meeting at the district level and the extended caste meeting beyond a particular district.

Structure of the Urban Caste in Coastal Gujarat

The Urban Caste as the Primary Collective at the Town Level

CASTE RULES REGULATING MARRIAGE AND COMMENSALITY

The existence of another type of caste in coastal Gujarat, quite different in nature from the rural caste in the Deccan, came to light merely through such English documents as civil decisions of courts of law established by the British in the Bombay Presidency. Notably medieval Marathi documents have scarcely shed any light on this type of caste. This caste in coastal Gujarat, categorized as the urban caste in this chapter, was commonly called 'Jamaut' (from the Arabic-Persian term '*jamā'at*' meaning a group, party or assembly), and the caste rule of those castes was referred to as 'Bundobust' (from the Persian term '*bandobast*'). The distinctive features of the urban caste were most clearly reflected in these Bundobusts. Under the early Bombay administration, caste rules registered at courts of law were regarded as having the same legal force as the law enacted by the state, such that many caste rules of various castes were registered at courts, especially in coastal Gujarat where British colonial rule began much earlier than in the Deccan.

The Surati (residents of Surat city) collective of the 'Ahmudabadee Beesa Khundaita Bunyuns' (specifically Ahmadabadi Visa Khadayata Vania. As to the romanizing of the caste name, I follow those rendered by Enthoven throughout this chapter.), as an example, registered the following rules regarding marriage at the district court of Surat in 1805.

> That any one giving his daughter in marriage to a man beyond the walls of Surat should be deemed an offender against the Government, and against their tutelar Deity Sree Kotha Rungjee, and should be held responsible to the Cast for such act, together with all aiding and abetting him, and that neither the giver, receiver, nor abettor, should be allowed to hold connexion with the Cast.
>
> That all Konkunees who had already betrothed their children in Surat should, when the marriage was celebrated, pay the usual sum of Rupees 150, at the Munder of Sree Kotha Rungjee, and give a dinner

to the Body corporate of the Cast (Sahjun Muhajun [from *sāhjan mahājan* in Gujarati meaning merchant gentlemen]) who should then attend the wedding procession.

That visitor (Pahona [from *pāhuṇā*]) Members of the Cast coming from Kulyan and other parts of the Konkun, or from Goojurat, or other country, should be entitled to attend the Feast without any hindrance.

That since many persons now took more as Dowry, than Rupees 262, the old established amount customarily taken on both sides the river Tappee, a full meeting should be held for the purpose of settling it.

That any one henceforth taking a bribe for the fixing of a marriage, should not hold connexion with the Cast.

That if the Bunyuns of Vesma, within the jurisdiction of Surat, gave their daughters in marriage to other than Vesma, or Surat, people, the Cast at Surat would cut them. That no one coming from another place to live at Surat should be allowed a share in Luhana [from *lahāṇī* in Gujarati meaning distribution of gifts] until he had been five years resident here, and had given Rupees 5 for the benefit of the fund for Cast cooking utensils, &c.

That any one coming from the Konkun to reside at Surat and paying these dues, should be allowed to receive Luhana.

This caste rule of the Surati collective of the Ahmadabadi Visa Khadayata Vania bore signatures of 146 members while the remaining 13 members did not sign for some reason or other.

Shumbhoodas Raeechund, one of the 13 members who did not sign, was excommunicated after the registration of this caste rule by reason that he married a daughter of his cousin to a man residing outside Surat city. He then filed a suit for damages of a thousand rupees on the plea that he was not able to marry her to a man, as the only man who could give her hand in marriage was her father and that he himself was not to be bound by this caste rule as he had not signed it. The defendants (the caste as a 'Body corporate') refuted that the caste made this rule on the grounds that poor members found difficulty in marrying their daughters due to the prevailing bad habit of rich members seeking brides outside Surat city by giving money, and that in spite of this the plaintiff married a small girl of his cousin less than two and half years of age taking Rs. 1,300, so that they temporarily excluded him from such formal association of the caste as attendance at the formal caste meeting but not from private association such as privately taking a meal together with him. The defendants thus claimed that no damage was caused to the plaintiff by their action.

The Bombay Sadr Divani Adalat, then located in Surat, decreed on appeal in favour of the plaintiff but at the same time recommended him and the other 12 members who had not signed the caste rule 'to become parties to it', 'viewing the object of the Bundobust as highly beneficial' (1 B.S.D.A. 347. 1808).[8]

Similar caste rules were made relative to the commensality as well. In one case, the Soni (caste of goldsmiths) of Surat city (the Surati Soni), belonging to the 'Ahmudabadkur Shreemalee' (Ahmadabadkar Shrimali Soni), made a caste commensal rule under the following circumstances. In 1809, a dispute broke out in this caste over the manner on the occasion of the caste commensal meeting. One Hurjeevun Lukmeechund of this caste held a commensal meeting at his home when some participants asked to have an abundance of food on a banana-leaf plate, and then tried to take home the leftovers. Hurjeevun Lukmeechund refused to allow it, which resulted in a dispute. On this, the caste headmen (Seth from '*śeṭ*' in Gujarati, in this case three in number) appealed to the Nyat Gour (from '*jñāt guru*' or '*jāt guru*' in Gujarati meaning a caste mentor or caste priest) to hold a caste meeting of all of the caste members (Ruyut from '*ra'īyat*' in Arabic-Persian). The caste meeting was thus held for two days and developed the following commensal rule after making a vow in one voice to Wagheshwuree, the tutelary god of this caste:

> 1st. That any Seth, or Ruyut leaving broken victuals at a Feast, pay a fine of 4 pice.
>
> 2d. That the fine to be taken from a person carrying away any Victuals, be, from one of the three Setheeas, or Head men, Rupees 2.5 and from a Ruyut Rupees 1.25. The Host wishing to send away Victuals to any one is to do it the next day.
>
> 3d. That no person be allowed to distribute the Victuals, but those requested to do so by the Host. Any person interfering in it without being asked, to pay a fine of Rupees 1.25.
>
> 4th. That the men of the caste do not go in until the Women have got up from Dinner, and the ground has been swept and cleansed, and the Host has called in the men. Any person offending against this, to be fined Rupees 1.25.
>
> 5th. That Lassee (a particular sort of food) be allowed to be left.
>
> 6th. That each person, on going to dinner, take one patul [from *pātal* in Gujarati meaning a dish made of banana leaves] and two Dhurreeas only, under a penalty of 4 pice.

7th. That the persons who undertake to wait upon the Cast during dinner, shall hand salt, water, and vegetables, to every person requiring them, under a fine of Rupees 1.50 on refusal.

8th. That the Cast commence eating on permission from the Brahmun.

9th. That any person Seth, or Ruyut, refusing to pay the fine prescribed for his fault, be excluded from future dinners till he pay the amount.

10th. That any person, of whatever rank in the Cast, deviating from this agreement, forfeit 51 Rupees to Government, and lose Cast for a whole year.

11th. That this paper be lodged in the Temple of Wagheshwuree, and that Bhaee Tooljaram be bound to give a sight of it to any member, under penalty on refusal of a fine of Rupees 5.

This caste rule bore signatures of 173 members who could be regarded as the entire membership of the Surati collective of the Ahmadabadkar Shrimali Soni. A suspicious point of this caste rule was, however, that some of the signatures seemed not to be signed by the members themselves, but by the Nyat Gour on their behalf. This caused trouble when a dispute broke out among the caste members over the commensality. One Kuhandas and another 19 members of this caste held a commensal meeting on the ocassion of the festival of Wagheshwuree without the sanction of the Nyat Gour. The caste headmen accused them of violating the caste commensal rule against which Kuhandas and the others refuted that this commensal rule had not been made with the consent of all of the caste members, as the caste headmen had made the Nyat Gour sign the names of the members who opposed this rule.

The Bombay Sadr Divani Adalat decreed on appeal that this commensal rule could not be recognized as legal since the caste rule was required to be made with the consent of the majority, if not all, of the caste members. The court, however, regretted that the caste headmen could not establish this caste commensality rule which was 'calculated for the order and regularity of their Cast meetings' (1 B.S.D.A. 108).

From these above-cited caste rules, the following characteristics of the urban caste which were quite distinct from those of the rural caste in the later medieval Deccan, can be deduced:

1. The primary collective of the urban caste was united together townwise. In other words, each town constituted the primary unit of the collectivity of the urban caste. The number of families constituting

this primary collective was roughly around one hundred to two hundred inferrable from other cases as well.[9]

2. The urban caste as the primary collective accepted members of other towns on condition of the lapse of a prescribed time after the arrival of the new member and payment of a prescribed amount of the admission fee to the caste fund.[10]
3. The urban caste possessed the property in the form of the caste temple, caste fund, cooking utensils for the commensal meeting and most probably something like the caste hall in which the caste meeting was to be held and cooking utensils and other caste properties were to be stored.[11]
4. The urban caste as the primary collective had its own tutelary god installed in the caste temple maintained by the caste under the management of a Brahman priest.[12]

RELATIONSHIP BETWEEN THE YAJMAN CASTE AND GURU CASTE

Another important characteristic of the urban caste, in addition to the above-mentioned four characteristics, was the existence of the Nyat Gour. The urban caste had its own caste mentor or caste priest called Nyat Gour (from '*jñāt guru*', '*jāt guru*' in Gujarati) who belonged to a specific Brahman caste. This was a hereditary relationship between a caste who employed the Nyat Gour (hereafter, the *yajmān* caste) and a specific Brahman caste (hereafter, the *guru* caste) who sent certain members of the caste to be the Nyat Gour of the *yajmān* caste.

In one lawsuit in the early part of the nineteenth century filed in the Bombay Sadr Divani Adalat (1813), 250 members of the Surati collective of the Dussa Shreemalee Bunyuns (Dasa Shrimali Vania) claimed that the defendant (the respondent in the court of appeal) did not have the right to collect certain fees, such as the marriage fee, payable to the Nyat Gour which accrued from each family of the Yujmans (*yajmāns*). The defendant conversely pleaded to have the hereditary right to officiate as the Nyat Gour at ceremonies in the home of the members of this caste. The point of issue in this case turned out to be whether the *yajmān* caste had the right to remove the Nyat Gour from office or not. The Bombay Sadr Divani Adalat, on appeal, finally decreed in favour of the defendant (respondent) holding that 'according to that custom [of this part of the country], the office was hereditary, and the holder of such a position could not be removed at will, but by unanimous consent of the whole caste; and the wish for a change in this instance was not unanimous, because there was a party in favour of the defendant' (1 B.S.D.A. 80).

In another case in the latter half of the nineteenth century, the Auditch (Audich) Brahman caste of Ahmadabad used to send several members of the caste to Surat as the Nyat Gour of the Mochi (caste of ornaments makers) of Surat city (the Surati Mochi). On one occasion, however, there were so many marriage ceremonies among the Mochi of Surat at the same time that the Audich Nyat Gours sent by the caste to Surat could not manage to officiate at all of the marriage ceremonies by themselves. Being enraged at this, the Mochi of Surat dismissed the Audich Brahman caste of Ahmadabad from the office of the *guru* caste of the Surati Mochi. Opposing this, the Audich Brahman caste of Ahmadabad filed a suit for the recognition of its hereditary right to act as the *guru* caste of the Surati Mochi. The Bombay High Court on appeal decreed against the plaintiffs (the Audich Brahman caste of Ahmadabad) holding that the defendants (the Surati Mochi) had the right to change their Nyat Gour (20 B. 784. 1895).[13]

As these cases demonstrate, the urban caste in coastal Gujarat had a hereditary relationship with a specific Brahman caste who sent its members as the Nyat Gour of the *yajmān* caste to officiate at such ceremonies and rituals as marriages and commensal meetings. This relationship between the *yajmān* and *guru* castes in the towns of coastal Gujarat was quite distinct from the relationship between the villager and village *vatandār* Joshi in the medieval Deccan as discussed in the previous section.

This seems to mean that the town in eighteenth-nineteenth century Gujarat did not form a community constituted on the communal division of labour, or the caste division of labour, including the division of ritual labour in such community festivals and ceremonies as Dasara, as was the case with the village community of the medieval Deccan.[14] In other words, the town in coastal Gujarat was something like a grouping of castes, each of which formed its respective relationship with a specific Brahman caste (*guru* caste) who did not belong to the same town in which the *yajmān* caste reside.

This generalization of the nature of the town in eighteenth-nineteenth century coastal Gujarat, however, needs much more exhaustive and detailed investigation.

Secondary Network of the Urban Caste

MULTI-STRATA CONSTITUTION OF THE URBAN CASTE

The above-cited cases of the Bombay Sadr Divani Adalat are highly suggestive of the constitution of the urban caste as well.

Figure 1

Stratum	
	Gujarati Vania (40 caste groups)
4	Khadayata Vania
3	Ahamadabadi Khadayata Vania
2	Ahamdabadi Visa Khadayata Vania
1	Surati collective of Ahmadabadi Visa Khadayata Vania (159 families)

In the first case, the Ahmadabadi Visa Khadayata Vania (159 families) constituted, so to say, the lowest stratum of the entire constitution of the caste as shown in Figure 1. The so-called Gujarati Vania comprised in all 40 caste groups, one of which was the Khadayata Vania. The Ahmadabadi Khadayata was one section of the Khadayata Vania who regarded Ahmadabad as its headquarters, or legendary place of origin. Visa (*vīsa*, 20) was the term applied to the majority group or superior branch of a caste that was split into two groups with the minority group or inferior branch designated as Dasa (*dasa*, 10). Should a further split have taken place, the term Punch (*pāñc*, 5) was used to denote the most minor or inferior branch. Thus, the Ahmadabadi Visa Khadayata was the majority group or superior branch of the Ahamadabadi Khadayata, of which the Surati collective was one of the basic units.

In the second case, the Ahmadabadkar Shrimali Soni had a similar multi-strata constitution with the primary collective of Surat city (173 families) at the bottom of the entire constitution. The Shrimali Soni was one of the Gujarati Soni castes, and Ahmadabadkar Shrimali Soni was one section of the Shrimali Soni who regarded Ahmadabad as its headquarters or legendary place of origin. The multi-strata constitution of this caste is shown in Figure 2.

This multi-strata constitution was a distinctive characteristic of the urban caste in coastal Gujarat which was quite different from the twofold structure of the rural caste in the medieval Deccan as discussed in the previous section.

Figure 2

Stratum	
3	Shrimali Soni
2	Ahmadabadkar Shrimali Soni
1	Surati collective of Ahmadabadkar Shrimali Soni (173 families)

CASTE RULE BEYOND THE PRIMARY COLLECTIVE

As time passed under British colonial rule, the caste collectivity at the secondary network stratum, rather than at the primary collective stratum, became stronger. This would remain a general tendency throughout the Indian subcontinent to which the Bombay Presidency was not an exception.[15]

As an example, the Pathare Prabhu in the Bombay area which they called Desh (country), strengthened its collectivity at the Desh stratum forming the Kshatria Union Club under which there were five primary collectives of Girgaum, Mazgaon, Parel, Mahim and Warli, collectively known as Chargram (four villages).[16] In 1887, the Pathare Prabhus held a general caste meeting at the Desh stratum and drew up the general caste rule purporting to stop inviting *naikins* (*nāikīṇ* in Marathi, dancing girl) on the occasion of the *muñjī* (*upanayana*) and marriage ceremony for the purpose of reducing ceremonial expenses. The preamble of this caste rule reads as follows:

> Every family in the caste is to act according to these rules and if any transgression of these rules, on the part of any one, be proved, he shall be considered as an offender of the caste.

In 1889, one Raghunath Damodar of the Girgaum gram broke this caste rule by inviting naikins to sing a song at his nephew's marriage ceremony. The Girgaum gram, therefore, held a caste meeting and decided to deprive him of the right of the 'man-pan invitation' (the right to receive *mān-pān*, that is, the honours and presents) and to notify the Desh and other grams as such. The Girgaum gram also distributed a circular of this purport to its members (gramastha, *grāmastha* meaning villagers). Raghunath Damodar, opposing this, filed a suit claiming damages of Rs. 5,000 for defamation of character and reputation. The Bombay

High Court on appeal decreed against the plaintiff (Raghunath Damodar) holding that it was a 'caste question unconnected with property or legal rights', as the 'man-pan invitation' was merely a 'social priviledge' and not considered a legal right (15 B. 599).[17]

As shown in this case, the Pathare Prabhu of the Bombay area (Desh) formed a strong higher-level organization named the Kshatria Union Club, claiming Kshatriya status for themselves in the so-called *varṇa* ranking and using the English terms for appeal to the British administrators. As a result of this strengthening of the secondary network of the caste, the caste rule at the secondary organizational level began to develop in the latter half of the nineteenth century.[18]

Conclusion

From the discussion above, the following points of comparison between the rural caste in the Deccan and the urban caste in coastal Gujarat can be drawn:

1. The primary unit of collectivity of the rural caste was a district (*pargaṇā*) while that of the urban caste was a town.
2. The rural caste had a twofold structure with the secondary network of primary collectives outstretching the boundary of a district while the urban caste had a multi-strata constitution with the higher-level organization ever strengthening its control over the primary collectives in the latter half of the nineteenth century.
3. The rural caste was incorporated into the communal division of labour of the village community while the urban caste did not constitute a part of the communal division of labour of a town. In other words, the town in eighteenth-nineteenth century Gujarat was not a community in the same sense as the village community in the medieval Deccan. This was most clearly reflected in the difference of the ritual or priestly relationships, namely, the difference between the villagers-village Joshi relationship in the Deccan and the *yajmān* caste-*guru* caste relationship in coastal Gujarat.
4. The urban caste possessed property in the form of the caste temple, caste fund, cooking utensils for the commensal meeting, and perhaps something like the caste hall to hold the caste meeting and store such caste properties as cooking utensils while such caste property was not known to exist in the case of the rural caste in the medieval Deccan. The urban caste of eighteenth-nineteenth century

Gujarat acted, in this sense, as a sort of corporate body or juristic person while the rural caste in the Deccan constituted a part of the rural communal structure.

Notes

1 Cf., as examples, Dirks 1987, Raheja 1988b and Quigley 1993. See Introduction of Chapter 9 as to some discussion on the problematic points raised by these authors.

2 By the High Courts Act of 1861, the Bombay Sadr Divani Adalat, Bombay Sadr Faujdari Adalat and Supreme Court of Bombay were united to constitute the Bombay High Court. Thus, the Bombay High Court had the appellate civil and criminal jurisdiction over the whole areas of the Bombay Presidency as well as the original jurisdiction covering the Presidency Town of Bombay which was taken over from the Supreme Court of Bombay.

3 As for the function and authority of the Dharmadhikari, see Chapter 9.

4 As for *doṣa-patra* and *śuddhi-patra* issued by the Dharmadhikari, see Chapter 9.

5 As for the concept of *anuloma-pratiloma*, cf. Kane: II 51-54.

6 In classical law books of India, rules regulating the giving-taking of food had not, it seems, so developed as in the case of the later medieval Deccan. Cf. Kane: II 791.

7 This document was formerly discussed by the late Prof. H. Fukazawa from the perspective of the relationship between the caste and the state ['The State and Caste System (Jati)', Fukazawa 1991: 100-1].

8 As this case denotes, the caste was recognized as a sort of autonomous body (a 'Body corporate') which had the right to make rules ('Bye Laws' in British administrative terminology) corresponding to the law of the state under the Bombay administration, so that a caste member who violated the caste rule could be legally excommunicated. This policy of the Bombay government ultimately led to the well-known 'caste autonomy' policy under the Elphinstone Code system. For further details, see Chapter 5 of this volume.

9 For example, the Surati collective of Shravak Visa Osval Vania consisted of 250 families (1 B.S.D.A. 35), while the Surati Valand (barbers) comprised only 67 families (2 B.S.D.A. 473).

10 Refer also to the following decisions of the Bombay Sadr Divani Adalat: 1 B.S.D.A. 356, 1 B.S.D.A. 365, 1 B.S.D.A. 390 and 1 B.S.D.A. 420. The late Prof. H. Fukazawa once discussed this topic in his article, 'The Artisan Trades in Nineteenth Century Western India', which was written in Japanese and unfortunately not translated into English.

11 Refer to the following decisions of the Bombay Sadr Divani Adalat and

Bombay High Court: on cooking utensils, 2 B.S.D.A. 323, 3 B.S.D.A. 108, 4 B.H.C.R. (A.C.J.) 110, 5 B. 83, 11 B. 534, 19 B. 507, and on caste funds, 12 B. 225, 34 B. 467.

12 It is not certain whether the Brahman priest of the caste temple and the Nyat Gour were identical or not.

13 The difference between the above-mentioned decision of the Bombay Sadr Divani Adalat (1813) and this decision of the Bombay High Court (1895) reflects the change in judicial judgement in regard to the hereditary rights which had been enjoyed under former governments. In the latter half of the nineteenth century, various hereditary rights began to be abolished through various administrative and judicial procedures such as the 'commutation' and 'resumption' of *vatans*. It was the case with the hereditary right of the *guru* caste in coastal Gujarat as well. For details of 'commutation' and 'resumption' of *vatans*, see Chapters 7 and 8 of this volume.

14 As to the division of ritual labour in the village community in the medieval Deccan, see Chapter 9.

15 Cf., for example, Carroll 1975 and Carroll 1978. She discussed the development of the caste network, 'caste(s) associations' in her terminology, of the Kayastha and several other castes (*jātis*) in north India in relation to British colonial rule.

16 The term Chargram (four villages) seems to show that there had existed only four original collectives of the Pathare Prabhu caste in the Bombay area (Desh), with a new one being established and added afterwards, though it is not certain which of the five was the new one.

17 As to the 'caste question', see Chapter 5 of this volume.

18 The Kutch Dasa Osval of the Bombay area, as another example, formed a committee of 35 members which subsequently decided not to employ the Brahman at such ceremonies as marriages (19 B. 507).

5

The 'Caste Autonomy' Policy in the Nineteenth-Century Bombay Presidency

Introduction

The caste, being treated as a sort of body corporate, has been well known to have been granted a considerable degree of autonomy under British colonial rule (Mulla 1901; Kikani 1912; Aiyar 1918). This caste policy, the so-called 'caste autonomy' policy (Galanter 1989: 151-54), was first formulated in the Bombay Presidency during the early part of the nineteenth century under the governorship of Mountstuart Elphinstone (in office 1819-27).[1]

On 1 January 1827, M. Elphinstone promulgated, in all, 27 regulations (Bombay Regulations I-XXVII of 1827) revising the former somewhat irregular enactments. These regulations were collectively known as the Elphinstone Code and formed the basis of the Bombay administration. The regulation pertaining to the caste autonomy policy was Regulation II of the Elphinstone Code which defined the constitution of civil courts and the powers and duties of their judges. Section XXI, clause 1 of this regulation reads as follows:

> The jurisdiction of the Civil Court shall extend to the cognizance of all original suits and complaints between natives and others (*not British-born subjects*), respecting the right to moveable or immoveable property, rents, Government revenues, debts, contracts, marriage, succession, damages for injuries, and generally of all suits and complaints of a civil nature, it being understood that no interference on the part of the court in caste questions is hereby warranted, beyond the admission and trial of any suit instituted for the recovery of damages on account of an alleged injury to the caste and

> character of the plaintiff, arising from some illegal act or unjustifiable conduct of the other party.
>
> (Clarke 1851: 10)

Thus, Bombay Regulation II of 1827 excluded, in principle, the 'caste questions' from the jurisdiction of civil courts established by the East India Company in the Bombay Presidency. In other words, the caste questions were left to the disposal or discretion of the caste as a sort of body corporate under the Bombay administration.

This caste policy of the Bombay government stood in contrast to that of the Bengal and Madras governments at least in the first half of the nineteenth century. Bengal Regulation III of 1793, Section VIII included the caste questions within the jurisdiction of civil courts on the same footing with 'the succession or right to real or personal property, land-rents, revenues, debts, accounts, contracts, partnerships, marriage, ..., claims to damages for injuries' (Clarke 1854). This was followed verbatim by Madras Regulation II of 1802, Section V (Clarke 1848). This means that the caste policy of the Bengal and Madras governments was considerably changed by the Bombay government in the early part of the nineteenth century.

This chapter aims, first, to trace the historical process of formation of the caste autonomy policy in the Bombay Presidency down from the conquest of the Maratha kingdom in 1818 by the army of the East India Company to the Elphinstone Code and, second, to ascertain the actual extent of autonomy allowed to the caste in the Bombay Presidency in comparison with the Bengal and Madras Presidencies.

The Panchayat System

Elphinstone on the Panchayat System

On 25 October 1819, M. Elphinstone, the then Deccan Commissioner, submitted a lengthy report to the Governor-General concerning the so-called Conquered Territories, that is to say, the territories conquered from the Maratha kingdom (Peshva government) in 1818 as a result of the third Anglo-Maratha War.[2] Elphinstone referred in this report to the question of the suitable system of civil jurisdiction to be introduced in the Bombay Presidency as follows:

> It is necessary to examine the native system of civil justice with

> attention, and ascertain its success in affording protection to men's rights. If this should prove even moderate it will scarcely be thought advisable to attempt any alteration; but if the plan be found inadequate to the end required, it will be necessary to see whether any alterations can be introduced to render it more efficient without changing its fundamental principles, or whether it is necessary to set it aside altogether, and to introduce a new system in its room.
>
> (R.E.I.H.: IV 188)

Bearing this question in mind, Elphinstone made inquiries into the system of civil jurisdiction under the Maratha administration and found that the so-called *panchayat* had been playing an important role in it. The *panchayat* was a very popular institution for settling disputes or confirming rights or privileges in the local society, though the term *sabha* was more common in the medieval Deccan. Various types of *panchayat* such as the village *panchayat*, district *panchayat* and caste *panchayat* were held according to the nature of problems to be addressed.[3]

Elphinstone understood that these *panchayats* of various natures and levels had in combination been sustaining the system of civil jurisdiction under the Marathas. At the same time, however, he found many 'defects and abuses' inherent in the *panchayat* system. Chief among them were: (1) a lack of a formal legal procedure for filing suits and appeals; (2) a lack of the principle of not debating the same matter twice; (3) a lack of uniformity of the decision, due to its being based on the local practises or usages; (4) occurrences of such unlawful acts as bribery; and finally (5) a lack of the apparatus for enforcing the decision.

After enumerating these defects and abuses of the *panchayat* system, however, Elphinstone continued as follows:

> But with all these defects the Maratha country flourished, and the people seem to have been exempt from some of the evils which exist under our more perfect government; there must, therefore, have been some advantages in the system to counterbalance its obvious defects, and most of them appear to me to have originated in one fact, that the Government, although it did little to obtain justice for the people, left them the means of procuring it for themselves. The advantage of this was particularly felt among the lower orders, who were most out of reach of their rulers, most apt to be neglected under all governments. By means of the punchayet they were enabled to effect a tolerable dispensation of justice among themselves, and it happens that most

> of the objections above stated to that institution do not apply in their case.
>
> (R.E.I.H.: IV 194)

Elphinstone then proceeded to compare this *panchayat* system with these merits and demerits to the so-called Adawlut (Adalat) system, that is, the English type of judicial system that had been introduced in the Old Provinces already acquired by the East India Company before 1818 mainly in coastal Gujarat. The Adawlat system, he found, had many advantages. First, substantive regulations were enacted and made known to the people. Second, the decisions of civil courts were based on the same principle such that the people could foresee the result of their cases. Third, the procedure of filing suits and appeals was established. Fourth, the prompt dispensation and enforcement of justice was ensured. Finally, the judges were fair and impartial, and their fairness was guaranteed by the system of appeal. In spite of these advantages, however, he continued:

> it appears that although the Regulations are promulgated, yet as they are entirely new to the people of India, a long time must pass before they can be generally known, and as both they and the decisions of the courts are founded on European notions, a still longer period must elapse before their principles can be at all understood;....
>
> (R.E.I.H.: IV 197)

Thus, Elphinstone realized that it could not be an easy task to create a faultless judicial system either from the Adawlut system (English type system) or the *panchayat* system (native system). 'If this be the case', he thought, 'it becomes of the first consequence to cherish whatever there is good in the existing system, and to attempt no innovation that can injure the principle now in force, since it is so uncertain whether we can introduce better in their room' (R.E.I.H.: IV 198).

Finally Elphinstone came to the conclusion that the *panchayat* system should be preserved as the basis of the civil jurisdiction in the Conquered Territories:

> I propose, therefore, that the native system should still be preserved, and means taken to remove its abuses and revive its energy; such a course will be more welcome to the natives than any entire change, and if it should fail entirely it is never too late to introduce the Adawlut.... Our principal instrument must continue to be the

> punchayet, and that must continue to be exempt from all new forms, interference, and regulation on our part.
>
> (R.E.I.H.: IV 198)

Elphinstone thus proposed to make the most of the *panchayat* system as the basis of civil jurisdiction in the Bombay Presidency. He himself pointed out in his report that there existed various types of *panchayat*, enumerating, first, the village *panchayat* that used to be convened by the Patil to settle all sorts of disputes within a village, second, the *panchayat* of 'trades' (merchant castes or artisan castes in a city) represented by the headmen ('Shaitees'), third, the district *panchayat* to be held under the leadership of Daismooks (Deshmukhs) and Daispandies (Deshpandes) to settle such disputes as the boundary dispute between villages that could not be dealt with by the village *panchayat*, and several others. In the same vein, Elphinstone wrote as follows with regard to disputes within a caste:

> Disputes about caste were settled by the caste, unless when a complaint of unjust expulsion took place, when the government ordered a punchayet of respectable persons of the caste from an unprejudiced part of the country.
>
> (R.E.I.H.: IV 191)

Elphinstone understood that ordinary disputes within a caste were settled by the caste *panchayat* of the caste concerned, but that in the case of such disputes as unjust expulsion from a caste in which the caste as a sort of body corporate itself was involved as one party to the case, a *panchayat* composed of caste elders of other parts of the country was summoned.

Thus, the fundamental principle of Elphinstone's administration was to preserve these various types of *panchayats* intact, so far as possible, and make them the foundation of civil jurisdiction.

'Rules respecting Punchayets'(1822)

M. Elphinstone was appointed Governor of Bombay on 1 November 1919, just one week after he had submitted the aforementioned report to the Governor-General of Bengal, and left Poona (Pune) to proceed to Bombay. The office of the Deccan Commissioner was taken over by W. Chaplin, formerly the Principal Collector of Dharwar. W. Chaplin also followed the policy of Elphinstone to make use of the *panchayat* system in civil jurisdiction and made inquiries into the defects inherent in it for seeking a solution to them. On 20 August 1822, Chaplin submitted a long report on revenue and civil administration to the Bombay government to which were appended various 'enclosures'. Among these enclosures was a memorandum entitled 'Mr. H. Borradaile's Note upon Punchayets' which contained an important proposal with regard to the *panchayat* system. In his 'Note', H. Borradaile wrote on the caste *panchayat* as follows:

> Matters relating to caste or depending upon the customs of them, or of any particular trade or business, are far best settled by a punchayet composed of members chosen from the trade or caste. Indeed every decision upon such points must partake somewhat of the nature of a caste punchayet, for the evidence of the members of it is essential to enable the judge of the case to decide;.... Decisions by members chosen from the caste too, are, in my opinion, more unbiassed than almost any other. For this reason I would recommend that where a punchayet is given on matter relating to caste as above, neither party should be allowed to claim choice of members out of it, unless he could prove that there was a general enmity to him in it.
>
> (R.E.I.H.: IV 604)

Based upon this observation, Borradaile proposed the following categories of 'cases in which punchayets might be considered the legal and fixed mode of decision' (R.E.I.H.: IV 605):

1. Points of religion
2. Customs of the country, caste, or trade
3. Division of property
4. Old and intricate accounts
5. Cases of wuttuns [*vatans*] and hucks [*haqqs*]
6. Disputes for maintenance

After many inquiries and discussions on the *panchayat* system having been conducted, the following 'Rules respecting Punchayets' were drawn up in 1822:

1. Causes relating to the internal regulations of particular castes shall be exclusively settled by punchayets composed of members of the caste concerned.
2. All causes relating to the following subjects shall be referred to

punchayets for adjustment, unless the parties shall agree to bring their suit before a Moonsiff, and shall state their wish in writing before witnesses.

1. Religion
2. Marriage
3. Peculiar customs of places
4. Wuttuns, or hucks
5. Division of property
6. Maintenance
7. Old and intricate accounts
8. Disputes between two inhabitants of the same village within the sum of fifty rupees personal property or value
9. Suits for damages for alleged personal injuries, and for personal damages of whatever nature
10. Boundary disputes

(R.E.I.H.: IV 864)[4]

The most important point pertaining to these 'Rules' was that 'causes relating to internal regulations of particular castes' were separately treated from all other causes to be referred to the decision of *panchayats*. From the aforementioned report of Elphinstone onward, the caste questions had always been lumped together with other various causes to be decided by *panchayats*. The 'Rules respecting Punchayets', however, provided in the separate clause that the caste questions were only to be settled by 'punchayets composed of members of the caste concerned'. This was a step forward to the caste autonomy policy.

Formation of the 'Caste Autonomy' Policy

'Committee for the Revision of the Regulations'

While inquiry into the *panchayat* system was still in progress, M. Elphinstone, the Governor of Bombay, was pondering over the possibility of formulating the comprehensive civil code to be uniformly applied to both the Old Provinces and Conquered Territories. He organized for this purpose the 'Committee for the Revision of the Regulations' with a membership of three.[5] The task of this committee was to revise regulations already promulgated and enforced in the Old Provinces so as to make them applicable to the Conquered Territories as well. This was not an easy task to accomplish since it included the basic problem involving the legislative principle of British india.

In the field of civil jurisdiction, the leading principle of the British administration had been laid down by Warren Hastings, the then Governor of Bengal, in 'A Plan for Administration of Justice' formulated in 1772 after the Court of Directors of the East India Company signified its decision to take direct charge of the Divani of the Mughal provinces of Bengal and Bihar in 1771.[6] Section XXIII of this 'Plan' reads as follows:

> That in all Suits regarding Inheritance, Marriage, Cast, and other religious Usages or Institutions, the Laws of the Khoran with respect to Mahometans, and those of the Shaster with respect to Gentoos, shall be invariably adhered to: On all such Occasions, the Moulavies or Brahmins shall respectively attend to expound the law, and they shall sign the Reports, and assist in passing the Decree.[7]

This plan was immediately sanctioned by the Court of Directors to be enforced in the Bengal Presidency and later extended to other presidencies as well.

The term, 'Shaster' (Shastra, a generic term for the classical law books) to be applied to the 'Gentoos' (Hindus), however, was quite ambiguous, as there existed many classical law books such as the *Manusmṛti* and *Yājñavalkyasmṛti* as well as many commentaries on these classical law books of later periods with different provisions for the same case. Moreover, in actual disputes the customs and usages of particular localities or communities seemed to have weighed much more heavily than the written law of any kind.

Thus, it was necessary not only to revise the existing regulations of the Bombay government but also to try to overcome such an actual state of affairs in the field of civil laws in India as mentioned above for preparing the comprehensive civil code applicable to everyone irrespective of regional and communal differences. In this respect, Elphinstone wrote in his report dated 22 July 1823 as follows:

> There are but two courses by which a remedy can be applied, — the first is, to make a new Code founded entirely on general principles, applicable to all ages and nations, — the second is to endeavour to compile a complete and consistent Code from the mass of written law and the fragments of tradition, determining on general principles of jurisprudence those points where the Hindoo books and traditions

> present only conflicting authorities, and perhaps supplying on similar principles any glaring deficiencies that may remain when the matter for compilation has been exhausted. The 1st of these courses, if otherwise expedient, is rendered entirely impracticable here by the attachment of the Natives to their own institutions, and by the degree to which their laws are interwoven with their religion and manners. The 2d plan is therefore the only one which it is in our power to pursue. The first step towards the accomplishment of its objects, appears to be to ascertain in each district whether there is any book of acknowledged authority either for the whole or any branch of the law: the next is to ascertain what exceptions there are to the written authorities, and what customs and traditions exist independent of them. The best modes of conducting these inquiries are, 1st, to examine the Shastrees, Heads of Castes, and other persons likely to be acquainted either with the law, the customs of Castes, or the public opinion regarding the authority attached to each; and 2d, to extract from the records of the Courts of Justice the information already obtained on these subjects in the course of judicial investigations.
>
> (Steele 1827: II-III)

Thus, Elphinstone proposed two types of investigation as the prerequisite for compiling 'a complete and consistent Code from the mass of written law and the fragments of tradition' which had been inherited in this part of India. The first investigation, that is to say, inquiries from 'Shastrees, Heads of Castes, and other persons' was conducted in the Conquered Territories. The Committee for the Revision of the Regulations prepared a questionnaire for this purpose, and in accordance with this questionnaire more than one hundred castes in the areas around Pune were actually investigated. Further, the Committee sent the same questionnaire to Principal Collectors, Collectors and Residents posted in native states and asked them to respond. Based on information thus accumulated, A. Steele published a voluminous semi-official book entitled *Summary of the Law and Customs within the Dekhun Provinces Subject to the Presidency of Bombay, Chiefly Affecting Civil Suits* (Bombay, 1827). Reference was often made to this book in civil courts in the Bombay Presidency when the parties of a suit contended about whether or not a particular custom was prevailing in the caste concerned.

On the other hand, the second investigation, that is, the extraction from judicial records of information regarding laws and usages among Indian people, was conducted in the Bombay Sadr Divani Adalat, the predecessor of the Bombay High Court existing until 1862. Most of the legal documents extracted were, therefore, those pertaining to the Old Provinces, especially coastal Gujarat. The cases thus collected were compiled by H. Borradaile into two extensive volumes entitled *Reports of Civil Causes adjudged by the Court of Sudur Udalut, for the Presidency of Bombay, between the Years A.D. 1800 and A.D. 1824, divided into Two Parts* (abbreviated in this volume as 1 B.S.D.A. and 2 B.S.D.A.).

The results of these two types of investigation played an important role in the formulation of the so-called Elphinstone Code system of Bombay administration, of which the caste autonomy policy was one of the most characteristic features.

Castes in Civil Courts

The casebook of the Bombay Sadr Divani Adalat compiled by H. Borradaile especially afforded much information for the formulation of the caste autonomy policy of the Bombay government. Several important cases decided by the Bombay Sadr Divani Adalat in close relationship with this problem will be discussed here.

The first case (1 B.S.D.A. 347) involved the Surati (residents of Surat city) collective of the 'Ahmudabadee Beesa Khundaita' (Ahmadavadi Visa Khadayata Vania). The Surati collective of this Gujarati merchant caste made a caste rule (Bundobust, *bandobast*) pertaining to the caste commensal meeting in 1805 and registered it at the district court of Surat.[8] This caste rule bore the signatures of 146 caste members but 13 other members did not sign it for one reason or another. Shumbhoodas Raeechund, one of these 13 members, was excluded from the social association with other caste members on the grounds that he married a daughter of his cousin to a man residing outside the city walls of Surat in violation of this caste rule. He then filed a suit against the caste headmen and other members of the caste for damages of Rs. 1,000 on the plea that he could not have married this girl as he was not her father and that he should not be bound to abide by this caste rule as he had not signed it. The defendants responded in defence of this caste rule that 'it was intended as a remedy for an evil custom daily increasing, that of rich persons sending to other parts of the country for wives (on account of the debauchery of Surat?) whereby the daughters of many poor people were left unmarried', and maintained 'that Appellant's (plaintiff's) brother's signing the Bundobust was the same as if Appellant (plaintiff) himself signed it, and that he had broken another article of it by receiving Rupees 1,300, from the person to whom the Girl, only two and half years' old was betrothed' (1 B.S.D.A. 347 at 349). Further the defendants argued that they only temporarily excommunicated him, as indicated by the fact that they ate with him at private dinners.

In this case the Surat District Court held that this caste rule was

> ... deserving of support from the Magistry, in as much as they tended to lessen and to regulate the expense of marriages, and to put a stop to that extravagance and profusion which led many families in difficulty. Government had directed the Judges to exert all proper influence, with due regard to the prejudices of the Natives, for the attainment of this desirable object. Appellant had not been turned out of Cast, but merely excluded from its General assemblies as having offended against the Body corporate, and it was in his power by making certain concessions, to get readmitted to all his privileges. His claim to damages was therefore dismissed.
>
> (1 B.S.D.A. 347 at 350)

On appeal, the Bombay Sadr Divani Adalat in turn changed the decision of the lower court as follows:

> Viewing the object of the Bundobust as highly beneficial, Appellant as well as twelve others who had hitherto withheld their consent, were recommended to become parties to it. This he agreed to do, and the decision was, that on his signing the Bundobust, he should be restored within one month to his full privileges, or that Respondents, who now agreed to this arrangement, should on their refusal to receive him after his submission, pay the damages sued for, Rupees 1,000.
>
> (1 B.S.D.A. 347 at 351)

Thus, the civil courts as well as the Bombay government itself regarded this caste rule as 'deserving support' and 'beneficial' for regulating the internal order of the caste.

The second case (1 B.S.D.A. 108) concerned the Surati Soni (goldsmith) collective of the 'Ahmudabadkur Shreemalee' (Ahmadabadkar Shrimali). In 1809, a dispute over the manners pertaining to the caste commensal meeting occurred in this caste. On the occasion of a caste commensal meeting held by Hurjeevun Lukmeechund, some guests tried to take the leftovers home but he disallowed it. This caused a dispute in the caste. Then, the caste headmen (Seths) asked the caste priest (Nyat Gour, *jñāt guru*) to summon a caste meeting. The caste meeting was held for two days and a caste rule regarding the caste commensal meeting was made.[9] This caste rule bore the signatures of 173 members which seems to be the total members of the Surati collective of this caste. Some signatures, however, were not written by the persons themselves but by the Nyat Gour. This turned out later to be the cause of a further dispute. In this same year, Kuhandas and 19 other members of this caste held a caste commensal meeting on the occasion of the festival of their tutelary god, Wagheshwuree, without sanction of the caste headmen. The caste headmen regarded this act as a violation of the caste rule and 'called upon the court to enforce the obedience' of them. The lower court held that this caste rule could not be valid, as 'according to the verbal opinion of their Shastrees the consent of the majority of a Cast, at least, if not all the members, was necessary to make any act or Rule binding among them'. The Bombay Sadr Divani Adalat affirmed this decision of the lower court, 'regretting at the same time that Appellants [the caste headmen] should fail in establishing Regulations calculated for the order and regularity of their Cast meetings' (1 B.S.D.A. 108 at 110).

In this case, the civil courts placed a high value on the caste rule which was calculated to establish order in the caste commensal meeting and regretted that the courts held it invalid due to some signatures not being bona fide.

These two cases revealed the intention on the side of the colonial administration to make use of the autonomous potentiality of the caste in maintaining societal order to the advantage of colonial rule, practically treating the caste as the smallest unit of the administrative organization.

The following two cases more clearly demonstrate this intention by their sanctioning the 'caste jurisdiction' and expecting the castes' effective functioning in maintaining societal order.

In one case Hurrukchund Moteechund was excommunicated by the Surati collective of the 'Shravuk Beesa Ooswal Bunyuns' (Shravak Visa Osval Vanias) on the grounds that he had been suspected of his wife's murder. He therefore filed a suit for damages of Rs. 1,000 against the caste headman and 10 other caste *panchayat* members. At the hearing, the plaintiff claimed that he had been imprisoned on suspicion of his wife's murder two years before but was released as not guilty. In spite of this, the defendants did not readmit him into the caste by not inviting him to marriages and funeral ceremonies. Moreover, as his daughter was already 14 years old, it was mandatory for him to marry her off. He thus claimed that he filed this suit purposing to summon the caste seniors to the court and made them readmit him into the caste. The defendants put forth three refutations against this. First, the plaintiff had been excommunicated by the will not only of the caste *panchayat* members but also of all of the caste members. Second, his children were not excommunicated. Third, the caste meeting had been held twice at the house of the caste headman to discuss whether he be readmitted into the caste or not but could not reach a decision. The district court judge held that the defendants had no reason to excommunicate him, awarding damages of Rs. 1,000 to the plaintiff. The defendants (caste *panchayat* members) proposed that the caste members should readmit him to evade payment of Rs. 1,000 for damages. The caste meeting composed of all members of 250 men, however, rejected it. Hurrukuchund Moteechund (the plaintiff) sued again for damages of Rs. 1,183 against Dhurmuchund Abeela and 21 other members of the caste whom he deemed the leaders of his opponents. In this suit damages of Rs. 1,000 were also awarded to him.

The defendants of these two suits, totaling in all 33, lodged an appeal at the Bombay Sadr Divani Adalat. They claimed that the caste had the right to refuse 'common intercourse with a man guilty of any crime' and that they obtained sufficient proof to allow them to believe that the plaintiff had committed the murder, 'though the evidence might not be conclusive enough in the opinion of the Court of Session to warrant his conviction'. They further maintained that:

> ... the investigation in the Cast was not with a view to change the sentence of the Court, but was in exercise of a privilege possessed for ages, of preserving the Cast free from the contamination and disgrace of associating with a man conscientiously by them believed to be guilty of a crime, as in the present instance, of having murdered his own wife, and this right of choosing their own associates being inherent in the Cast individually and as a body, notwithstanding any previous trial of the Criminal, the decrees of the lower Courts, depriving the whole Cast in fact of their privileges, were unjust and ought to be reversed.
>
> (1 B.S.D.A. 35 at 39)

Threipland, the Advocate General of the Bombay government, being asked his opinion on this case, submitted the following report to the Bombay Sadr Divani Adalat which strongly influenced the judgement of the court:

> On grounds of publick policy nothing can be more obious than that the jurisdiction which is exercised by Casts in this country, ought as little as possible to be interfered with. It is a power which experience does not prove to be liable to much abuse, and its proper exercise is of such eminent utility in the prevention of misconduct on the part of our native fellow subjects, that whatever tends to weaken its authority must be accounted as an evil of considerable magnitude....
>
> [And ...] it often happens that the very Court which finds itself compelled to acquit, is impressed with a consciousness, only short of absolute conviction, of the Prisoner's guilt, and hence the celebrated phrase of 'acquitted Felon' is that by which many, who escape the laws of their Country, may, after all, most properly be designed....
>
> It is precisely in such cases that the benefits of an ulterior Cast Jurisdiction are most likely to be felt. By its means, Offenders, against whom there may not be sufficient proof to warrant a conviction which would subject them to the loss of their lives, may still be made amenable to penalties and deprivations, the dread of which cannot fail to operate with salutary influence, and are so far from being subversive of the authority of a regular Court, that they are rather to be viewed as coming in aid of that authority, and by making men anxious to avoid the appearance of guilt, cannot fail on many occasions to prevent the reality....
>
> The question in short is, whether Casts, in determining who are fit persons to continue of their respective Bodies, are compellable to see only with the eyes of a Court of Law, and to hear with its ears. If it were sound policy to endeavour to effect the abolition of all such native Jurisdiction, I should recommend this restraint being put upon them; but if their authority is to be maintained, I should advise their acts to be only called in question where they plainly proceed from revengeful or malicious motives, not where they are ascribable to a conscientious, even though it should be a mistaken, opinion of crime.
>
> (1 B.S.D.A. 35 at 40-42)

Threipland's opinion that the jurisdiction exercised by the caste or the 'ulterior Cast Jurisdiction' should be preserved intact so far as possible was accepted by the Bombay Sadr Divani Adalat.[10] Accordingly, the Bombay Sadr Divani Adalat ordered the lower court to collect the opinion of members of this same caste residing in other parts of the country than Surat, complying with the request of the defendants.[11] To this inquiry, the Ahmadabad collective of the same caste replied as follows:

> As you mention that the people of the Cast of Surat have excommunicated him, it appears to be a dispute of the Cast; He must therefore satisfy them before his re-admittance, without which it cannot be allowed.
>
> (1 B.S.D.A. 35 at 45)

Accepting this opinion of the Ahmadabad collective of the same caste, the Bombay Sadr Divani Adalat finally decided in favour of the defendants, reversing all of the decisions of the lower courts (4 November 1811). Thus the plaintiff finally failed to get his readmission to the caste through legal procedure.

This decision of the Bombay Sadr Divani Adalat holding that 'a dispute of Cast' could only be dealt with by the caste concerned, bestowing extensive discretion on the caste in such matters as excommunication of a member from the caste, came quite close to the acknowledgement of the 'caste autonomy'.

In the following case (2 B.S.D.A. 473), the principle that civil courts should not interfere in the decision of the caste *panchayat* as far as possible was stated more clearly. This suit involved the barber caste of Surat (Surati Valand) in which the plaintiffs were Meetha Kuchura and his sister and the defendants Bhana Mungul and all of the other members of this caste. Meetha Kuchura began to live together with a woman of the carpenter caste who had been excommunicated by the caste by reason of immorality. The caste members warned him not to continue such improper conduct but he paid no heed to it, resulting in his excommunication from the caste. At the hearing, he claimed that he had received her only as a lodger living upstairs while he and his sister were living downstairs, and that he had never taken food prepared by her as he and his sister used to cook themselves. Against this, the defendants produced evidence to prove 'criminal intercourse' between them and further submitted three caste rules. One of the caste rules dated 25 April 1820 (registered at the district court on 20 May 1820) gave three leaders of this caste the authority to excommunicate or fine the caste members who violated the caste rule prohibiting the caste members to take into the home a woman of other castes. The district court decided in favour of the defendants judging that 'every circumstance tended to establish that a criminal intimacy and connexion did exist, and therefore the Cast was justfied in the exclusion'.

On appeal, the judge of the Bombay Sadr Divani Adalat took the following view:

> The principles on which Punchayut disputes should be judged, were now generally admitted to be those which authorized the least interference with the institutions which those classes of the community, using such mode of control over the members, had established for themselves. On such principles it would require clear and decisive proof of malice and violence combined to justify an interference with the act of the expelling Members.
>
> (2 B.S.D.A. 473 at 477. 11 March 1823)

The judge thus dismissed the appeal, holding that in this case the caste had not excommunicated the plaintiff by 'malice and violence'. Thus, the principle that the act of the caste *panchayat* should not be interfered with by the civil court so far as it was not motivated by 'malice and violence',[12] was established by this decision of the Bombay Sadr Divani Adalat. It practically amounted to recognition of caste autonomy.

The Caste Autonomy Policy in the Elphinstone Code

The *panchayat* policy cherished by Elphinstone and followed by Chaplin and the inquiries into caste practises conducted in the areas around Pune as well as the compilation of decisions handed down by the Bombay Sadr Divani Adalat materialized, as a result, in Regulations II and VII in the Elphinstone Code. Regulation VII of 1827 was titled 'A Regulation to facilitate the amicable Adjustment of Disputes of a Civil Nature by means of Arbitrators (a Punchaet)', the preamble of which reads as follows:

> Whereas it is desirable, for the easy and amicable settlement of disputes of a civil nature, that the parties should have the means of adjusting them by arbitration, without being obliged to resort to a court of law, and that an award duly pronounced in such arbitration should have the force of a decree of court;... the following Rules are therefore enacted,....
>
> (Clarke 1851: 83)

With regard to the method of arbitration, Section I of this regulation provided that 'Any such matter as is cognizable in a civil court may, for the purposes specified in this Regulation, be referred, by mutual consent of the parties, to one or more arbitrators, chosen in such manner as may be agreed on by the said parties.' Regulation II of the Elphinstone Code, however, laid down that the caste questions were, in principle, not cognizable by civil courts. These two regulations read together, the caste questions were, without doubt, excluded from the disputes which could be adjusted by 'one or more arbitrators' since only 'such matter as is cognizable in a civil court' could be referred to the arbitrators. In other words, such disputes of civil nature as those on 'the right to moveable or immoveable property, rents, Government revenues, debts, contracts, marriage, succession, damages for injuries' (Bombay Regulation II of 1827) could either be sued in civil courts or referred to 'arbitrators', while the caste questions could only be decided by the caste itself.

Thus, the caste questions were accorded special treatment in the Elphinstone Code system which later came to be known as the caste autonomy policy.

What are the 'Caste Questions'?

Cases not Cognizable in Civil Courts

In the Elphinstone Code, however, no substantive definition of the caste question was provided. What are the caste questions or what is the extent of caste questions? This was rather a tricky question to be answered only through judicial judgements passed by civil courts. By the last decades of the nineteenth century, however, the outline of cases not cognizable in civil courts (the caste questions) had become fairly well demarcated through legal decisions of the Bombay Sadr Divani Adalat and Bombay High Court (Mulla 1901; Kikani 1912; Aiyar 1918). The well-known Indian judge of the Bombay High Court, M.G. Ranade (Justice Ranade) pointed out in one decision handed down by him as follows:

> Claims between rival factions of the same caste to common caste property, claims to leadership of caste, claims to require voluntary offerings and honours and presents to be paid to particular members, claims to officiate as priests against the consent of the caste, claims for compulsory invitations to dinners, &c.... These are matters which affect the internal autonomy of the caste and its social relations, and suits in regard to them have been properly held to be barred by s. 21 of Regulation II of 1827 and similar enactments in other parts of India.
>
> (23 B. 122 at 129-30. 21 February 1898)

Thus, Ranade enumerated five categories of the caste questions not cognizable in civil courts. The first category of the caste questions included disputes over such 'common caste property' as the caste fund and cooking utensils that were possessed by castes, especially in coastal Gujarat cities, for preparing food on the occasion of a caste commensal meeting. In one case, the Ghanchi caste of Broach split into two factions as a result of the dispute over marriage fees. As the one faction monopolized all of the cooking utensils of the caste, the other faction filed a suit suing for half of the cooking utensils or money equivalent to them. On appeal, the Bombay High Court dismissed it, holding that this case was included in a category of the caste questions (5 B. 83. decided in 1880). Though cases pertaining to 'common caste property' were, in principle, held not to be cognizable in civil courts, civil courts could interfere in cases that the right of the caste to its property would likely be violated. In one such case, one member of the Katchia caste of Broach that split into two Tad (factions), changed sides from one faction to the other as a result of a difference of opinion, but he did not return the former faction's cooking utensils in his custody. The former faction thus filed a suit for the recovery of the cooking utensils. The Bombay High Court remanded this case to the lower court, holding that this case should have been decided in the civil court as the caste had the right to protect its own property against infringement (11 B. 534). The Bombay High Court thus judged that the civil courts could interfere in case the right of caste was violated.[13]

'Claims to leadership of caste' and 'claims to officiate as priests against the consent of the caste' which constituted other categories of the caste questions, included such cases as those pertaining to the office of *guru* of the Mahar caste (6 B. 725), the right of the Audich Brahman caste of Ahmadabad to officiate at rituals in the homes of the Surati Mochis as Nyat Gours (caste priests) (20 B.784) and perhaps the office of *aya* of the Hiremath of Kamalapur, Dharwar (34 B. 455).

Cases involving excommunication of a caste member from his caste were the most difficult suits to be judged in civil courts. There seems to be two categories of the excommunication case. One was, so to speak, casual or informal excommunication such as temporary exclusion from social association or relationships within a caste, often resulting in 'claims to require voluntary offerings and honours and presents' and 'claims for compulsory invitations to dinners' in Ranade's sentence. Actual cases of this category of excommunication included exclusion from distribution of presents on the occasion of a marriage or funeral ceremony (for example, 10 B. 661), from 'man-pan invitation' (15 B. 599) and from mutual aid on the occasion of a funeral (18 B. 115). This category of informal excommunication was held to be a problem of 'social etiquette' or 'social privileges', or, in other words, 'a caste question unconnected with property or legal rights' (15 B. 599) which was not cognizable in civil courts.

Formal Excommunication Cases

Formal excommunication from a caste, on the other hand, constituted one of the most intricate legal points at issue to be decided in civil courts over which the judgements of the Bombay High Court often differed from those of the Calcutta and Madras High Courts. As mentioned in the last paragraph of the above-cited sentence of Ranade, 'the internal autonomy of the caste' had also been sanctioned by the middle of the nineteenth century in other parts of India than the Bombay Presidency. Still the difference of opinion or stance pertaining to the problem of the caste autonomy lingered on between the Bombay Presidency and two other presidencies. This difference was revealed in the decisions of the Bombay High Court on the one hand and the Calcutta and Madras High Courts on the other. The focal point of difference was whether or not the caste could legally be treated as a sort of club or voluntary association in England, or, in other words, whether or not the precedent of the decisions of English courts relating to clubs or voluntary associations was applicable to the cases involving excommunication of a caste member from his caste. Over this question, the Bombay High Court and the other two high courts criticized each other as exemplified in the following case.

In the areas around Bombay, there had been residing a small Jewish community called the Beni Israel.[14] At the end of the eighteenth century, the headman (*mukadam*) of this community, Samuel Ezekiel Devakar by name, constructed a synagogue in Bombay. This synagogue was the common property of this community, but the descendants of Devakar had been managing it as the headmen of this community. In the 1870s, however, considerable members of this community began to harbour a grievance against the headman's management of this synagogue and split to form a separate faction. Thereafter, these two factions were reunited under the leadership of the former headman as a result of a compromise. In 1884, however, 300 among 400 members of this community held a meeting and resolved to dismiss him from the office of headman. The headman did not agree to his dismissal, however, holding it as invalid. Thus, the opposition party filed a suit suing for the confimation of their resolution (11 B. 185). The point at issue in this case was whether or not the meeting of 300 members, by the decision of which the headman was dismissed, could be acknowledged as a regular community meeting.

On this point, the Bombay High Court held on appeal that though this community was not the caste to which Section XXI, Bombay Regulation II of 1827 should be applied, this community was a 'private and voluntary religious society resting upon a consensual basis', and that the law relating to such societies could be summarized as follows: 'The members may make rules for themselves, and may constitute a tribunal to enforce the rules, and the decision of that tribunal is binding when it has acted within the scope of its authority and in a manner consonent with the general principles of justice' (11 B. 185 at 194-95). In this judgement, the Bombay High Court judge often referred to cases in England pertaining to 'dismissal of a member from a club' in which it was held that 'the proceedings [of dismissal] must have been conducted with fairness'. In accordance with this, the Bombay High Court judge finally decided that the proceeding of dismissal of the headman of the Beni Israel community was not fairly conducted, as he had been given no previous notice that his dismissal would be discussed at the meeting.

The Calcutta High Court criticized in the following case (21 C. 463, decided in 1893) this decision of the Bombay High Court for its treating the Beni Israel community as a 'private and voluntary society ... resting upon a consensual basis' exactly on the same footing with clubs and voluntary associations in England. This Calcutta High Court suit was raised by some members (*bhakats*) of a *satra* (a religious fraternity belonging to the Vishnu sect) in Assam who were excommunicated from the *satra* on the grounds that they had received *mantra* from a man of another sect. The defendants (leaders of this *satra*) pleaded that civil courts 'had no jurisdiction to interfere with the decision of the majority of the *bhakats*, by which the plaintiffs had been excluded from the prayer-hall' (21 C. 463 at 468-69), referring as the precedent to two English cases as well as the above-mentioned Bombay High Court case (11 B. 185). On appeal, the Calcutta High Court handed down the following sentence:

> The English cases cited are cases of expulsion from clubs or voluntary assiciations which people are free to join or not,.... The case, however, is very different with regard to castes or religious fraternities like the one before us. As a rule, people do not join them as a matter of choice; they belong to them as a matter of necessity; they are born in their respective castes or sects; and the consequences of exclusion from caste or sect are far more serious and affect a person's status in a far greater degree than those of expulsion from a club. The protection of

> Courts of Justice, even though presided over by Judges of a different religious persuasion, against expulsion seems, therefore, to be much more needed in the one case than the other.... The Bombay case (Advocate-General of Bombay v. Haim Devakar [11 B. 785]) is no doubt more in point, but as it is opposed to the decision on this side of India (See Gopal Gurain v. Gurain [7 W.R. 299] ....), with all respect for the learned Judge who decided that case, we must follow as we are bound to do so, the decisions of our own Court in preference to it.
>
> (21 C. 463 at 470)

Thus, the Calcutta High Court held that civil courts could interfere in the decision involving excommunication of a member of such private associations as this *satra*, in such cases, first, that the rules of the associations were contrary to 'natural justice', second, that the decision was against the rules of the association, and third, that the decision was not bona fide. This means that the Calcutta High Court took a stricter stance with regard to the question of the caste autonomy than did the Bombay High Court. This judgement of the Calcutta High Court was followed by that of the Madras High Court in a case involving excommunication of a member from a caste.[15]

In the following decision of the Bombay High Court (26 B. 174), the well-known Indian judge, N. Chandavarkar, strongly refuted this line of judicial judgement on the side of the Calcutta and Madras High Courts. This case involved the Visa Osval Vania caste residing in Zanzibar, east Africa which was then treated as a district of the Bombay Presidency. Around the end of the nineteenth century a dispute occurred in this caste. Some members of this caste received an invitation to a feast from one member of the Lovana (Lohana) caste and actually attended it, in spite of the order of the caste headmen (*shettias*) to forbid attendance at the feast. The caste headmen, therefore, summoned the caste meeting and decided to excommunicate them, without calling on them for explanation. Against this, the excommunicated members brought a suit praying for a declaration that their excommunication be illegal, and that they be still members of this caste. They also claimed damages for defamation. On appeal, the Bombay High Court held that in such cases as this in which the only cause of action was the 'loss of dignity and social privilege' which had been enjoyed as a member of a caste, civil courts could not interfere as 'the question raised was entirely a caste question'. It did not matter in these cases, it was judged, if a caste member was excommunicated without having been heard in defence by his caste.

In the sentence, Chandavarkar pointed out the difference of judicial opinion between the Bombay and Calcutta High Courts over the problem of the caste as follows:

> They [judges of the Calcutta High Court] think that as the institution of caste in the form in which it prevails in this country is different from clubs and voluntary associations, the law held in the English decisions to be applicable to the latter cannot apply to the former, and that a Civil Court has jurisdiction, not only to entertain claims to property or office involving caste questions, but to determine whether a rule laid down by a caste is reasonable or not. It is true, in a sense, that a member of a caste belongs to it by birth, whereas a member of a club enters it voluntarily. But I fail to see how that can make any difference as to the legal aspects of either. It is just as competent for a man to leave his caste as it is competent for a member of a club to resign his membership. Though a man belongs to his caste by birth, it can hardly be said on that account that he belongs to it by necessity, for it is the man who himself determines the necessity. Though born in it by necessity, he continues by volition in it. He can go out of it whenever he likes–the caste cannot compel him to be in it. The caste is as much a voluntary association as a club–the one can frame rules for its guidance and revoke them and make fresh rules as well as the other. It is equally within the power of a caste to admit into its fold men not born in it as it is within the power of a club to admit any one it likes as its member. To hold that the membership of a caste is determined by birth is to hold that the caste cannot, if it likes, mix with another caste and form both into one caste.
>
> (26 B. 174 at 186-87)

This judicial judgement of Chandavarkar to attribute the same voluntary nature as that of clubs of England to the caste might give the impression that he went too far in the legal logic. Nevertheless, there is no doubt that Chandavarkar followed suit of the traditional line of policy in the Bombay Presidency to grant as wide autonomy as possible to the caste or any other bodies resembling it, as indicated by the historical fact that the caste autonomy policy had first been formulated in this presidency. Taking this legal tradition of the Bombay Presidency into consideration, it was rather natural that the Bombay High Court had been critical of the judgements on the caste questions of the Calcutta and Madras High Courts.

Conclusion

The caste autonomy policy was, as discussed above, a policy designed for incorporating autonomous potentiality to maintain societal order inherent in castes into the colonial ruling system. For the state in general, without doubt, the most important problem is how to mobilize voluntary participation of the people to maintain order and stability. In the case of a colonial state like British India in particular, this was of crucial importance. As the British colonial administration found in the caste the most effective native organization for maintaining societal order and stability, it was no wonder that the policy to bestow as wide autonomy as possible on the caste was formulated under British colonial rule.

There existed, however, a certain degree of difference in the caste policy between the Bombay Presidency on the one hand and the Bengal and Madras Presidencies on the other. This was revealed in the difference of the judicial judgement between the Bombay High Court and the Calcutta and Madras High Courts with regard to the caste questions. This difference seems to be caused by the different local circumstances prevalent in each of the presidencies such as the nature of the communal structures of each of the societies as well as the difference of the period of colonization and the trend of political ideas then prevailing in England (Stokes 1959).

The caste autonomy policy, in historical perspective, gave ever stronger vitality to the caste under British colonial rule than it used to enjoy under former governments. Being sustained by the caste autonomy policy, the caste *panchayat* was flourishing, while other types of *panchayat* such as the village *panchayat* and district *panchayat* gradually fell into disuse. Moreover, many castes extended the caste linkage or network by uniting together many caste collectives of similar nature which were formerly scattered over wide areas in relative isolation. The so-called caste cluster or caste association (Carroll 1975; Carroll 1978) on the upper level of caste union began to be organized, and often made the caste rule binding upon the lower level organizations of the caste. The Pathare Prabhu in the areas around Bombay, for example, formed the upper caste organization named the Kshatriya Union Club and made a caste rule that they should not invite *naikins* on the occasion of ceremonies like *munji* and marriage (15 B. 599. 1891). In the case of the Kutch Dasa Osval of Bombay, a committee of 35 members was set up and made a caste rule prohibiting the asking of Brahmans to officiate at their marriage ceremonies (19 B. 507. 1895). These trends indicate that many castes began to develop a stratified and extended structure with their own binding rules under British colonial rule, being prompted, at least partly, by the caste autonomy policy.[16]

Notes

1 Mountstuart Elphinstone (1779-1859) was employed by the East India Company in 1795 and immediately proceeded to India. He was appointed the Resident of Poona (Pune) in 1811 and then the Deccan Commissioner in 1818 to administer the so-called Conquered Territories that were taken over from the Maratha kingdom as a result of the third Anglo-Maratha War. In 1819 he was promoted to the Governorship of the Bombay Presidency and founded the basis of the Bombay administration. See further Colebrooke 1884; Stokes 1959: 148-49.

2 This report of Elphinstone was first printed in R.E.I.H. Vol. IV, pp. 139-206 and later published in book form under the title of *The Territories Conquered from the Paishwa* (Bombay, 1872). As this later edition (2nd ed.) in book form, however, contains many misprints, I draw on the original report printed in R.E.I.H. Vol. IV.

3 As to caste meetings of two levels, that is to say, the district (*pargana*) level caste meetings and extended caste meetings beyond a district, see Chapter 4 of this volume. The village *panchayat* was mainly constituted by the Patil, Kulkarni, *vatandar* Kunbis and *bara balute* and the participants of the district *panchayat* included the Deshmukh, Deshpande, Patils, Kulkarnis and caste headmen (*mhetars*) of various castes. (See also Chapter 1 of this volume.)

4 Ballhatchet mistakenly attributes these 'Rules' to the hand of M. Elphinstone. He also neglects clause 1 of these 'Rules' with the result of undervaluing the importance of these 'Rules' for the formulation of the caste autonomy policy in the Bombay Presidency (Ballhatchet 1957: 197 f.n. 1).

5 The members were Babinton (chairman), W. Erskine and A. Robertson. Babinton was later replaced by C. Norris. Cf. Colebrooke 1884: II 123, 134; Kumar 1968: 75-76; R.E.I.H.: IV 870.

6 The East India Company was granted the Divani (the office of the Divan) of the Bengal and Bihar Provinces by the Mughals in 1765 as a result of the battle at Baksar in 1764 but it did not immediately proceed to take direct charge of the Divani, appointing two Indian 'Naib Duans' (Nayeb Divan, deputy Divan) respectively in Bengal and Bihar. In 1771, however, the Court of Directors of the East India Company decided to 'stand forth as Duan' with its own officials, dismissing two deputy Divans. Thus, the letter to this purport of the Court of Directors dated 28 August 1771 was sent to the President and Council at Fort William (Sixth Report from the

Committee of Secrecy appointed to enquire into The State of The East India Company, 26 April 1773, in *The Reports from Committees of the House of Commons 1715-1801*, Vol. 4, p. 299).

7 'A Plan for the Administration of Justice extracted from the Proceedings of the Committee of Circuit, 15 August 1772', Seventh Report from the Committee of Secrecy appointed to enquire into The State of The East India Company, 6 May 1773, in *The Reports from Committees of the House of Commons 1715-1801*, Vol. 4, p. 350. According to this section, 'Moulavies and Brahmans [or more commonly Shastris]' were actually posted in each civil court to assist British judges in their interpreting Islamic and Hindu laws up to the 1860s. See, further on Shastris posted in civil courts, Chapter 11 of this volume.

8 As to the structure of this caste and their caste rule, see Chapter 4 of this volume. Under the Bombay administration, caste rules duly registered at the courts had the same legal power as that of the regulations or acts of the government. Thus, many castes registered various caste rules at the district courts in the Bombay Presidency, especially in coastal Gujarat. The caste rule was called 'Bundobust', being derived from the Persian term *bandobast*, of which the administrative term in English was 'Bye Law'.

9 As to the structure of this caste and their caste rule, see Chapter 4 of this volume.

10 In another case suing for damages for injury (loss of caste), for example, the court confirmed the right of caste 'to maintain its purity by refusing communion with a suspected person', referring to 'the sentiments of Mr. Threipland, approved by the Sudur Udalut [Sadr Adalat]' (1 B.S.D.A. 84 at 88).

11 This procedure of inquiring into the opinion of members of the same caste residing in other parts of the country was quite often resorted to when the caste group of a locality itself was the party of the case. See, also, the opinion of M. Elphinstone on the caste *panchayat* quoted above (R.E.I.H.: IV 191).

12 In other judgements, the term 'malice and violence' was often substituted by the term 'malice and ill-will'. See, for example, 1 B.S.D.A. 35 and 1 B.S.D.A. 81.

13 See further, 19 B. 507 and 34 B. 467.

14 The Beni Israel is a Jewish community that originally migrated around the sixth century from Aden or the Persian Gulf area to the western coast of India. Their population in 1901 was 10,864 (5,465 males and 5,399 females). They had been assimilated into Indian cultures and adopted Marathi as their mother tongue. In the nineteenth century, however, they began to strengthen their self-consciousness as Jews under the influence of Christianity which developed in India under British colonial rule. See Enthoven 1922: I 67-77.

15 The judgement passage in 33 M. 67 reads as follows:

> A caste, no doubt, is a voluntary association of persons for a certain purpose. It is open to a person to leave it, but, every Hindu, at any rate the majority of them, are born into some caste or other. Their status and their relations towards the other castes are defined and fixed by the caste to which they belong. Their matrimonial relations, their laws of inheritance and generally their religious and social rights and duties also are determined by their caste.... A person cannot be deprived of the membership of the caste except in accordance with caste usage. The caste as a body, or the majority of them, may no doubt expel him, but if they do so without giving him an opportunity of explanation, the Civil Courts will interfere.... The decided cases [of the Madras High Court] show that their procedure must be in accordance with usage and that the excommunication must not be opposed to natural justice (33 M. 67 at 69).

16 Shahid Amin refers to interesting caste rules made in an area in northern India under the influence of Gandhian politics of the time as follows:

> On 27 January 1921 the sweepers, washermen and barbers of Naugarh, in neighbouring Basti, meeting in *panchayats* of their various brotherhoods, decided that 'anyone who partakes of meat, fish and liquor would have to pay a fine' of Rs 51 towards the upkeep of vagrant cows (Amin 1995: 102-3).

II

Discrimination and Privilege

6

Ati-Shudra Castes in the Later Medieval Deccan

Introduction

This chapter aims at shedding light on the reality of Ati-Shudra castes in the later medieval Deccan through the medium of Marathi public and private documents. Medieval Marathi documents cover chronologically from the fifteenth to the early nineteenth centuries and geographically the western Deccan and Konkan to which the coverage of this chapter also corresponds. More strictly, this chapter focuses on the seventeenth-eighteenth century Deccan under the Maratha kingdom (Peshva government). Thus, the social life of Ati-Shudra castes under the Peshvas is the main theme of this chapter.

Discrimination against Ati-Shudra Castes

The caste system is well known to have been marked by severe discrimination against the Ati-Shudra castes. Although discrimination towards classes like the Chandala (*Caṇḍāla*) was widespread in ancient India, it does not seem likely that the members of these classes were grouped together to form a distinct social stratum (*varṇa*). Furthermore, the percentage of discriminated classes is considered to have been rather small in ancient India (Yamazaki 1997: 15). Conversely, in the medieval Deccan, discriminated castes were grouped together as Ati-Shudra and treated as a distinct social stratum. Moreover, the percentage of discriminated castes was also much higher than in ancient India. This means that the medieval discrimination which was quite different from its ancient predecessor was formed during this period. Nonetheless pinpointing the exact period of formation of this medieval discrimination is very difficult; the period between the eighth and twelfth centuries might reasonably well be presumed as being this formative era. It is known, in fact, that Indian society in general began to change from the bottom in the seventh or eighth century, what is referred to as the post-Gupta period, and that this social transformation gave rise to the predominant features of medieval India such as the village community and the caste system by the twelfth century.

The shaping of medieval discrimination in the Deccan was also an unmistakable part of the general social transformation depicting this period, and, in particular, discrimination against Ati-Shudra castes in the later medieval Deccan was a direct development of this medieval system of discrimination (Yamazaki 1997: 15-16).

Sparśa, Sparśāsparśa and Saṃsarga

Contact with an Ati-Shudra was regarded as bringing impurity upon oneself and this impurity was considered to be transmittable from the person directly touched by an Ati-Shudra to other persons who happened to come into contact with the contactee. Fundamentally then, what indeed did the word 'contact' (*sparśa*, *sparśāsparśa* or *saṃsarga* in Marathi) mean? Some examples may suffice.

In one instance, a Brahman named Bajirao Moreshvar had stayed in the *vāḍā* of Anandrao Gopal Joshi with his family for four months. Afterwards, a *kuṇbīṇa* (female slave) of this family was found to be a woman of the Chambhar caste. This meant that Anandrao, Bajirao and their families had become impure through contact (*saṃsarga*) with the *kuṇbīṇa* so that they had to undergo the following purification ceremony:

48 *prājāpatye* for each Brahman,
24 *prājāpatye* for each woman,
24 *prājāpatye* for each Brahman child,
4 *prājāpatye* for each Shudra.

(S.P.D. XXXXIII 92. 1795)

In another instance there was a *baṭīka* (female slave) in the family of a Mamledar, Balaji Mahadeo, who was a Prabhu by caste. As she was found to have committed *vyabhicāra* (adultery) with an *antyaja* (Ati-Shudra) man, she was regarded as having become as impure as an Ati-Shudra. She had been working in the family for nearly two and a half years, sweeping, smearing the floor with a wash of cow dung, brushing kitchen utensils, cutting vegetables, making beds and engaging other duties. Thus, all of the members of this family had necessarily come into contact (*saṃsarga*) with her so that all of them were considered to have become impure. They were therefore ordered to undergo the following purification ceremony:

> 135 *prājāpatye* for the mother of the Mamledar,
> 270 *prājāpatye* for the Mamledar himself,
> 135 *prājāpatye* for the child of the Mamledar.

In practise, however, one *prājāpatyā* could be commuted for two rupees, with the money thus collected being distributed among Brahmans. In addition, as the house and the land on which the house stood was also regarded as impure, it had to be purified as follows:

> House land: To be dug up and purified by letting a cow walk on it,
> Earthernware and metallic utensils: To be purified by fire,
> Wooden floor and door: To be destroyed because it can not be purified.
>
> (S.S.R.P.D. VIII 1125. 1781-82)

These instances denote that contact with an Ati-Shudra did not necessarily mean bodily touch, but it included indirect contact (association) through living together in the same house. Indirect contact was termed *saṃsarga* in contrast with *sparśa* (*sparśāsparśa*) meaning physical contact with an Ati-Shudra (e.g. *Manusmṛti* edited by G. Jha, XI-180).

Importantly as well, bodily touch with an Ati-Shudra was likely to occur in a crowded place like the pilgrimage centre of a sacred place.

A good example of this concerned Pandharpur on the Bhima River, a tributary of the Krishna, situated nearly 300 km south-east of Pune which has remained the celebrated sacred place of Vithobha (Vitthara) where a great number of pilgrims gathered every autumn. They were known as the *vārkarī* and formed the main body of the Deccan *bhakti*. *Bhakti* was open to every man including Ati-Shudras, and even a Mahar saint Chokhamela had been enshrined in Pandharpur. Thus, a considerable number of Ati-Shudras (Mahars and others) joined these pilgrimages to Pandharpur. However, if an Ati-Shudra came near the Vithoba temple when it was over flowing with pilgrims, bodily touch with him was quite likely to occur. Brahmans were so much afraid of this that they appealed to the government (Peshva government) to keep Ati-Shudras away from the Vithoba temple. The government resultantly decreed as follows:

> There is a stone image of Chokhamela to the north of the Vithoba temple and Ati-Shudras make their pilgrimage to it. The place neighbours the road frequented by pilgrims so that they happen to come in touch with an Ati-Shudra [*sparśāsparśa*]. This is against [the *dharma* of] Brahman. Therefore, Ati-Shudras should worship the image of Chokhamela by the side of the lamp-pillar in front of the Vithoba temple or in the *Mahārvāḍā*. Ati-Shudras must not approach the Vithoba temple itself. If they violate this edict, they must be punished.
>
> (S.S.R.P.D. VIII 1129. 1783-84)

As this case denotes, physical contact with an Ati-Shudra (*sparśa*, *sparśāsparśa*) was regarded as an incident to be avoided at all cost (cf. *Manusmṛti* V-84). In villages where villagers knew each other well, physical contact with an Ati-Shudra was not likely to occur, of course, but in towns or at sacred places where unknown people gathered, the possibility was certainly not unlikely.

In Nasik, a Budhalakar (an Ati-Shudra caste, skin vessel [*budhalā*] makers) asked a barber (Nhavi) who was sitting on the bank of the Godavari River awaiting clients. The Budhalakar did not inform the barber that he was a man of an Ati-Shudra caste as the latter did not ask him his caste. Just as the barber began to cut his hair, another member of the barber's caste happened to come along and told him that he should not have cut the hair of an Ati-Shudra. The barber who had thus made bodily touch with this Ati-Shudra was excommunicated from his caste. Having been embarrassed, the barber acknowledged his sin (*doṣa*) and asked the Dharmadhikari of Nasik to free him from his sin through an adequate ceremony (A.S.S. I 193. 1795).

Restriction of Dwelling Place

To prevent any physical contact with Ati-Shudras the places where they could dwell were restricted. In the medieval Deccan, these Ati-Shudra dwelling places were generally called *Mahārvāḍā* and were situated just outside the village walls.

As a case in point, in the village Katraj, Karyatmaval District, the homes of Mahars, Mangs and Chambhars were thought to be neighbouring too near the village site (*pāṇḍhara*). It was therefore decided to destory and rebuild their homes in a place more remote from the village site. The following sums of money were granted for this relocation of their homes:

For Mahars [22 families]: Rs. 207
For Mangs [two families]: Rs. 14
For Chambhars [two families]: Rs. 30.

In addition, the government gave them in all 300 pieces of timber for rebuilding their houses (S.S.R.P.D. VIII 1142. 1789-90).

In another case, in the village Baner, Pune Province, the *Mahārvāḍā* was situated to the east of the village wall. Through the *Mahārvāḍā* a rivulet flowed where Mahars used to wash their skinned hides. When Shahaji, the father of Shivaji, came to hold this village as *jāgīr* his minister Dadaji Kondadeo planned to draw water from this rivulet but so long as the Mahars continued to dwell there, water thus drawn could not be used. Thus, the *Mahārvāḍā* there was destroyed and rebuilt on the opposite side of the village behind the shrine of Bairoba (S.P.D. XXXI 65).

These cases demonstrate that the dwelling places of Ati-Shudras were occasionally changed to suit the needs of the village to which they were affiliated.

Duties and Perquisites of Ati-Shudras

In the medieval Deccan, many castes were classed as Ati-Shudra but the most numerous in number among them were the Mahar, Mang and Chambhar. Members of these castes who were incorporated into the village system of the division of labour (the Vatan system) as village servants were respectively called the *vatandār* Mahar, *vatandār* Mang and *vatandār* Chambhar. Although it is inopportune here to dwell on this Vatan system, in a word, this system constituted the most fundamental social relationship in the medieval Deccan which penetrated the village community as well as the *parganā* (district) community. Notably, the *vatandārs* of the Ati-Shudra castes were an indispensable element of this system and invariably included in the *bārā balute* (12 types of village servants).[1]

As a case pertaining to the perquisites of Ati-Shudra *vatandārs*, a dispute broke out between Mahars and peasants cum Mangs in Parner District. The Mahars subsequently made the following appeal to the government:

1. When bulls and other cattle [*baela va ḍhoreṃ*] die in the village, it is the custom that we Mahars take their hides [*kātaḍī*] except

for those of the plough bulls [*dhurecā baela*], even though the peasants have begun to dispute with us over this matter.

2. On the occasion of Dasara, Mangs go from door to door asking for alms and we Mahars take *pāñc naevedya* [an offering] and *pāñc paise* [a money offering] but Mangs have begun to quarrel over this.
3. On the occasion of Pola, we Mahars take the offering made to bulls, but now Mangs say that they should take it.
4. When bulls and other cattle [*ḍhora*] of a Mang's house die, it is the custom that we Mahars take them and that Mangs should not interfere with this.
5. On the occasion of the *śānti* ceremony in Dasara, we Mahars let a buffalo [*ṭoṇgā*] walk around the village boundary and we walk before it carrying a pot of *peḍhā* [sweetmeats] in hand. After the *śānti* ceremony is over, we Mahars take the buffalo and *peḍhā* but now Mangs are asking for a half of the *peḍhā*. Mangs must not be allowed to ask for this.
6. We Mahars take the offering made to Jarimari [the *devī* of cholera] but now Mangs are making trouble over it and say that they should take it.
7. On the occasion of a marriage ceremony, the bridegroom of the Mahar caste rides on a horse [*ghoḍā*] and goes in a procession but the bridegroom of the Mang caste must ride on a bull. Now, Mangs are making their bridegrooms ride on a horse, so please order them to make their bridegrooms ride on a bull as in the past.[2]

Receiving the appeal from the Mahars, the government conducted an inquiry, and the statement by the Mahars proved to be true. Therefore, a government order was issued to the district officials, Deshmukhs, Deshpandes and Patils of Parner and other districts to the effect that they had to behave in accordance with the long-standing custom and must not make trouble (S.S.R.P.D. VI 816. 1776).

Disposing of the carcasses of dead cattle was one of the main duties of *vatandār* Mahars and, as a reward, they could take the hides of the disposed cattle except for those of plough bullocks which they had to hand over to the former owner of the cattle. The first and fourth clauses of the above-cited document indicate that there were occasionally disputes between Mahars and peasants or Mangs over the right to take the hides of dead cattle.[3]

On the occasion of Dasara, Pola and other festivals, it was customary to worship the *devī* by offering buffaloes or goats as a sacrifice. This ceremony was known as *śānti* and, especially on the occasion of Dasara, the *śānti* ceremony used to be performed to pacify the *devī*. When cholera or other plagues broke out, the offering of sacrificed animals was also made to Jarimari, the *devī* of cholera, to appease her anger. In the *śānti* ceremony Ati-Shudras, especially *vatandār* Mahars, played the leading role. In reward for this, they had the right to take sacrificed animals, offerings and money offerings, after the ceremony was over. Disputes occasionally arose over this right between Mahars and Mangs (the third and sixth clauses of the above-cited document). (For further details of *śānti*, see below.)

Disputes of a similar nature often occurred in various places. The headman (*mhetar*) of the Mahars of Karepathar District appealed to the government as follows regarding the right to take the sacrificed buffaloes on the occasion of Dasara:

> As the custom dictates, we make a buffalo walk around the village boundary and we walk before it with a pot of *peḍhā* in hand. After that we sacrifice the buffalo by the side of the house of *mulāṇā* [Islamic teacher] and skin the hide for making a drum. Mangs stretch the hide over the drum. When cattle [*ḍhora*] die in the families of Mang, we Mahars take them but now the Mangs say that they should take them.
>
> (Oturkar 77)

In another instance in the village Pargav, Karepathar District, a dispute between Mahars and Chambhars broke out with regard to the right to take *pāñc naevedya* of Holi. The Patil of the village gave the following evidence (1778-79):

> Since the time of my grandfather, *pāñc naevedya* of Holi had been given to the Chambhars but at the time of my father Mahars began to quarrel over it. But even after that *pāñc naevedya* has been given to Chambhars.
>
> (Oturkar 70)

Thus disputes over perquisites among various Ati-Shudra castes, especially between Mahars and Mangs, does not seem to have been a rare occurrence in the later medieval Deccan.

Headman (*mhetar*) of Ati-Shudra Castes

In each village there usually dwelled several families of some Ati-Shudra castes, and each Ati-Shudra caste formed a tight-knit community within a *parganā* community generally composed of 20 to 100 villages which constituted a district (*parganā* or *ṭappā*).[4] Each caste in the *parganā* community had its own headman (*mhetar*) whose duty was to represent the caste to the state and other castes. In reward for this, the caste headman had the right to take perquisites from caste members within the *parganā* community. His office was also a *vatan* to be held hereditarily.

The headman of the Chambhar caste of Supe District presented himself at the office of Shahaji (the father of Shivaji) who held the district as *jāgīr* and made the following statement:

> Chambhars of this district used to pay tax every year in kind using shoes and not in cash. However, this year officials did not take the shoes as tax and made us pay in cash by commuting a pair of shoes for one and a half *ṭake*. Owing to this we are now in a deplorable condition. Therefore, please take the tax in kind in the form of shoes as before and stop taking it in cash.

Shahaji acknowledged his statement as true and the following order was issued to the official of Supe District:

> It has been decided not to take the tax from Chambhars in the form of cash. Therefore do not take even one *rukā* from them. Instead of it, take the tax in kind as before.... Order all Chambhars of this district including Baramati Sub-district to obey the headman Mal and if not, make them obey by force.
>
> (M.I.S. XX 12)

As this document shows, the headman of a caste played the role of representing the caste to the state (in this case, *jāgīrdār*) and of defending its interests for the discharge of which he could make the caste members obey him. The reason why the state (*jāgīrdār*) ordered the caste members to obey him was that tax from a caste was collected by caste headman so that for the state too it was necessary to support the authority of the caste headman over the caste members.

Perquisites of the headman of the Ati-Shudra castes were somewhat different from those of the headman of other castes. For example, perquisites of the headman of Mahars of Sasvad District were enumerated as follows:

1. Hooves and heads of cattle [*gurācā śīrā va khuravitā*].
2. *Poḷī* [plain wheat cake] of Holi.
3. *Taśrīf* [grant of a dress of honour] from the government.
4. *Nāikī* [*vatan* of *nāik*] of *ṭhāṇa* [soldier-police station].
5. Music [to be played in front of the house on the occasion of festivals].

(S.C.S. VII 43. 1657)

As mentioned before, one of the main duties of *vatandār* Mahars was to dispose of the carcasses of dead cattle, and the 'hooves and heads' of cattle (*gurūṃ*) thus disposed of became the perquisite of the Mahar headman. The Mahar headman's right to take *polī* offered to the fire of Holi was relative to the Mahars' duty to bring the fire of Holi to the festival site (A.S.S. III 127). *Nāikī vatan* of *ṭhāṇa* was related to the military or police role of the Mahars. A certain section of Mahars and other Ati-Shudra castes was posted in the station (*ṭhāṇa*) set up in the main town of a district as soldier-police. Their office was called *nāikī* and was a *vatan*. Ati-Shudra castes like the Mahar had been, in part, hillmen who had played a great role as a military force in the process of state building by Shivaji. *Nāikī vatan* of *ṭhāṇa* held by the Ati-Shudra castes was related to this character of these castes. (For further details, see below.)

Caste-Ranking among the Ati-Shudra Castes

In the medieval Deccan, there were various castes grouped together as Ati-Shudra but they were not on an equal footing with each other. The above-cited document regarding the dispute between Mahars and peasants cum Mangs indicates that stratified caste-ranking existed even among the Ati-Shudra castes. Once again the last clause of the document runs as follows:

> On the occasion of a marriage ceremony, the bridegroom of the Mahar caste rides on a horse and goes in a procession but the bridegroom of the Mang caste must ride on a bull. Now, Mangs are making their bridegrooms ride on a horse, so please order them to make their bridegrooms ride on a bull as in the past.

The reason why a dispute occurred over this problem of on which animal the bridegroom of each caste was to ride was that the social status of a caste was indicated by the kind of animal on which the bridegroom of the caste rode. Specifically, the caste the bridegroom of which rode on a horse was considered to be higher in social (caste) ranking than the caste of which the bridegroom rode on a bull. Thus, Mahars claimed that they were higher in social (caste) ranking than Mangs by saying that their bridegrooms rode on a horse while Mang bridegrooms were to ride on a bull. As stated before, this claim of Mahars was recognized by the government.

Social (caste) ranking among the Ati-Shudra castes was expressed in other forms too. In Pune and Junnar Provinces, a dispute broke out between the Chambhars and Buruds (bamboo workers) over the problem of whether or not Chambhars had to make shoes (*payepośa*) for Buruds. Finally, it came out that Chambhars had not made shoes for Buruds in the past so that it was decided that from now on as well Chambhars did not need to make shoes for them (S.P.D. XXII 306. 1735). This means that Chambhars were regarded as being higher in social (caste) ranking than Buruds.

Social ranking between Ati-Shudra castes thus expressed in various forms accumulated and formed a social status chain like a staircase onto which all the Ati-Shudra castes were to be placed.

Ati-Shudras and *Devī*

Boundary Disputes

In the later medieval Deccan, boundary disputes between villages often occurred and on those occasions *vatandār* Mahars played an important role. The boundary dispute between the villages Malshiras and Pisarven in Pune Province was, for example, very long-standing. In-between, arbitration was tried several times but it took a long time to reach a final settlement.

This boundary dispute began in the early seventeenth century when the Nizam Shahi dynasty was under the sway of Malik Ambar. When the boundary dispute occurred, Patils of these two villages asked Malik Ambar to intervene. Accordingly, it was decided that both parties were to go to the *kasbe* Harsul and undergo an ordeal (*divya*). The *huddedār*, Deshmukh, *śeṭa* and *mahājana* of the *kasbe* Harsul gathered together in the *kasbe* Harsul and made preparations for the *divya*. However, the Patil of Pisarven declared that there was no need for the *divya* since the rivulet which flowed from the direction of the village Tekavdi had served as the boundary between two villages and it continued to do so. Therefore, the government order was issued to the *kārkūn* to demarcate the boundary according to the statement of the Patil of Pisarven.

With the *farmān* to this effect, both parties returned to their respective villages, but soon afterwards Pisarven began to make trouble again. This time the Patil of Malshiras went to Pune and asked for arbitration. As a result, it was decided to resort to trial by *divya* at the Vateshvar Temple in the *kasbe* Sasvad, and for this purpose the *kārkūn*, Deshmukh and others were sent to Sasvad. The *vṛttikār* (*vatandār* Mahar) Kana bin Dhondi of Malshiras was to undergo the *divya*. All of them went to the disputed boundary, and according to the statement of the villagers of Malshiras, 27 boundary marks (mainly stones, cf. *Manusmṛti* VIII-248) were recorded down and soil of the boundary was gathered. Then all of them proceeded to the Vateshvar Temple. The *divya* was to be done using an anvil (*aerṇī*). In the first place, a hand of Kana was cleansed and the characteristic points of the palm were noted down. Subsequently, Kana took up the red-hot anvil heated by charcoal in his hand and passed over seven circles (*maṇḍala*)[5] drawn on the ground and threw the anvil onto a heap of hay that blazed up. Kana's hand was then covered by a *khaletī* (*khalitā*, small bag or purse) and sealed. After three days all of them gathered again and unsealed Kana's hand to examine it. His hand turned out to be unburnt. Thus, it proved that Kana was successful in the *divya* and the boundary marks recorded down previously according to the statement of the villagers of Malshiras were acknowledged as being true.

This boundary dispute did not come to an end even with this trial though. Thereafter it became more complicated as the village Tekavdi was also involved in it. To bring this long-standing boundary dispute to a final settlement, the *nivāḍpatra* (deed of decision) of Peshva Bajirav was issued (S.G.R.A.O. Sanads and Letters II 39. 1723-24).

As this case indicates, a meeting of the *parganā* community with the attendance of local officials, Deshmukh, Deshpande, Patil, Kulkarni and other *vatandārs* was held when a boundary dispute occurred but it was not easy to reach an amicable settlement even through such meetings. On such occasions, the ordeal known as *divya* for hearing the divine will was used to be resorted to. There were various types of *divya* but the most popular was the so-called *agni divya* which was resorted to in the above-mentioned case, and *ravā divya*. In the latter case, a small piece of iron called *ravā* was used. The *ravā* was put in a vessel filled with boiling oil and *ghī*. The man who was to undergo the *divya* put his hand into it and took the *ravā* out, and if his hand was not scalded he was proved to be successful in the *divya*.[6]

As stated above, on the occasion of the *divya*, *vatandār* Mahars played an important role. The following is another example.

In the boundary dispute between Ghatan and Bhosar, the *vatandār* Mahars of these two villages underwent the *divya* by hot anvil. At first, the nails of these two Mahars were pared and their hands were cleansed with soap and then the characteristic points of their palms were written down on a paper. Afterwards, their hands were sealed by *piśvyā* (*piśvī*, purse or small bag). The complainant (*agravāḍī*) village made leaves of *pīpal*, threads of *kovarī* (a kind of tree) and *dahībhāt* (mixture of curd and boiled rice) its witness. On the day of the *divya*, charcoal was brought from both the villages which was used to heat an anvil. The hands of the two Mahars were unsealed and then both of them were purified by ritual bathing. The Mahar of the complainant village touched the red-hot anvil first. Local officials and the other attendants put 7 leaves of *pīpal*, threads of *kovarī*, 19 *śer* of *dahībhāt* and 9 *śer* of butter on his palm. And then his hand was sealed again. After three days, his hand was unsealed and examined. It came out that his palm was burnt and the inner side of his thumb was also blistered. On the other side, the hand of the Mahar of the defendant (*prativāḍī*) village was found to be clean. Thus, the Mahar of the defendant village was acknowledged as being successful in the *divya* and he walked along the boundary line he assumed to be correct to determine it (S.G.R.A.O. Sanads and Letters II 6).

These cases illustrate that *vatandār* Mahars usually played the role of undergoing *divya*. Why was it then that Mahars who were in everyday life discriminated against in various ways could play the role of hearing the divine will through *divya*? Who was the god whose will Mahars asked to hear? He (or She) could not be an orthodox Brahmanical god under whose authority Mahars and other Ati-Shudras were discriminated against. Thus the only conceivable deity was a goddess called *devī*. In the understratum of Brahmanical religions there existed the thick stratum of the animistic religious world that had not been totally assimilated into orthodox Brahmanical religions. It might have been a pre-Aryan religious heritage rooted deeply into Indian soil, and the deity in this religious world was a goddess called *devī*. The divine ruler of the soil of the Deccan was not an orthodox Brahmanical god but a *devī* and the village boundary was also under the sway of *devī*. Therefore, the will of *devī* was requested in the case of boundary disputes.

Mahars and other Ati-Shudra castes, in general, were assumed to be the *ādivāsī* who had been living in the Deccan from the pre-Aryan period. They had not been totally assimilated into the Aryan culture and still continued to retain their own peculiar culture. The reason why Mahars, who were counted in the class of Ati-Shudra, were called *bhūmiputra* might be attributed to the popular belief that the Deccan was originally the land of Mahars (Mate 1933: 32-42). Therefore, the *devī* who was ruling the soil of the Deccan was presumed to be, in origin, the goddess of Mahars. The fact that Mahars played the role of receiving the will of *devī* on the occasion of boundary disputes could be attributable to this reason.

Śānti

The religious ceremony known as *śānti* shows even more clearly that the divine ruler of the soil of the Deccan was not an orthodox Brahmanical god but a *devī*. *Śānti* was performed when either plagues like cholera and smallpox broke out or extraordinary natural phenomena like earthquakes and thunderbolts occurred. These phenomena were considered to be caused by the *devī*'s anger so that the ceremony of *śānti* was performed to pacify this anger whenever these phenomena took place.

Even without the occurrence of an extraordinary phenomenon, the *śānti* ceremony was performed as, so to speak, a yearly event on such festive occasions as Dasara. In this ceremony of *śānti*, buffaloes or goats were sacrificed as offerings to the *devī*. In *śānti* Mahars and Mangs played a leading role as this ceremony belonged to the animistic religious world of *devī*. Then how in practise was the ceremony of *śānti* performed? A document relative to the *kasbe* Karad (1735-36) which might refer to *śānti* performed on the occasion of Dasara recorded the specific procedure of *śānti* as follows:

1. To walk around the village boundary while swinging *iraḍa* [pieces of wood taken from forest].
2. A Mahar proceeds with a pot of *peḍhā* in hand and a Mang follows him also with a pot of *peḍhā* in hand. Both of them walk around the village boundary.
3. A buffalo decorated by turmeric and garland is made to walk around the village boundary.

   Iraḍa is held at the head of the procession, then the Mahar and Mang with pots of *peḍhā* in hand and then the buffalo walk around the village boundary.

4. A *ratha* [float] made by the Sutar is decorated and drawn to the place of the Kumbhar. An idol of the goddess made from clay by the Kumbhar is placed on the *ratha* and drawn to a temporary *maṇḍapa* in front of the Hanuman temple with music playing. The idol of the goddess is installed in the *maṇḍapa* and the *ratha* is cleansed and put by the side of the idol.
5. The Mahar worships the buffalo which has come to the *maṇḍapa* after walking around the village boundary. The offering including betel leaves to the idol are to be taken by the Mahar and Mang.
6. The buffalo is taken before the idol and his head is to be cut on a certain line by the Mahar and then is to be cut off by the Mang.
7. For three days the idol is worshipped. All the villagers, old and young, are to bring offerings to the idol.
8. Afterwards, the lamp on the head of the buffalo installed in front of the idol is to be taken out and buried in the ground of the Patil and Kulkarni.
9. On the fourth day, the idol is to be brought to the village boundary and thrown out of the village. The *maṇḍapa* is then burnt down.

(M.I.S. XXII 215)

As this document denotes, an important part of the *śānti* ceremony was to walk around the village boundary in a procession. The *iraḍa* at the head of the procession might have relevance to animistic worship of the tree. While walking around the village boundary with a pot of *peḍhā* in hand, the Mahar and Mang assumably threw *peḍhā* one by one out of the village, since evil spirits were expected to go out of the village with the *peḍhā*.[7]

Thus, the important role played by Mahars and other Ati-Shudra castes in boundary disputes and *śānti* presents a striking contrast to the discrimination levelled against them in daily life.

Ati-Shudra and *Ādivāsī*

Although Ati-Shudra castes were discriminated against in various ways in the later medieval Deccan, it would be improper or at least one-sided if one were to look upon them as deplorable beings only to be depressed. As mentioned before, they played an important role in the animistic religious world of *devī*. In other words, their existence was ambivalent in the sense that discrimination in everyday life and spiritual superiority in the animistic world counterbalanced each other in their very existence.

Moreover, Ati-Shudra castes, especially Mahars and Mangs, had a mode of existence which differed markedly from the one which the word Ati-Shudra conjures up in our imagination. They had been, on the other hand, hillmen (*ādivāsī*) and often daring mountain soldiers. Shivaji, the founder of the Maratha kingdom, relied on them as military force especially in the earlier period of his state building.

Sarnāik and Nāik of Forts and Ṭhāṇas

In the Deccan, numerous forts (*gaḍ*) were built on the mountain tops. In each of these hill forts, some *nāiks* (the head of guards) and a *sarnāik* (the head of *nāiks*) were each posted with tens of guards. The *sarnāik* and *nāik* offices were *vatans* to be held by the hereditary patrimony of a certain family, strange as it might sound. The fort was one of the most important power apparatuses of the medieval state. Accordingly, it would be rather difficult to understand the reason why the fort's *sarnāik* and *nāiks* were not appointed by the state under whose rule the fort was held. Yet the Vatan system which formed the backbone of the medieval society in the Deccan had penetrated so deeply into the power apparatus of the state that even the *sarnāik* and *nāik* offices had become *vatan*.

In the mountainous area of the Ghat, hillmen like the Koli and Ramoshi had been dwelling in great numbers. A large portion of the Mahar and Mang whom one casually tends to regard as Ati-Shudra were also hillmen like the Koli and Ramoshi. The holders of the *vatan* of *nāik* were mostly such hillmen.

Purandhar had been an important fort situated nearly 20 km to the south of Pune whose *nāiks* used to be Kolis and Mahars. Around the end of the seventeenth century a dispute between the *sarnāik* of Purandhar, a Brahman named Ganesh Nilkantrao, and *nāiks* of Koli and Mahar broke out. As regards this dispute Nilkantrao made a statement to the government asking for arbitration (S.C.S. I 92).

Under the Bidar dynasty (in the late fifteenth century), since this area had been in a troubled condition, it was decided to build a fort here. Accordingly, the Deshmukh of this district was dispatched for this purpose and succeeded in building the Purandhar Fort. On him was bestowed the *sarnāik vatan* of this fort. To assist him, a *nāik* with 60 guards and two other Koli *nāiks* with 15 guards respectively were also posted in it. Subsequently the Bidar dynasty collapsed, and this area was brought under the control of the Nizam Shahi. However, the Adil Shahi who had been a rival of the Nizam Shahi sieged the Purandhar Fort, and Kolis, taking advantage of this, began to devastate this area. Therefore, Mahadaji Nilkantrao, the grandfather of Ganesh Nilkantrao, summoned the Kolis and bestowed on them the deed (*kaul*) appointing them to the office of *nāik.* At the same time, as the bravery of Mahars had been well known in this area, Mahadaji bestowed a *nāik vatan* of the Purandhar Fort on two Mahars with 40 guards each. After Mahadaji died, four of his sons quarrelled with each other and weakened as a result of which the Purandhar Fort was captured by Shivaji. Thereafter, Ganesh Nilkantrao succeeded to the *sarnāik vatan* of the Purandhar Fort, but Koli and Mahar *nāiks* had become powerful by then and often brought trouble to Ganesh. Ganesh therefore begged the government for arbitration.

The Purandhar Fort was brought under the control of the Mughals after they captured and pitilessly killed Sambhaji, the eldest son of Shivaji. But Maratha *sardārs* gathered under the banner of Rajaram, a half brother of Sambhaji, began to counterattack the Mughals. They tried to recapture the fort when Sarjarao Jedhe, the Deshmukh of Bhor, made it known to Rajaram that Kolis and Ramoshis were eager to occupy it. In response to this, the *abhaya patra* (deed of assurance) of Rajaram was issued to order Kolis and Ramoshis to occupy the Purandhar Fort for a bounty in case success was met (M.I.S. XV 352).

In 1747, when Madhavrao, a later Peshva, was born, 10 *cāvara* (nearly 300 hectares) of land was granted to Kolis, Ramoshis and Mahars of the Purandhar Fort as tax-free land (S.P.D. XXXI 182).

As these documents indicate, *nāik vatans* of the Purandhar Fort used to be held by Kolis, Ramoshis and Mahars under whom many hillmen were posted as guards. *Nāiks* of the Rohida Fort were also Mahars. In 1746, a dispute over the *nāik vatan* of this fort arose. One party in this dispute, Khandnak Mahar, made a statement to the government as regards this dispute.

Under the Adil Shahi and Nizam Shahi, the *nāik vatan* of the Rohida Fort was jointly held by an uncle of Khandnak's father and another Mahar. After both of them had died, Khandnak's father went to Raigad to see Shivaji at which time the latter bestowed on him the *sanad* (deed) of the *nāik vatan.* With the *sanad* of Shivaji, Khandnak's father returned to the Rohida Fort and began to serve as the *nāik.* After his death, Khandnak succeeded to both the Mahar *vatan* of the village Karanjiye and the *nāik vatan* of the Rohida Fort. Being unmarried, he then married a daughter of Bhojnak of Vadi, Utroli District. Thereupon, Bhojnak proposed to him to leave the Mahar *vatan* of the village Karanjiye to Bhojnak taking the *nāik vatan* of the Rohida Fort himself as it would be difficult for him to discharge the duties of two *vatans* at the same time. Thereby a dispute between Khandnak and Bhojnak began (S.C.S. III 609).

Thus it is unquestionable that the *nāiks* and guards of the hill forts were mostly hillmen like Kolis, Mahars and Ramoshis.

In the later medieval Deccan, however, these hillmen were unable to continue their style of living in mountains free of any relationship with the settled agricultural society in the plain. For example, a portion of Kolis had been incorporated into the Vatan system of the village as water carriers. In some villages, those Kolis were counted as one of the *bārā balute* (12 types of village servants) (Oturkar 139). A section of Ramoshis had become watchmen of the village. When the *kasbe* Supe was infested with robbers, a Ramoshi head watchman and 3 Ramoshi watchmen were posted (S.S.R.P.D. VIII 954. 1773-74). There were 3 *vatandār* Ramoshis in the village Garade, Karepathar District, who watched the village gate (Oturkar 78). In the *kasbe* Satara, there were 33 watchmen of the Ramoshi and Mang castes whose charge was defrayed by the money collected from leading merchants of Satara (S.S.R.P.D. VIII 958).

Thus hillmen like Kolis and Ramoshis were living outside as well as inside the settled agricultural society and *nāiks* and guards of the hill forts were positioned exactly in-between these two groups.

The Mahar and Mang whom we are accustomed to assume to be of Ati-Shudra caste also had not been totally absorbed into the settled agricultural society. Even in the later medieval age a large number of them were still hillmen, and in-between the hill and village there were hill forts posted with Mahar and Mang *nāiks* and guards.

In principal towns of the Deccan there were *ṭhāṇas* (soldier-police station) posted with *nāik*. The office of *nāik* of *ṭhāṇa* was also a *vatan* whose holder was generally a Mahar. The Mahar who possessed the *nāik vatan* of the *ṭhāṇa* in the *kasbe* Paithan had the right to take numerous perquisites from the inhabitants of Paithan as well as merchants and others who brought commodities into the market of Paithan. The following are some of them:

1. For every cart of brinjal, 10 [*śer*] to the village watchman [*veskar*] and 15 [*śer*] to the Mahar.
2. For every cart of sugarcane, 10 [*śer*] to the village watchman and 15 [*śer*] to the Mahar.

3. For every bullock-load of banana, 7 [*śer*] to the Mahar.
4. For every loom of Koshti [weaver caste], 5 *rukā* and a piece of cloth to be divided by the watchman and the Mahar.
5. For every oil-press of Teli, half [*śer*] of the oil.
6. A Chambhar is to give two pair of shoes to the Mahar every year.
7. A Dhangar is to offer a goat on the occasion of Dasara and two goats on the occasion of Divali to the Mahar for sacrifice.

(M.I.S. XX 174)

Thus it is brought to light that in the later medieval Deccan the so-called Ati-Shudra castes like the Mahar and Mang assumed various modes of existence including that of a hillman, *nāik* and guard of hill fort or *ṭhāṇa* and village *vatandār* making it improper to look upon them only as Ati-Shudras who were merely to be discriminated against.

Dispute between Mahar and Brahman

Although Mahars in the later medieval Deccan functioned in various capacities, they did not form separate groups according to their respective modes of existence. On the contrary, all of them still held a strong nexus and acted as a body whenever any matters concerning them all occurred.

In 1784 Mahars of Paudkhor District appealed to the district official as follows:

> It was the custom that *vatandār* Joshi officiates as the priest at the marriages of us Mahars. In other districts too, a Brahman is to officiate at the marriages of Mahars. However a dispute over the transaction [*deṇeṃ gheṇeṃ*] between us and Joshis arose and Joshis stopped officiating at our marriages. This state of affairs has been continuing for some 15 or 20 years. So we beg you to restore the matter as before, taking the custom of other districts into consideration.

Receiving the appeal, the district official made an inquiry and reached a conclusion that *vatandār* Joshis were to officiate at the marriages of Mahars, and, as a matter of fact, *vatandār* Joshis continued to officiate at the marriages of Mangs and others, making it improper for them to refuse to officiate at the marriages of Mahars only. Thereupon, the district official ordered *vatandār* Joshis to officiate at the Mahar marriages (A.S.S. I 74).

However, the *vatandār* Joshis of Paudkhor District refused to obey his order and presented a statement of the following purport to the government asking for intervention.

The offices of Joshi, Upadya and Dharmadhikari of Paudkhor District had been *vṛtti* (*vatan*, patrimony) of their families. Although it was the custom for them not to officiate at the marriages of Mahars, the latter began to complain in this regard to the district official. As a result, the district official ordered them to officiate at the marriages of Mahars merely on the ground that earlier the *havāldār* of the Korigad Fort had once made their uncle of 10 to 15 years officiate at the marriage of a Mahar *nāik* of the fort since the priest of the Mahar caste (*meḍhyā* Mahar) was not available.

Meanwhile, Mahars demanded *vatandār* Joshis to officiate at their marriages on the ground of the order of the district official, but Joshis refused to comply. The district official thus levied a fine of Rs. 10 and forced them to officiate. Thereupon Joshis presented a statement to the district official to the effect that they were only assumed to inform Mahars of the auspicious time for a marriage of the Mahars but not to officiate at the marriage. The district official did not acknowledged this, however, and confiscated their *vṛtti* saying that they must not officiate at the marriages of Shudra castes either. Such being the case, *vatandār* Joshis of Paudkhor appealed again to the government to intervene and order the district official to restore the *vṛtti* to them.

Receiving the appeal, the government conducted an inquiry and came to the following conclusion. It was not the custom for *vatandār* Joshis to officiate at the marriages of Mahars. It might be the custom of some other districts but it was not the case in Konkan. Here there were the Mahar priests (*meḍhe* Mahar) in the Mahar caste to officiate at their marriages. Joshis of Junnar too wrote to the government that Joshis did not officiate at the marriages of Ati-Shudras in Junnar as the priest of Ati-Shudra castes (*ḍhegomego*) was present and he officiated at their marriages. Formerly Mahars in the service of hill forts (*kilyāce cākarmāne*) and Mahars in the province (*prāntāntīl*) , in all several thousand, had gathered together and caused a disturbance. They had appealed to the then ruler of the Deccan, Aurangzeb, to make *vatandār* Joshis officiate at their marriages. But Aurangzeb had decided that Joshis were not to officiate at the Mahar marriages taking the long-standing custom into consideration. Even under the Mughal rule (*Moglāī*), the long-standing custom was respected so that it was very improper to start a new custom under the *Svarājya*, abandoning the old. Therefore, the custom that *vatandār* Joshis only officiate at the marriages of castes other than Ati-Shudra castes should have been respected. According to this conclusion, a government order to the district official of Paudkhor District was issued to the effect that he must not force Joshis to officiate at the marriages of Mahars (S.S.R.P.D. VIII 1132).

As this case shows, thousands of Mahars of various positions including *nāiks* and guards of hill forts and *vatandār* Mahars of agricultural villages acted as a body to push their claim through. They failed, in the result, to accomplish this but nonetheless it is clearly evident here that Mahars of various circumstances struggled in a united front against discrimination.

Conclusion

The reality of Ati-Shudra castes in the later medieval Deccan which impresses us most strongly is the fact that their existence was ambivalent. They were discriminated against in various ways in daily life but at the same time they played an important role on the occasions of boundary disputes and the ceremony of *śānti*. They were *vatandārs* of villages but at the same time they were mountain soldiers and town police, with all of them still retaining a strong nexus with their fellow caste members in the hills. These facts clearly indicate the ambivalence of their existence. But, at the same time, they were so deeply incorporated into the caste system that various castes assumed to belong to Ati-Shudra quarrelled with each other over the problem of social (caste) ranking among them. In this sense too, their existence was ambivalent.

Notes

1 For the Vatan system and the *bārā balute*, see Chapters 1 and 2 of this volume as well as Kulkarni 1969: 24-55.

2 H. Fukazawa formerly translated this document into English in relation to *balute haqqs* of *vatandār* Mahars (Fukazawa 1991: 224). His translation seems, however, not to be a complete one.

3 See Chapter 7 of this volume for the law suit filed in the Bombay Sadr Divani Adalat (6 B.S.D.A. 68. 1849) pertaining to a dispute between Mahars and peasants cum Mangs of the similar nature in the nineteenth-century Bombay Presidency. In this suit, both parties admitted that the hides of bullocks skinned by *vatandār* Mahars should be handed over to the owners of the bullocks as a reward for which Mahars were to be remunerated by a certain weight-load of corn.

4 As to the definition and structure of the *pargaṇā* community in the later medieval Deccan, see Chapter 1 of this volume. See also Chapter 4 of this volume for the communal structure of 'rural castes' in the Deccan including those of Ati Shudras.

5 Kane describes the *maṇḍalas* in the fire ordeal as follows drawing on classical law books including the *Yājñavalkyasmṛti* and even the *Mitākṣarā*, a commentary on the *Yājñavalkyasmṛti*:

> Nine circles [*maṇḍalas*] with cowdung are to be drawn from west to east, they being meant for Agni, Varuṇa, Vāyu, Yama, Indra, Kubera, Soma, Savitṛ, and all gods. The *śodhya* [person undergoing the ordeal] should stand in the first circle facing the east. ... Then the *śodhya* holding in both his hands the red-hot piece should walk from the first to the eighth circle not hurriedly but slowly and at ease. Having reached the 8th circle he should throw the red-hot iron piece on to the 9th circle (Kane: III 370-71).

Yājñavalkyasmṛti II-106, however, prescribes 'seven *maṇḍalas*' for the fire odeal instead of nine (Stenzler 1970: Sanskrit text 56).

Kane also refers to the ordeal of fire performed in the presence of the Peshva 'on the tank of the Godavari River' in 1745 in which 'an iron ball of 50 palas ... was heated red-hot and the *śodhya* carried it across seven circles and threw it in the 8th circle on flour and bundles which begn to burn' (Kane: III 378).

6 For various methods of *divya* in the later medieval Deccan, see Gune 1953: 90-99.

7 This can be inferred from the similar ceremony performed for village gods in south India in which, though flesh of sacrificed animals, instead of *peḍhā*, was thrown out of the village while walking around the village boundary (Whitehead 1916: 46-52). *Peḍhā* might be a less offensive substitute for animal flesh quite commonly used in the later medieval Deccan.

7

Conflict and Controversy over the Mahar Vatan in the Nineteenth-Early Twentieth Century Bombay Presidency

Introduction

As mentioned in Chapter 6, the Mahar *vatan* in the medieval age had been a kind of hereditary patrimony to be safeguarded within the framework of social relations in the village community and *pargana* (district) community as well as the state power apparatus. Under British colonial rule, various types of *vatan* underwent divergent changes. Some types of *vatan* were abolished at an earlier stage, for example, while still some others were maintained tenaciously. It depended mainly on the necessity or expediency of British colonial rule and partly on the changing social relations within Indian society itself.

What then was the destiny of the Mahar *vatan*? The Mahar *vatan* was one of the most tenaciously maintained *vatans* which was only to be abolished by the Bombay Inferior Village Watans Abolition Act of 1959 after India gained its independence. This chapter aims at clarifying the reason why the Mahar *vatan* was maintained so persistently by tracing the conflict and controversy over it in the nineteenth-early twentieth century Bombay Presidency. The conflict and controversy over the Mahar *vatan* used to occur, on the one hand, between the *vatandar* Mahars and peasants (Kunbis) of the same village, often involving *vatandar* Mangs as the secondary participants taking sides with peasants. The focal point of legal issue of this type of contention was the right to take the hides of dead cattle of the villagers, the carcasses of which were to be skined and disposed of by the *vatandar* Mahars. On the other hand, the heavy burden of the official as well as unofficial duties imposed on the *vatandar* Mahars by the government and village community were the main cause of the conflict and controversy over the Mahar *vatan* in and outside the Bombay Legislative Council, especially after the so-called Montagu-Chelmsford Reforms in 1919.

Vatans in the Early Administrative System of the Bombay Presidency

Vatandars and the State

The Maratha kingdom (Peshva government) was overthrown by the army of the East India Company in 1818 and most of its territories, the so-called 'Conquered Territories', came to be incorporated into the Bombay Presidency which formerly included only the narrow coastal areas of Gujarat and Konkan. The foundation of the administrative system of the enlarged Bombay Presidency was laid by the then Governor of Bombay, M. Elphinstone, who rearranged and consolidated regulations issued earlier by the Bombay government into the so-called Elphinstone Code.[1]

In the Elphinstone Code, *vatan* was translated as the 'hereditary office' and allowed to continue to be enjoyed by the former holder. But the denomination of '*vatandar* Kunbi' was discontinued so that the category of 'hereditary office' holders included only village establishments (Patil, Kulkarni, *bara balutedars* and some others) and district officers like Deshmukh and Deshpande. Bombay Regulation V of 1827 (Chapter I, Section I, First) provided a prescription of 30 years with regard to the immovable property which included 'lands, houses, hereditary offices, or other immoveable property'. Thus, *vatans* (hereditary offices) were acknowledged as a kind of immovable property by the Elphinstone Code.

However, the Bombay government did not deal with all *vatans* alike. It paid special attention to *vatans* which had a direct connection with the collection of taxes, especially land tax, and police administration in the village and district. In the Maratha administration, the Vatan system had had the twofold function of regulating the social relations within the village community and *pargana* community as well as of substituting for the local administrative system of the state. Thus, *vatandars* had had the dual standing as a member of the village and district establishment and as a local officer of the state. But all the *vatandars* did not share alike in this dual standing. *Vatandars* whose qualification as local officers of the state had been stronger than others were district officers like Deshmukh and Deshpande and village officers like Patil and Kulkarni. The *vatandar* Mahar who had served as the assistant to Patil in tax collection, the village police and other duties had the standing of the 'inferior village officer'. Thus, *vatans* to which the Bombay government gave special consideration were those of district and village officers including the *vatandar* Mahar whose knowledge of the district and village it had the intention to utilize for local administration.

The Bombay government defined Deshmukh and Deshpande as 'hereditary district officers' and Patil, Kulkarni, *vatandar* Mahar and others as 'hereditary village officers'. Bombay Regulation XVI of 1827 stipulated the duties and powers of the Collector of which Chapters III and XVII-XXVII laid down rules regarding the 'hereditary district and village officers'. The duties and powers of the Collector with regard to the appointment and dismissal of the hereditary district and village officers were provided in Chapters XVII and XVIII which were later rescinded by Section I of Act XI of 1843 to strengthen the powers of the Collector in this regard. Section II of the same act had the following provision:

> ... that all hereditary officers, of whatever denomination, belonging to, or employed in the management of the land revenue, or of the customs or town duties, or excise, or other revenue, or in the police, or in the civil administration of the country, shall render the usual services of their respective offices, as far as the same may be required by the collector, or other officer under whose control they may be placed by usage or the orders of Government.[2]

It follows that the Collector had the power to dismiss these hereditary district and village officers when he found their services to be needless or useless. Thus, these hereditary district and village officers came to have strengthened their character as the local state officials under the control of the Collector than before, even though their offices were still hereditary.

Bombay Regulation XVI of 1827, Chapter XIX provided the duty of the Collector to keep records of the 'land and allowances attached to hereditary district or village offices'. The 'land' meant the service *inam* land of *vatandars* which was, as a rule, exempted from the payment of land tax, but in the usual cases, was made to pay a small sum known as *judi*. By Chapter XX of the same regulation, the allowances and emolument attached to the hereditary offices were prohibited to be taken away from the family of the office holders. These provisions were aimed at eliminating any danger of the duties of these offices not being properly executed due to the transfer to others of the land or allowances attached to them. Under the Maratha administration, the land or allowances affixed to *vatans* could have been divided, transferred or sold as property. However, the Bombay government restricted this as far as the *vatan* of the hereditary district and village officers was concerned for the sake of ensuring efficient local administration through these hereditary officers.

Thus, under the early administrative system of the Bombay Presidency based on the Elphinstone Code, *vatandars* closely connected with the collection of taxes and police administration were placed under the strong control of government as hereditary district and village officers. As a result, the *vatandar* Mahar was also placed under the strong legal restriction as the most important inferior village officer.

Balutedars and Peasants

The regulations of the Bombay government, however, did not embody the power to regulate *vatandars* totally. As mentiond before, the Vatan system had the twofold aspects of regulating the social relations within local communities and substituting for the local administration system of the state. The Bombay government paid attention only to the latter aspect of the Vatan system and its former aspect, that of regulating social relations within local communities, was left wholly uninfluenced by any legal control imposable by the Bombay government. Thus, relations between *vatandars* and peasants did not change even under the early Bombay administration because these social relations were set outside the legal restriction as private relations between private individuals. Under the Elphinstone Code system, the Vatan system was divided distinctly into two aspects, namely, the public aspect (relation between *vatandar* and state) and the private aspect (relation between *vatandar* and peasant) of which only the former was subject to the strong legal control exerted by the Bombay government.

In the village, *vatandars* other than Patil and Kulkarni were also known as *balutedars* or collectively, *bara balute*, meaning 12 earners of *balute* (a perquisite) in which were included artisan *vatandars* such as the Lohar, Sutar and Kumbhar and service *vatandars* like the Joshi, Nhavi and Parit as well as untouchable *vatandars* such as the Mahar, Mang and Chambhar.

What then was the relationship between these *balutedars* and peasants in the early administration of the Bombay government and how did it change in the course of time? These are questions examined hereafter in the light of legal decisions passed by the Bombay Sadr Divani Adalat (up to 1862) and the Bombay High Court (from 1862 onward).

On 29 September 1840, the full bench of the Bombay Sadr Divani

Adalat passed a decree on a case between Hunnappa, the *vatandar* Lohar of the village Hosour, Dharwar Zillah, and a fellow villager, Hunmunna. The plaintiff, the *vatandar* Lohar, sued for the payment of *balute* (a perquisite) for the year 1838 from the defendant which consisted of '11 phalies of jowaree and 1.5 ruts of kurbee'. The Moonsiff of Roan (Gondoo Temajee) held that the 'plaintiff, as the hereditary ironsmith of his village ... was entitled, by the custom of the country, to receive from the defendant, a fellow villager, his bullootee hucks, whether the defendant employed the plaintiff as an ironsmith or not'. The defendant appealed to the Judge of the Zillah Court (J.A. Shaw) who reversed the decree of the Moonsiff on the ground that 'it rested with the Ryots whether they employed the Plaintiff as an ironsmith, and paid him his hucks or not'. The Zillah Judge did not acknowledge the obligatory character of the *balute* payment for the villagers. On this, the plaintiff asked the admission of a special appeal to the Bombay Sadr Divani Adalat which was subsequently allowed. In the hearing the Sitting Judge, G. Giberne, pointed out as follows:

> ... the Zillah Judge had taken an erroneous view of the subject, and that his decision tended to upset a custom universally acknowledged, and endangered the constitution and foundation of all village communities established from time immemorial.

The Sitting Judge, despite these observations, still referred the case to the full bench of the Bombay Sadr Divani Adalat due to the importance of the subject for all of the *balutedars* and villagers. The full bench which consisted of three Judges including the Sitting Judge himself confirmed the judgement of the Sitting Judge in favour of the plaintiff, the *vatandar* Lohar of the village Hosour (4 B.S.D.A. 8).[3]

As this was the decision of the full bench of the Bombay Sadr Divani Adalat, this judgement was treated as the precedent for binding the judgements on the similar cases to be filed in all of the courts in the Bombay Presidency. Viewed in a more general perspective, this decision made it clear that the villagers (peasants) were obliged to pay the *balute haqqs* to village *balutedars* even though they did not request the *balutedars*' services. In other words, *balutedars* had the hereditary right to ask for the payment of *balute haqqs* irrespective of whether or not they rendered their respective services to the villagers. This system of the division of labour within the village community was regarded as 'the constitution and foundation of all village communities established from time immemorial' and respected as such by the Bombay Sadr Divani Adalat.

This standpoint was confirmed by yet another famous decision of the Bombay Sadr Divani Adalat in 1857. The *vatandar* Joshi of the village Amberee, Krishnumbhut, sued for the payment of the equivalent sum of money which three villagers paid to the other Brahman whom they had asked to perform several ceremonies. In the judgement in favour of the plaintiff, the Bombay Sadr Divani Adalat pointed out as follows:

> Whether certain religious ceremonies, which are optional or others which are obligatory are performed, the person entitled hereditary right to perform them is entitled to be paid his fee, whether he performs them or not.
>
> (11 B.S.D.A. 111)

Although this had been the fundamental line of the judgement of the Bombay Sadr Divani Adalat regarding the relationship between *balutedars* and peasants, it became more and more contradictory to the concept of freedom of the individual (freedom of contract) which the British had brought into India, and conflicts between *balutedars* and peasants began to occur more often than in the past.

The *vatandar* Mahar being one of the *balutedars* had the right to receive the *balute* payment from peasants under the early administration of the Bombay government just as the *vatandar* Lohar and *vatandar* Joshi did. For the *vatandar* Mahar, however, conflict with peasants was more likely to occur due to the peculiarity of his office. The major problem often responsible for conflict between *vatandar* Mahars and peasants was the right to take the skins of peasant's dead cattle as mentioned earlier in Chapter 6.

As an example, on 23 March 1849, the Bombay Sadr Divani Adalat decided not to admit the special appeal of Suntoo and three other *vatandar* Mahars suing for their right to take dead animal skins. Suntoo and the others initially brought a suit for damages to the Moonsiff's court on the ground that Babajee and other peasants had made village Mangs skin their dead animals and appropriated the skins even though *vatandar* Mahars had the right to take all the skins of the village's dead animals. The peasants argued that they had *vatandar* Mahars skin the draught bullocks when they died in the village and deliver the skins to the former possessors of bullocks giving the fee of 5 seers (*śer*) of grain for bigger bullocks and 4 seers (*śer*) for smaller ones and that they made

Mangs process the skins into ropes and other implements for agricultural purposes. They alleged that this had been the custom of the country by the time *vatandar* Mahars began to reject delivering the skins of draught bullocks to peasants. Thus, they claimed, they were obliged to win Mangs over and made them skin their dead bullocks as a countermeasure to what *vatandar* Mahars were doing. Therefore, it was against this action taken by the peasants that *vatandar* Mahars brought their suit.

The Moonsiff who tried the case decided in favour of the plaintiffs, *vatandar* Mahars, but in an appeal on this decision the Assistant Judge reversed it. The plaintiffs then appealed to the Zillah Judge who too dismissed it. As a last resort, *vatandar* Mahars prayed for the admission of a special appeal to the Bombay Sadr Divani Adalat which was admitted on the ground that the decisions of the two lower courts were 'opposed to the usage of the country'. But during the hearing, it became clear that the plaintiffs (*vatandar* Mahars as special appellants) did not object to the right of peasants taking back the skins of the draught bullocks, and peasants did not prevent the plaintiffs from conveying away the skins of other animals. The upshot of this was thus that there was nothing to adjudicate for the Bombay Sadr Divani Adalat (6 B.S.D.A. 68).[4]

This conclusion was in consonance with the decision of the Maratha (Peshva) government on the subject referenced in Chapter 6. It had been the custom of the country since the Maratha period that the skins of dead draught bullocks belonged to their former possessors whereas the skins of all other animals that died in the village went to *vatandar* Mahars. This custom had been maintained by the decisions handed down by the Bombay Sadr Divani Adalat by the middle of the nineteenth century. In the second half of the century, however, this custom began to decay and a new custom that the skins of all dead animals were the property of the former possessors of the animals began to take shape.

In this regard, in a suit brought by two *vatandar* Mahars of the village Bedzurgi, Bijaour Taluka, against two other *vatandar* Mahars of the same village concerning distribution of the perquisites of Mahar *vatan* among them, the Bombay High Court pointed out as follows in 1870:

> ... it has been repeatedly decided in this court, in suits for proceeds of the carcasses of dead cattle between the Mahars and the ryot owners of the cattle, that the person who owned the cattle while alive has also a right to the property in the dead carcasses of such cattle, and may dispose of it to anybody he pleases.
>
> [8 B.H.C.R. (A.C.J.) 28]

As this case denotes, in the course of the nineteenth century conflicts often arose between *vatandar* Mahars and peasants over the problem of who should be awarded possession of the skins of dead cattle. In these cases, the parties to the conflicts frequently resorted to taking legal action. Through these actions a new precedent came to be consolidated in that the owner of the animal while alive was also the owner of the skin of the animal when dead.

Under British colonial rule, the relationship between *balutedars* and peasants began to change as one part of the general change in the framework of medieval Indian society, and this change was most prominently reflected in the conflict between *vatandar* Mahars and peasants.

The Bombay Hereditary Offices Act and its Aftermath

The Bombay Hereditary Offices Act of 1874

The Bombay Hereditary Offices Act (Bombay Act III of 1874) was an outcome of the policy of the Bombay government to readjust the concept of the hereditary office to the changing situation in the second half of the nineteenth century. The Bombay government had been trying to put under legal control the hereditary officers closely connected with tax collection as well as the village police, but the situation surrounding them began to change in the course of the nineteenth century.

One of the most important changes in local administration during this period was the dismissal of most Deshmukhs and Deshpandes (hereditary district officers) from their office through the procedure called 'commutation'. As a result of the Summary Settlement Act (Bombay Act II of 1863), it became possible to dismiss the Deshmukhs and Deshpandes of the Conquered Territories from their duties on the condition that a reduced rate of tax be levied on their *inam* land. This was because the establishment of the state administration system had made their services redundant. The procedure of commutation of Deshmukh and Deshpande *vatans* was first started in the Southern Division (Southern Maratha Countries) by S.J. Gordon making it known as the Gordon Settlement. Since then, the process of commutation was extended to the Central and Northern Divisions also as a result of which the commutation of Deshmukh and Deshpande *vatans* was completed in 10 of the 12 Collectrates of the Bombay Presidency by 1873. Thus, most Deshmukhs and Deshpandes had ceased to be hereditary district officers by the time the Bombay Hereditary Offices Act was enacted.

The first bill of the Bombay Hereditary Offices Act (Bill III of 1873) was introduced into the Bombay Legislative Council by A. Rogers on 23 July 1873. Declaring his bill being concerned only with the hereditary village officers, Rogers divided these officers into two distinct categories, Patil and Kulkarni on the one hand and inferior village servants represented by *vatandar* Mahars on the other, to underscore the inherent problems of the respective categories. As regards Patil and Kulkarni he indicated the principal problem to be that their duties were performed through the so-called rotation system in which each shareholder of the *vatan*, when the *vatan* was shared by several shareholders as was often the case, officiated by turns according to the share of each shareholder. Because of this rotation system, a shareholder of the *vatan* who was not deemed sufficiently competent to carry out the duties of the *vatan* happened to become the officiator of the *vatan*, thereby often inhibiting the efficiency of local administration. Thus, Rogers made it clear that his bill was aimed at abolishing the rotation system among shareholders of Patil and Kulkarni *vatans*.

With regard to the inferior village servants represented by *vatandar* Mahars, Rogers indicated the principal problem to be the disputes arising between *vatandar* Mahars and peasants of which the main cause was the fee which *vatandar* Mahars received individually from peasants. Rogers remarked as follows:

> ... our system of revenue surveying has rendered the registration of land so perfect that there is very little use for the service of some of these hereditary officers, that the villagers who have been in the habit of paying them with grains or some small perquisite now refuse to pay them anything at all; and it is suspected that the mhars [Mahars], seeing no probability of recovering their rights, or what they imagined to be their rights, except by the expensive process of going to law, have resorted to the poisoning of cattle. This section [Section IV] will provide a simple means for remedying this state of affairs. By it a punchayet will be appointed, and the matters in dispute will thus be satisfactorily settled.
>
> (P.C.G.B. 1874. XII 94)

Thus, troubles culminating in the poisoning of cattle of peasants by *vatandar* Mahars made new legislation to regulate their relationship an urgent necessity.

Rogers's first bill met with strong opposition on the ground that it totally minimized the hereditary district officers attaching importance only to the hereditary village officers, and was consequently withdrawn. On 25 September, Rogers again introduced a renewed bill (Bill XII of 1873) with some amendment to his former bill into the Bombay Legislative Council. The main point of his amendment was to make it applicable to Deshmukhs and Deshpandes who still retained the office of hereditary district officer. The new bill was discussed and then passed as the Bombay Hereditary Offices Act of 1874 which was translated into Marathi, Gujarati and Kannada so as to make the Indian people familiar with it.

The Bombay Hereditary Offices Act defined the hereditary office as follows:

> 'Hereditary office' means every office held hereditarily for the performance of duties connected with the administration or collection of the public revenue, or with the village police, or with the settlement of boundaries, or other matters of civil administration [Section 4].[5]

By this definition, the only *balutedars* who were included in the category of the hereditary village officers were *vatandar* Mahars and some other *balutedars* directly connected with tax collection, the village police and certain other duties. Thus, this act was not applicable to the other *balutedars* like *vatandar* Sutars. Ever since enforcement of the Elphinstone Code, the Bombay government had been trying to divide various *vatandars* into two distinct categories, that is, *vatandars* who were closely connected with local administration and others who were not so, placing only the former under the strict legal control. In this historical context, the Bombay Hereditary Offices Act constituted the process of completion of this policy of the Bombay government. This Act was also inapplicable to Deshmukhs and Deshpandes whose *vatans* had been commuted by the Summary Settlement.

Section 15 of the Bombay Hereditary Offices Act provided the procedure of commutation by which the Collector could dismiss *vatandars* from their offices with the consent of *vatandars* under mutually agreed terms. This procedure was also applicable to village *balutedars* but Section 16 of the same Act provided that commutation of their *vatans* should not be 'held to affect any right of individuals or village communities to exact such service as may be customary from village servants who have been relieved by Government of liability to perform such service to the State'. Thus, the procedure of commutation changed the relationship between *balutedars* and the state but not that between *balutedars* and peasants which had been left outside the concern of the state as a private social relation within their respective village communities.

The most important sections of the Bombay Hereditary Offices Act directly related to the inferior village servants were Sections 18 and 64. Section 18 stipulated the procedure to award disputes between the inferior village servants represented by *vatandar* Mahars and peasants. The following were the main purposes of Section 18:

1. 'When all or any of the property of a village-watan of lower degree than that of Patel and Kulkarni consists of a right to levy in money or kind directly from individuals', the Collector can constitute a panchayat of 5 men of whom 2 should be appointed by the villagers, another 2 by the watandars and the sar-panch (headman) by the Collector to define the 'nature and extent of such right and of the duties to be performed'.
2. The decision of the panchayat 'shall be in accordance with the opinion of the majority of the panchayat, provided that in case the villagers or watandars fail to nominate members within seven days, the Collector shall appoint such members'.
3. If 'the panchayat do not come to a decision within seven days from the appointment of the sar-panch, the Collector may himself pass a decision'.
4. 'The decision of the panchayat or the Collector ... shall be final and binding on all persons and classes ....'

The purpose of this Section was to relieve the civil courts from this kind of dispute between *vatandar* Mahars and peasants by leaving it to the *panchayat* comprising the representatives of *vatandar* Mahars and peasants or, in case of failure of the *panchayat*, to the discretion of the Collector.

Disputes concerning the perquisite of *vatandar* Mahars occurred and went to law courts so often that the duties of *vatandar* Mahar could not be performed properly. With this understanding foremost in mind, the Bombay government tried to devise a 'simple means for remedying this state of affairs'. This solution took the form of the *panchayat* provided in Section 18 of the Act. Specifically, this meant that the relationship between *vatandar* Mahars and peasants had become too strained to be left outside the government purview as a private social relation within the village community.

Section 64 of the same Act stipulated the registration of *vatandars* and appointment of the officiator among them with regard to *vatans* lower than that of Patil and Kulkarni. Clause (d) of Section 64 was 'to provide for and enforce the joint responsibility of the whole body for the neglect of duty or misconduct of any of their members or their representatives'. As for the 'misconduct of the whole body' of *vatandars*, it provided as follows:

> ... in cases where the crime of cattle poisoning is prevalent, with the sanction of Government, to attach, during the pleasure of Government the watans of the person whom he may have reason to believe to have been guilty of, or to have connived at, the commission of the crime.

As mentioned previously, Rogers noted the fact of cattle poisoning by *vatandars* Mahars when he introduced his first bill of the Bombay Hereditary Offices Act. However, Clause (d) of Section 64 which referred to cattle poisoning was inserted in his second bill in the course of discussion in the Bombay Legislative Council. F.S. Chapman summing up the purpose of the bill in the final discussion on 15 October 1874 remarked as follows:

> ... this principle of [joint] responsibility has been laid down for the first time in the case of the crime of cattle poisoning of which the mhars of the villages are often believed to be guilty, either from motives of revenge on account of non-payment of their dues, or in order to obtain the skins of the animals. This is a crime which is most difficult to detect and punish, and which entails the most ruinous consequences on the ryots. I believe the very guarded provision which we have made is most necessary, and I hope it may prove effectual.
>
> (P.C.G.B. 1874. XIII 56)

Thus, it seems that conflicts and disputes between *vatandar* Mahars and peasants had risen to such a high pitch as to make poisoning of peasants' cattle by Mahars a frequent occurrence.

Disputes between Vatandar Mahars and Peasants

Here, the process of the intensification of tension between *vatandar* Mahars and peasants is traced through the legal decisions handed down by the Bombay High Court concerning the Mahar *vatan*. Section 18 of the Bombay Hereditary Offices Act provided a procedure for granting awards by a *panchayat* with regard to disputes between peasants and village *vatandars* lower than Patil and Kulkarni. Still, however, some law suits were brought to civil courts based on various causes of action.

In 1885, four *vatandar* Mahars of a certain village in Belgaum District sued five *vatandar* Mangs and ten peasants of the same village for proclaiming a declaration to Mangs to the effect that the right to take *aya* (a perquisite) which had been wrongfully given to Mangs by the peasants belonged to *vatandar* Mahars and an injunction against the peasants to the effect that they should not give *aya* to *vatandar* Mangs. In opposition to this allegation, *vatandar* Mangs claimed that they were also *vatandars* of the village and performed the duties concomitant to their *vatan* so that they had the same right as that of *vatandar* Mahars to take *aya* from villagers. The peasants contended that *vatandar* Mangs had the same right to take *aya* as *vatandar* Mahars with some peasants giving it to *vatandar* Mahars and some others to *vatandar* Mangs. The Judge in the first instance held that *vatandar* Mangs were intruders on the right of *vatandar* Mahars and that *vatandar* Mahars were entitled to the relief claimed. From this decree, the defendants appealed to the district court of Belgaum on the ground that this suit was not cognizable by the civil courts under the provisions of the Bombay Hereditary Offices Act. The District Judge held that the suit was barred under Section 18 of the same Act which provided a *panchayat* as a means of giving awards in cases of disputes of this kind and reversed the decree of the lower court. Standing against this decree, the plaintiffs appealed to the Bombay High Court which confirmed the decree made by the District Judge (13 B. 83).

This dispute seemed to take place owing to the action of peasants to exclude *vatandar* Mahars from their office by taking *vatandar* Mangs to their side when tension between *vatandar* Mahars and peasants heightened. The remarkable point of this decision reached by the Bombay High Court was that not only disputes between *vatandar* Mahars and peasants but also those between *vatandar* Mahars and *vatandar* Mangs were held to be awarded by a *panchayat* or at the discretion of the Collector. This must have been due to the understanding of the court that the main confrontation was between *vatandar* Mahars and peasants involving *vatandar* Mangs as the secondary participants. As mentioned in Chapter 6, the confrontation between *vatandar* Mahars and peasants cum *vatandar* Mangs had been rather the usual pattern of contention since the Maratha period.

In 1892, all of the peasants of the village Chinchodi, Ahmadnagar District, decided to remove *vatandar* Mahars from providing the services to the village and to employ Mangs in their place. In 1894, after two years had passed under this state of affairs, a meeting of peasants was held at the house of the Patil to consider the restoration of *vatandar* Mahars to their duties. It was therefore agreed in the meeting that the latter should be restored on condition of payment of Rs. 300 for the repair of village temples. This payment was, in fact, the fine for suspected poisoning of certain cattle by Mahars during the period of suspension of their services. *Vatandar* Mahars also agreed with this condition and paid the sum to the Patil through a village Vani.

Thus *vatandar* Mahars were to be restored to their office but only after the Patil was prosecuted under Section 161 (bribery) of the Indian Penal Code (Act XXXXV of 1860) on his receiving this Rs. 300 from *vatandar* Mahars. The reason for his prosecution was that as it was part of the Patil's performance of official duties as a superior to restore *vatandar* Mahars to their office, the Patil who took Rs. 300 for this restoration was therefore considered to have committed the crime of bribery. Against this judgement, the Patil and villagers contended that they had excluded *vatandar* Mahars from their 'private services' to the villagers and not from their 'public services' as the hereditary village servants. And this time, they restored *vatandar* Mahars to their 'private services' so that this did not comprise the performance of official duties by the Patil even though he took part in the restoration of *vatandar* Mahars. In the Bombay High Court, the Patil was subsequently sentenced to pay a fine of Rs. 10 on the ground that *vatandar* Mahars' 'public services' and 'private services' could not be distinctly separated and, in fact, that the Patil had removed *vatandar* Mahars from the essentially public function of carrying the village revenue to the district office during the period of suspension. Thus, a reconciliation between *vatandar* Mahars and peasants through the payment of Rs. 300 by the former was broken (21 B. 517).

In 1911, a dispute between *vatandar* Mahars and peasants in the village Peth, Satara District, again involved Mangs of the village. *Vatandar* Mahars alleged that peasants of two hamlets (branch villages) of Peth had given the skins of dead animals to Mangs intruding on the rights of *vatandar* Mahars. On this allegation, *vatandar* Mahars asked for an award of the Deputy Collector of Satara District who ordered a Mamlatdar to inquire into the case and submit a report to him. The Mamlatdar asked for the Deputy Collector's sanction to constitute a *panchayat* for the award which was given. He appointed his Head Karkun as the *sar-panch* and ordered both parties to nominate two *panchs* respectively. The *vatandar* Mahars nominated them but the peasants rejected their nomination. Resultantly, the Mamlatdar nominated the *panchs* himself. On 22 January 1912, the *panchayat* awarded in favour of *vatandar* Mahars, and the Deputy Collector approved the award and ordered the Mamlatdar to take action in accordance with the award. But the legality of this procedure was examined in the civil courts and, in the end, the Bombay High Court decided that the award was invalid on the ground that the procedure for making the award did not substantially comply with the provisions of Section 18 of the Bombay Hereditary Offices Act (47 B. 95).

This case clearly denotes that the system of granting awards by a *panchayat* as spelled out in Section 18 of the Act did not function satisfactorily.

Towards the Abolition of the Mahar *Vatan*

Discussions in the Bombay Legislative Council

In the 1920s, various demands brought forward by *vatandar* Mahars were being discussed more often than before in the Bombay Legislative Council. Initially, the Council started with a small number of members as a kind of advisory body to the Governor of Bombay, but in the second half of the nineteenth century and the early part of the next, the Indian Councils Act was revised several times through which the Legislative Council of each of the Presidencies or States was enlarged to include Indian members recommended by various bodies. Through the Government of India Act of 1919 (the so-called Montagu-Chelmsford Reforms), representatives of the 'Depressed Classes' which included the depressed castes formerly known as the untouchables as well as tribes, were nominated to the Legislative Assembly of the Centre and the Legislative Council of each of the Presidencies or States. In the case of the Bombay Presidency, two members of the Depressed Classes were nominated by the Governor of Bombay. In January 1921, the first session of the new and enlarged Bombay Legislative Council was convened in which representatives of the Depressed Classes took their seats for the first time in the history of the Bombay Legislative Council. This resulted in the demands of *vatandar* Mahars being discussed in the Council with ever greater frequency. On 26 February 1923, D.D. Gholap presented a resolution to the Legislative Council which was very implicative though very short: 'That this Council recommends to the Government the commutation of the Maharki vatan' (B.L.C.D. VIII 369).

Gholap was a veteran leader of the Mahar community and as such became the first member from the Depressed Classes to be nominated to the Bombay Legislative Council. The 'commutation' referred to in his resolution, as an administrative term, meant the procedure for relieving hereditary officers of their duties in return for enhancement of tax levied on the lands which had been held by them as the service *inam* lands that had been the tax-exempt or privileged tenure. But what Gholap asked for was to relieve *vatandar* Mahars of their duties on condition that the full assessment be levied on the Mahar *vatan* lands the same as on the Raiyatwari lands of peasants. On Mahar *vatan* lands only a small sum called *judi* had been levied earlier. This procedure of relieving *vatandars* of their duties was, in administrative terms, known as 'resumption' and not 'commutation' as a Government member pointed out in the discussion. The 'resumption' meant the procedure to resume the *inam* lands which had been exempt from land tax or held on a nominal levy paid to the Government as ordinary Raiyatwari land under full assessment. The difference between commutation and resumption was that, in the case of commutation, a reduced rate of land tax was still levied on the commuted lands.

Gholap explained the reason of his presenting the resolution as follows:

> There is a tendency to be seen in all parts of the Presidency on the part of the ryots [*raiyat*] to say 'Mahars are Government servants, why should we pay them for nothing?' On the other hand, Government had declared that the Mahars are not full-time and salaried servants of Government, and that they do not come within the category of Government servants. But what is the real fact? The Mahars are not Government servants, neither do they serve the ryots: they serve the village officers and their relatives in the name of public business, rather than the Government.... They are engaged day and night in doing the private work of the Patil and talati, being under their influence.
>
> (B.L.C.D. VIII 370)

Gholap cited his personal experience as an example to illustrate that *vatandar* Mahars were busily involved with the private works of the Patil and Kulkarni. In 1910, Gholap had come to his village as his high school was on vacation when the Patil of his village called for his father, a *vatandar* Mahar of the village. As his father was busy with sowing in the field at that time Gholap presented himself before the Patil. The Patil ordered him to cut bamboos and carry them to his relative's place in a village nearly eight miles away. Bamboo was urgently needed for the Dasara festival to be held in the evening of that particular day. Accordingly Gholap hurried along a hilly road with his friends shouldering a bundle of long bamboos. But as it got dark halfway to the village, he missed a step and tumbled down from the edge of the road, badly injuring himself (B.L.C.D. VIII 371).

As this personal experience denotes, it was very difficult to separate the public duties of *vatandar* Mahars from the private service asked for by the Patil and others. Besides, *vatandar* Mahars were ordered to serve at any time, day or night, so that for them the concept of working hours was not applicable. Further, not only *vatandar* Mahars themselves but their family, wives and sons, were compelled to work. This state of affairs had made the life of *vatandar* Mahars a very difficult one.

Gholap finished the explanation of his resolution with the following remarks:

> The Vatandar Mahars are now quite tired of it and there is no resource left to them to defend themselves against their miserable state except the commutation of their watans. Government have commuted the Kulkarni watans of about 7,000 villages in the Central and Southern Divisions alone. Also a native state in the Deccan has commuted the Maharki watan by which the Mahars of that state are more happy than they were before. On the same basis, I beg to urge upon the Government the necessity of the commutation of the Maharki watan, as it is found that the duties of the Mahars, as part-time village servants, are too laborious, that their remuneration for these services is too low, and that the numbers generally requisitioned by the village officers to do the duties are too large.
>
> (B.L.C.D. VIII 373)

The commutation of the Kulkarni *vatan* mentioned here by Gholap was the policy of the Bombay government carried out rather forcedly in the closing decades of the nineteenth and early part of the twentieth centuries.

Vatandar Kulkarnis were dismissed from their hereditary offices and replaced by *talatis* who were employed by the Government without hereditary rights. By this time, as the existence of hereditary officers like *vatandar* Kulkarni had become undesirable even for local administration, the Bombay government endeavoured to get rid of them by means of commutating their *vatans*. It thus seems that due to a misunderstanding, Gholap referred to the commutation of the Kulkarni *vatan* as a boon to them since a majority of *vatandar* Kulkarnis complained about it.

Gholap also mentioned the commutation of the Mahar *vatan* in 'a native state in the Deccan'. He indicated by this the Princely State of Kolhapur where Shahu II, the famous leader of the Non-Brahman Movement in the Deccan, abolished the Kulkarni *vatan* in 1913 and then in 1918 relieved *vatandar* Mahars of their duties on the condition that the full assessment on the *inam* lands of *vatandar* Mahars be levied. Thus by this time, the Vatan system had begun to change in various ways and from various causes leaving only the Mahar *vatan* maintained intact under British colonial rule.

Gholap's resolution aimed at calling attention of the members of the Bombay Legislative Council to these points. His resolution was supported by many Indian members of the Council but was ultimately withdrawn in the face of stiff opposition from government members. The reasons for the opposition were, first, that the enforcement of the commutation of the Mahar *vatan* must be 'forcing upon the Mahars a policy which will be extremely hard to a majority of them', and, second, that if the commutation of the Mahar *vatan* were to be carried into effect, the government would have to employ a great number of 'stipendiary servants' to replace *vatandar* Mahars, which would be quite difficult for the government to accomplish due to the financial stringency prevailing at the time. Of these causes, the first was, to some degree, grounded since a certain portion of *vatandar* Mahars objected to the abolition of the Mahar *vatan*. The second cause meant that the Bombay government confessed inadvertently that they had been making *vatandar* Mahars work for a very undervalued rate of payment. This financial concern continued to be the greatest cause of opposition to the commutation of the Mahar *vatan*.

In the new session of the Bombay Legislative Council beginning in February 1924, R.S. Nekaljay played an active part as a representative of the Depressed Classes. On 24 July of the same year, several members asked questions such as the following, regarding the Mahar *vatan*:

Nekaljay: (a) Will Government be pleased to state whether they are aware of several resolutions passed at public meetings of the depressed classes requesting Government to grant an immediate increase in the monthly salary of every watandar Mahar in the Presidency? (b) Will Government be pleased to state the duties which a watandar Mahar is required to perform in a village and his working hours?

[Government :] (a) Yes. (b) The principal duties of Mahars are to watch boundary marks and village office (chavdi); to carry Government letters and remittance to the taluka treasury, to sweep the village roads, to keep an eye on all Government property, trees, etc., to serve as a village guide and to help Government officers passing through the village, and to obey the orders of village officers in the discharge of Government duties. The Mahars are not full-time servants of Government and therefore no working hours have been fixed in their case.

R.D. Shinde: Is it not a fact that all these multifarious duties take up the whole day?

[Government :] No; I don't think so.

M.D. Karki: Are they to watch the boundary marks of every village occupant?

[Government :] Yes; I believe so.

S.S. Dev: If the boundary marks are to be watched by them, will it not require their attention for full 24 hours?

[Government :] I do not think boundary marks easily disappear, so I do not think it requires full 24 hours' attention.

S.S. Dev: Are they to keep their eyes on the trees for 24 hours?

[Government :] During the time they are awake I think they have a chance of keeping an eye on them.

(B.L.C.D. XIII 291-92)

Through discussions it became clear that even the government did not grasp the exact extent of the duties of *vatandar* Mahars as the government corrected its answer by admitting that the watching of boundary demarcating lands of peasants was not a duty of *vatandar* Mahars but that of the peasants themselves (B.L.C.D. XVII 370).

Nekaljay presented various resolutions concerning the Mahars or the Depressed Classes and demanded that the government seek a solution to the problems pointed out in his resolutions. On 14 August 1925, he presented a resolution to the effect that: (1) 'a limited number of watandar Mahars should be kept in each district of the presidency and that they should be paid at the rate of Rs. 15 rising to Rs. 20 per month', and (2) 'the *inam* lands at present held by watandar Mahars in the various districts should be continued free of assessment to the present holders in return for the long and meritorious services rendered to Government by them and their ancestors' (B.L.C.D. XV 1383). The second demand meant that *vatandar* Mahars should retain their *inam* lands as tax-exempt lands even though their services were done away with. Thus, Nekaljay demanded a much more favourable dealing for *vatandar* Mahars than the commutation (resumption) of the Mahar *vatan* demanded by Gholap.

In a resolution also presented on 4 November 1925, Nekaljay asked the government to institute a semi-official committee to inquire into the problems concerning *vatandar* Mahars and Dheds of Gujarat (B.L.C.D. XVI 739). Nekaljay also presented another resolution asking the Bombay government 'to recommend to the Imperial Government to make necessary provisions as early as possible to form a full Mahar battalion or a Mahar company in each of the Indian regiments' (B.L.C.D. XVI 783). As mentioned in Chapter 6, Mahars acquitted themselves well as daring mountain soldiers and played an important role in the state building by Shivaji. Mahars were thus recruited in large numbers even in the early stage of British colonial rule. But by the end of the nineteenth century, recruitment of Mahars was suspended probably under the influence of the 'Martial Races' theory. During World War I, recruitment of Mahars was resumed due to the strained military conditions, but with the termination of the War this practise was again suspended. As the case of the father of Ambedkar indicates, improvement of the social status of Mahars largely depended on one's military career, so that the demand for resumption of recruitment was strong among Mahars.

On 5 November 1925, Nekaljay presented another resolution to the Bombay Legislative Council:

> The Council recommends to the Governor in Council to prohibit by law the practice prevailing among certain classes of eating the flesh of dead animals keeping intact the right to take out the skin of dead animals.
>
> (B.L.C.D. XVI 770)

Nekaljay had already presented a resolution with similar purport on 15 August 1925 focusing mainly on Mahars. As mentioned in Chapter 6, Mahars not only skinned the dead animals but made use of their flesh as food. By this time, however, a strong argument was put forward that the 'eating of the flesh of dead animals' by Mahars was the reason why they were discriminated against. For this reason, Nekaljay presented a resolution recommending that the government prohibit by law the eating of the flesh of dead animals.

All the resolutions presented by Nekaljay were withdrawn or voted down except one concerning the recruitment of Mahars. However, it should not be underestimated that the problems regarding Mahars or the Depressed Classes were discussed in almost all sessions of the Bombay Legislative Council. It must have been on this groundwork that Ambedkar was able to play an active role as the representative of the Depressed Classes in the new session of the Bombay Legislative Council beginning in January 1927.

Ambedkar in the Bombay Legislative Council

B.R. Ambedkar was nominated as the representative of the Depressed Classes of the Bombay Legislative Council in 1927. He focused his attention in the Council towards the revision of the Bombay Hereditary Offices Act for improving the living conditions of the *vatandar* Mahars. Ambedkar introduced a bill (Bill XII of 1928) to amend the Bombay Hereditary Offices Act on 19 March 1928. The 'statement of objects and reasons' of his bill ran as follows:

1. To make better provision for the remuneration of the officiating watandars.
2. To allow commutation of watans of inferior hereditary village servants.
3. To provide for the conversion of Baluta into a money cess.
4. To allow the holder of inferior watan to free himself from the obligations to serve the ryots.
5. To define the duties of officiating watandars.

(B.L.C.D. XVIII 1084)

This order of the 'objects and reasons' is somewhat confusing. When rearranged properly, they can be divided into two parts. The first part constitutes the second clause that demanded the commutation of *vatans* and the second part relates to the first, third, fourth and fifth clauses for improving the lives of *vatandars*. These two parts constitute separate and parallel demands.

Ambedkar made the concept of 'freedom of contract' the leading principle while dealing with the problems of *vatandar* Mahars:

> What my bill aims at is freedom of contract; if the ryots do not want to employ the Mahars, they ought to have perfect liberty not to employ them, and if the Mahars do not want to serve, the Mahars should have perfect liberty not to serve.
>
> (B.L.C.D. XVIII 718)

On this principle, he wanted to revise the Bombay Hereditary Offices Act in the dual direction of improving the conditions of *vatandar* Mahars who wished to be relieved of their duties as well as of those who wished to remain in *vatandar* Mahar office. Thus, he intended to meet the demand of the former category of *vatandar* Mahars through the commutation of the Mahar *vatan* (the second clause of his bill) and of the latter category through the first, third, fourth and fifth clauses of his bill.

With regard to the commutation of Mahar *vatan*, Ambedkar's bill proposed to insert a provision in Section 15 of the Bombay Hereditary Offices Act with the following objective. If 'the whole body of representative watandars or a majority of them' agreed, they could be 'relieved of their obligations to perform such services in perpetuity' by a written application to the Collector, and in that case they should be 'entitled to retain possession of the lands held by them if they agree to pay full survey assessment on such lands' (B.L.C.D. XVIII 1082-83). This was, in essence, the same as the purpose of the resolution presented by Gholap.

The ground for opposition by the government to the commutation (resumption) of the Mahar *vatan* was financial stringency as was the case with Gholap's resolution. J. Ghosal, the Commissioner of the Central Division, estimated the cost needed for the commutation of the Mahar *vatan* as follows. Roughly there were 10,000 villages in the Central Division in which there were in all nearly 50,000 officiating inferior village servants. This number could be reduced to the absolute minimum of 24,000 by replacing them with stipendiary servants. The cost needed to pay this number of stipendiary servants was about Rs. 29,00,000 at the rate of Rs. 10 per month per person. On the other hand, financial gains of the commutation (resumption) of the Mahar *vatan* constituted the balance (in administrative terms, *nuksan* meaning 'the loss') between the full survey assessment on Mahar *vatan* lands and the *judi* formerly paid by *vatandar* Mahars. This balance was estimated to be only Rs. 5,00,000. Thus, for the commutation of the Mahar *vatan* a new financial burden of Rs. 24,00,000 was needed in the Central Division alone which had to be met by levying a new cess on the lands of 'poor agriculturists' or by

Government finance. This burden was too heavy for the agriculturists as well as, it turns out, for the government (B.L.C.D. XVIII 723).

Regardless of the accuracy of his estimate, the point was that the government itself acknowledged the fact that it had been paying only Rs. 5,00,000 for the services of *vatandar* Mahars estimated to cost Rs. 29,00,000 if performed by stipendiary servants.

The Bombay government was, however, not favourably disposed to giving up its right to get this free service from *vatandar* Mahars. As this fact indicates, the Mahar *vatan* represented something like a miracle for the government. Thus, it was quite natural that Gholap, Nekaljay and Ambedkar repeatedly demanded the commutation (resumption) of the Mahar *vatan*.

However, Ambedkar was largely mistaken if he expected to be able to relieve *vatandar* Mahars of their services to the village community or villagers by the commutation of the Mahar *vatan*. As mentioned before, the commutation would serve to change the relation between *vatandars* and the state alone. To alter the relation between *vatandars* and the village community or the villagers, however, Section 16 of the Bombay Hereditary Offices Act had to be amended, but Ambedkar's bill did not include a provision for this amendment.

With regard to the demands of *vatandar* Mahars who wanted to remain in office, Ambedkar's bill proposed the revision of the following purposes to the Bombay Hereditary Offices Act corresponding respectively to the first, third and fourth clauses of his bill.

1. 'To make better provision for the remuneration of the officiating watandars', the transfer of Mahar *vatan* lands must be nullified even though it took place before the enforcement of the Bombay Hereditary Offices Act to cope with the situation that many Mahar *vatan* lands were transferred into the hands of money-lenders.

In the discussion held by the Council, strong opposition was put forward that it should entail a loss only to the present landholders after several transfers of the same lands. Ambedkar himself was forced to acknowledge this.

2. 'To provide for the conversion of Baluta into a money cess', the government should levy a money cess corresponding to *balute* along with other taxes and deliver it to *vatandar* Mahars since

balute taken directly from the villagers by *vatandar* Mahars has been the main cause of the disputes between these two parties.

In the discussion, it was argued that this procedure was too much trouble for the government and too heavy a burden for the villagers.

3. 'To allow the holder of inferior watan to free himself from the obligations to serve the ryots', it is expedient to separate the portion of the money cess which is supposed to be the reward for the services to the village community or villagers from that portion which is supposed to be the reward for rendering services to the state and to relieve *vatandar* Mahars from rendering services to the village community or villagers on condition that the former portion of the money cess be relinquished by *vatandar* Mahars.

In the discussion, an argument was put forward against this action that it was not practicable due to the difficulty of separating the two portions of the duties of *vatandar* Mahars.

Thus, Ambedkar's concrete proposals met with strong opposition. Furthermore, Ambedkar was criticized that he himself contradicted his own principle of 'freedom of contract' by keeping the interests of Mahars alone in mind without giving any attention to the interests of the villagers. Ambedkar himself accepted this criticism.

Despite the strong opposition and criticism, however, Ambedkar's bill was referred to the Select Committee. It was the general procedure of the Council to refer the bill to the Select Committee when agreement had been reached on the main portions of the bill even though the details were yet to be scrutinized. However, in the case of Ambedkar's bill, agreement on even the main portions of the bill had not been reached. In spite of this, his bill was referred to the Select Committee on his approval that he would accept even a modification of the principle of the bill that might be suggested during the discussion (B.L.C.D. XVIII 791). The Select Committee comprised 15 members which, besides Ambedkar, included government members such as three Division Commissioners and Indian members like S.K. Bole and P.G. Solanki. The Select Committee was to submit a report to the Council by the beginning of June 1929.

However, as this procedure of referring his bill to the Select Committee was too exceptional to produce a satisfactory result, Ambedkar was finally obliged to withdraw it. Thus, the first endeavour of Ambedkar to improve the living conditions of *vatandar* Mahars through the revision of the Bombay Hereditary Offices Act proved to be a failure. Subsequently, Ambedkar again introduced a bill with a similiar purpose to the Council in 1937, but under the stringent situation prevalent just before World War II he was compelled to suspend his activities. Thus, the problem of the abolition of the Mahar *vatan* was carried over to the post-independence period.

Conclusion

On 15 August 1947, India gained its independence though in the form of the Partition. On 29 August of the same year, the Drafting Committee of the Constituent Assembly started to function with Ambedkar as its Chairman. On 26 November 1949, the Constitution of India was passed by the Assembly and came into force on 26 January 1950 of which Article 17 provided the abolition of untouchability. In 1955, the Untouchability (Offences) Act was enacted to put into practise the constitutional abolition of untouchability. In line with this overall movement against social discrimination after gaining independence, the Mahar *vatan* was at last abolished by the Bombay Inferior Village Watans Abolition Act of 1959.

Notes

1 The Elphinstone Code, in fact an aggregate of 27 regulations, are printed in Clarke 1851: 1-324.

2 This Act is not an act of the Bombay government but of the Government of India. The two Presidency governments of Bombay and Madras were deprived of the independent legislative right by the renewed Charter Act of 1833. The legislative right of the Presidency governments was restored by the Indian Councils Act of 1861.

3 For the full text of this legal decision handed down by the Bombay Sadr Divani Adalat, see Chapter 3 of this volume.

4 This case bearing on the right of the *vatandar* Mahar to the skins of dead cattle is referred to in Chapter 3 as well.

5 The text of the Bombay Hereditary Offices Act is printed in Khandekar 1938: I.

8

Priesthood and the Non-Brahman Movement in the Bombay Presidency: Towards the Abolition of the Joshi Vatan

Introduction

As mentioned in previous chapters, there existed in the villages of the medieval Deccan various *vatandars* (*balutedars*) collectively known as *bara balute* (*bara balutedars*). The Joshi was also an indispensable member of *bara balute* who was prescribed to conduct village rituals on such occasions as Dasara, Holi and others. Village Joshis (*vatandar* Joshis) were Brahmans who primarily held the office of Kulkarni of their respective villages as well. The Kulkarni was the tax functionary of the state and, at the same time, was the accountant and scribe of the village community.

Further, in most cases, the village Joshi-Kulkarni simultaneously acted as the *gharopadhya* (*ghara-upadhya*, family priest) of villagers, in whose homes he officiated at such family ceremonies as marriages and funerals.[1] It was not uncommon, however, for several Joshi families of common descent or even different genealogies to coexist in one village. In these cases, Joshi families allotted among themselves the villagers to whom they should provide services as the *gharopadhya*. Respective villagers for whom respective Joshis performed ceremonies were designated as their *yajmans* (*yajmanas*). In the case of the village Diya, Sasvad District, for example, two Brahmans surnamed Pansi who shared the offices of Joshi and Kulkarni of this village with other Brahmans, also served as the *gharopadhya* of at least three substantial peasants, Jadhav by name, of this same village (Fukazawa 1991: 234-37).

Thus, the village Joshi enjoyed the twofold relationship in his village, that is to say, the holistic relationship with the village community as the Joshi-Kulkarni and the dyadic relationship as the *gharopadhya* with individual villagers who were his *yajmans*.

Significantly the village Joshi who usually held the office of Kulkarni and *gharopadhya* at the same time wielded a strong influence as the local intellectual over the material and spiritual life of the villagers in the medieval Deccan. But the tide began to turn in their disfavour under British colonial rule especially from the last decades of the nineteenth century. The offices of Kulkarnis, which had formerly been prescribed as the 'hereditary office' by the Elphinstone Code, began to be replaced one by one by the newly introduced office of *talati* that was not a hereditary one but was a stipendiary office appointed by the government. Accordingly, the hereditary office of the Kulkarni finally gave way to the bureaucracy in the 1910s resulting in a lessened authority of the Joshi-Kulkarni.

This chapter aims to trace the historical changes that occurred in the privilege and power of the village Joshi as *gharopadhya* under British colonial rule during the nineteenth and early twentieth centuries. It brings to light an important and hitherto unnoticed aspect of the overall disintegration of the Vatan system in which the communal rights of *vatandars* (*balutedars*) to take perquisites from their *yajmans* regardless of whether they actually provided services to them or not was legally abolished.

Legal Status of the Joshi and Kulkarni *Vatans*

The Joshi Vatan as Immovable Property

In the so-called Elphinstone Code which constituted the foundation of the administrative system in the Bombay Presidency, *vatan* was designated as the 'hereditary office'. The Bombay Regulation V of 1827 which provided the 'limitation of time for prosecuting civil actions', reads as follows:

> Whenever lands, houses, hereditary offices, or other immoveable property, have been held without interruption for a longer period than thirty years, ... such possession shall be received as proof of a sufficient right of property in the same (Chapter I, Section I, First).

Thus, *vatans* as hereditary offices were legally regarded as immovable property on the same footing with lands and houses by the Elphinstone Code. The Bombay government adopted the policy of continuing all *vatans* as they had been under the former governments, at least in the early phase of its administration.

The Bombay Regulation V of 1827 was repealed by the Limitation Act of 1859 (Act XIV of 1859)[2] which lacked the substantive enactment to prescribe *vatan* as immovable property. This caused the filing of several suits involving the issue as to whether *vatan* was immovable property or not. Of these suits, the one pertaining to the village Joshi *vatan* was the Special Appeal No. 238 of 1871 ruled by the Full Bench of the Bombay High Court. The plaintiffs of this suit were Purshotam Sidhshvar and his brother, the Joshis of a certain village in Pune District. They sued for the recovery of their fees for the previous five years due from a villager, Balvantrao by name. The defendant pleaded that this suit was barred on the ground that the limitation provided by the Limitation Act of 1859 for suits pertaining to movable property was six years, construing *vatan* to be movable property. In opposition, the plaintiffs claimed that *vatan* was immovable property, the limitation for which was 12 years. The Bombay High Court decreed in favour of the plaintiffs. Firstly, it held that the Limitation Act of 1859 did not purpose to deny the purport of the Bombay Regulation V of 1827 which prescribed hereditary offices (*vatans*) as immovable property. Secondly, it held that the new Limitation Act (Bombay Act IX of 1871), which was enacted while this suit was pending in the court, provided the limitation for suits pertaining to hereditary offices to be 12 years (9 B.H.C.R. 99).

This decision was to set the precedent for all subsequent suits in the Bombay Presidency concerning not only village Joshi *vatan* but all of other *vatans* as it was the decision of the Full Bench of the Bombay High Court.

Inam Lands of the Village Joshi

A common practise in the medieval Deccan was for *inam* lands to be granted to the village Joshi by the govenment or village community. The latter was generally known as *ganv nisbat inam*. *Inam* lands were either totally exempted from tax payment or had a reduced rate of tax called *judi* levied on them. With *ganv nisbat inam* lands, the taxes leviable on them were paid by the village community as a whole. Under the Maratha administration, *inam* lands were generously bestowed on Brahmans, religious institutions like temples, state officials, district and village hereditary officers and others as a religious grant, reward and remuneration. This was the case with the village Joshi as well.

The Bombay government that had gained control over the western Deccan in 1818 was forced to rearrange or curtail various *inam* lands for it had the land revenue as its financial basis. For this purpose, the office of Inam Commissioner was established in 1843 to investigate the title deeds (*sanads*) of the *inam* lands which were alleged to have been granted by the former governments as proof of privilege. The duty and power of the Inam Commissioner was provided by Act XI of 1852 (An Act for the Adjudication of Titles to Certain Estates Claimed to be Wholly or Partially Rent-free in the Presidency of Bombay), based on which the Inam Commissioner was to classify *inam* lands into two categories, that is, *inam* lands that were to be continued and those to be discontinued.

Regarding *inam* lands of the village Joshi, Schedule B, 8 of the above-mentioned Act provided as follows:

> All lands authorizedly held by an official tenure, which it is evident from local usage was meant to be hereditary and has been so considered heretofore, even though there be no sunnuds [*sanads*] declaring it to be so; for instance, Inams which form the authorized emoluments of any hereditary office, as of cazees, village joshees, &c., and are not merely personal, are to be continued permanently.

By this provision, *inam* lands of the village Joshi were classified into the category of *inam* lands which were to be 'continued permanently', at least at this point of time (1852).

Thus, under the early administration of the Bombay government, the village Joshi *vatan* was designated as the hereditary office which should have been treated as a sort of immovable property, and further *inam* lands of the village Joshi were prescribed to be continued permanently as remuneration for the hereditary public officer.

Commutation of the Kulkarni Vatan

The circumstances began to change, however, in the latter half of the nineteenth century. The Bombay Hereditary Offices Act (Bombay Act III of 1874) brought about overall changes in the legal status of various *vatans*. Through this Act, the village Joshi *vatan* was excluded from the category of 'hereditary offices' which were now restricted to such *vatans* directly connected with tax collection and village police as those of the

Patil, Kulkarni and Mahar. This did not mean that the village Joshi *vatan* and *inam* lands were immediately abolished. At the least, however, it meant that the office of village Joshi was legally recognized as not being indispensable for administrative purposes.

Moreover, the hereditary office of the Kulkarni itself was to be reorganized after the enactment of the Bombay Hereditary Offices Act. As the administrative system of the Bombay government became more and more complicated, ever greater efficiency on the side of the Kulkarni was required. Thus, Kulkarnis were now obliged to pass a certain sort of test, commonly known as the 'survey examination', to prove their efficiency in officiating in the capacity of Kulkarni. This test prescribed by such Government Resolutions as No. 603 dated 15 August 1883 and others, was a rather simple one that included among other things 'Reading and writing the vernacular of the district', 'Mathematics up to simple interest' and 'Knowledge of the account forms'. Government Resolution No. 10676 dated 8 November 1916, however, stipulated the Vernacular (or English) School Final Examination as an additional qualifying test for the officiating Kulkarnis. Though this move on the part of the Bombay government provoked a strong reaction against it in the Bombay Legislative Council, the government was adamant in its position (P.L.C.G.B. LVI 338-45).

Thus, from the 1880s the Bombay government began to select only those Kulkarnis whom they evaluated as being efficient to remain in the office, ever raising the standard of qualification. This necessarily resulted in dismissal of inefficient Kulkarnis from their office through an administrative procedure called 'commutation'. Commutation was, in principle, a procedure for abolishing hereditary offices (*vatans*) by commuting *inam* lands attached to those hereditary offices into a sort of privileged lands taxable by rates reduced below the 'full revenue assessment'. The offices (*vatans*) of hereditary district officers such as the Deshmukh and Deshpande had been mostly abolished in the 1860s utilizing this administrative procedure of the commutation, based on the Summary Settlement Act (Bombay Act II of 1863).[3] The office of the Kulkarni also began to be abolished through this same procedure of the commutation from the 1880s,[4] based on Section 15, Clause 1 (Commutation of service) of the Bombay Hereditary Offices Act that read as follows:

> The Collector may, with the consent of the holder of a watan, given in writing, relieve him and his heirs and successors in perpetuity of their

> liability to perform service upon such conditions, whether consistent with the provisions of this Act or not, as may be agreed upon by the Collector and such holder.

Though it prescribed to commute *vatans* 'with the consent of the holder of a watan', there is no doubt that this consent was often a 'forced consent' as was alleged by a member in the Bombay Legislative Council with regard to the Kulkarni *vatan* (B.L.C.D. XVIII 316).[5]

The Bombay government especially intensified the commutation of Kulkarni *vatan* from 1912 and finally in 1914 declared to 'have put forward a suggestion for the commutation of these Kulkarnis and to get rid of the hereditary system' (P.L.C.G.B. LII 908). As compensation for the commutation of the Kulkarni *vatan*, the government proposed to continue offering one-third of the cash allowances which Kulkarnis used to receive from the government. Many Kulkarnis resisted against this move of the government, but without any success. Thus, the hereditary offices of Kulkarnis were abolished one by one during the course of the 1910s and were replaced by the office of *talati*. This constituted the first step towards the abolition of the village Joshi *vatan* itself.

The Village Joshi and the Non-Brahman Movement

Disputes between Village Joshis and Peasants

The village Joshi traditionally had the hereditary right to receive the customary fees when he, in his capacity as *gharopadhya*, officiated at family ceremonies in his *yajmans*' homes. Disputes centring around this hereditary right of the village Joshi began to occur frequently in the course of the nineteenth century under British colonial rule.

In one such case, the Bombay Sadr Divani Adalat, the predecessor of the Bombay High Court, handed down the following decision in 1839. The plaintiffs of this suit, the Joshis of the village Newasa, Ahmadnagar District, sued for the recovery of their 'hucks' (*haqqs*, fees) from the defendant, Ababhat by name. The plaintiffs claimed that they performed 20 rituals out of 27 formally prescribed for the marriage ceremony on the occasion of the marriage of the defendant's sister. The defendant had paid, however, only 10 annas, while their fees for these 20 rituals were to be Rs. 2-10-0. As opposed to this, the defendant pleaded that the plaintiffs performed mere 8 rituals, for which their fees totalled only 10 annas, and that his 'domestic Opadhya' officiated at the remaining

12 rituals.[6] At the hearing, the defendant finally admitted that out of 27 rituals prescribed for the formal marriage, 18 were performed by the plaintiffs, and that he had paid the plaintiffs mere 10 annas for 7 rituals out of 18 actually performed by them. Thus, the Full Bench of the Bombay Sadr Divani Adalat decreed that the defendant was required to pay the fees for the remaining 11 rituals, the amount of which should be decided by the defendant himself, and further that in case the defendant would not pay the fees of his own accord, damages of Rs. 1-8-0 should be awarded to the plaintiffs (3 B.S.D.A. 174). In this case, a dispute occurred between the village Joshis and one of their *yajmans* because the *yajman* did not pay for the rituals actually performed by the village Joshis, though circumstances must have been considerably more complicated.

Disputes of a different nature, however, became prevalent in the latter half of the nineteenth century, that is to say, disputes caused by *yajmans* employing other priests to officiate at their family ceremonies to the exclusion of the village Joshi. With disputes of this nature, the legal point at issue was whether or not this action of *yajmans* constituted a violation of the hereditary rights of the village Joshi. The leading case of the suits pertaining to this issue in the Bombay Presidency was the Special Appeal No. 3574 of 1857 ruled by the Bombay Sadr Divani Adalat. The plaintiff in this case was Krishnumbhut who had 'a quarter share in the hereditary offices of Joshee (astrologer), and Oopadhya (priest)' of the village Amberee.[7] The defendants, three members of the Kulkarni family of this same village, employed another priest, Anunt Gungadhurbhut by name, to perform certain ceremonies in their homes and paid him the fees. In opposition to this, the plaintiff contended that the defendants should have asked him to perform these ceremonies as they were his *yajmans* and further that their action therefore constituted a violation of the hereditary rights of the village Joshi. The Bombay Sadr Divani Adalat decreed in favour of the plaintiff, ordering the defendants to pay the plaintiff the same sum of the fee as that paid to Anunt Gungadhurbhut who actually performed the ceremonies. The essential portion of the judgement read as follows:

> The Court finds that the Senior Assistant Judge [of the lower court] is in error in holding it to be the rule of the Sudder Dewanee Adawlut that 'all religious ceremonies are optional, and that a fee can only be claimed by a party who has the right to perform them, when he has been actually called on to perform them'. The rule of the Court has consistently been that certain ceremonies are optional; but that, when

> these or other obligatory ceremonies have been performed, the person entitled of hereditary right to perform them is entitled to be paid his fee whether he performs them or not.
>
> (11 B.S.D.A. 111, at 116-17)

The Bombay Sadr Divani Adalat made this case the precedent of suits involving hereditary offices in line with the judgement in the above-mentioned suit over the Joshi's hereditary right of the village Newasa as well as that of the Special Appeal No. 2791 of 1851 ruled by the same court. In the latter case, the Joshi of a certain village sued for the recovery of fees due from one of his *yajmans* who employed another priest to perform family ceremonies to the exclusion of the village Joshi and actually paid him the fees (11 B.S.D.A. 111, at 115).

According to this precedent thus established by the Bombay Sadr Divani Adalat, *yajmans* were forced to pay the village Joshi, who was their *gharopadhya*, the same sum of the fee as that paid to other priests who actually performed family ceremonies. This meant that *yajmans* were obliged to pay double fees, if they wished to employ priests other than the village Joshi as his *gharopadhya* to conduct their family ceremonies.

The Bombay Sadr Divani Adalat was thus quite unambiguous in respecting the hereditary right of the village Joshi to perform family ceremonies in his *yajmans*' homes. This stance of the Bombay Sadr Divani Adalat that was in line with the purport of the Elphinstone Code to continue *vatans* (hereditary offices) as they had been under the former governments presented a striking contrast to that of the Calcutta Sadr Divani Adalat. The Full Bench of the Calcutta Sadr Divani Adalat in 1850 held that 'Yujmans, requiring any religious ceremonies to be performed for their benefit by any Pooruhit [priest], are at liberty to choose the Pooruhit whom they may prefer for that purpose, and no other Pooruhit can, as a right, claim a share in the fees paid either from the Yujmans or from the Pooruhit who received the fees.' [8] This meant that the Calcutta Sadr Divani Adalat denied not only the exclusive right of the hereditary priest (Purohit) to perform ceremonies in his *yajmans*' homes, but also the right to receive compensation in case his *yajmans* would have employed other priests to officiate at family ceremonies. The Bombay High Court, the successor of the Bombay Sadr Divani Adalat, itself took congnizance of this difference. In one case, the village Joshis of a certain village in Pune District sued for the declaratory decree to the effect that they had the hereditary right to perform ceremonies in the defendants' homes with payment of the fees. One passage of the judgement handed down by the Bombay High Court in this case read as follows:

> The right of a village or town priest to maintain a suit against a yajman, who has employed another priest to perform ceremonies, though apparently denied by the Courts of Bengal and the North-Western Provinces, ... has been recognized here.
>
> (3 B. 9)

There thus existed a conspicuous difference between the Bombay High Court and the Calcutta High Court with regard to the hereditary right of priests (Joshi and Purohit). This would have resulted from different circumstances in respective Presidencies, of which the most essential must have been the difference in the communal structure of respective societies. In the medieval Deccan, specifically in Maharashtra, all offices of communities tended to become hereditary ones which were commonly called *vatan*. Representative examples were the offices of Patil, Kulkarni and *bara balute* in the village community, Deshmukh and Deshpande in *pargana* (district) community, and *mhetar* (headman) of respective caste communities. All of these *vatans* were hereditary property or patrimony which could be inherited, transferred, sold and divided. As mentioned before, the Bombay government recognized these *vatans* as immovable property in the early phase of its administration. That the office of the village Joshi was the *vatan* to be continued under the Elphinstone Code system seems to be the most essential factor that brought about the difference in stance between the Bombay High Court and the Calcutta High Court with regard to the hereditary right of the priest.

This policy of the Bombay government, however, involved one delicate problem, namely, the problem arising from the fact that this policy necessarily restricted freedom on the side of the villagers to choose the priest. In fact, the *yajmans*' right to choose their family priests was upheld in some judgements of lower courts respecting personal freedom of choice (e.g. 11 B.S.D.A. 111, at 115). Though all of these earlier decisions of lower courts in favour of *yajmans* were reversed in the Bombay Sadr Divani Adalat, this problem concerning freedom of choice of the priest on the side of *yajmans* became an ever more controversial issue in the latter half of the nineteenth century.

In one such case, the Joshi of a certain village in Belgaum District, Krishnabhat by name, brought a suit against his *yajmans* and another priest. The cause of action in this case was that two of his *yajmans*,

Rayakotepa (defendant 1) and his nephew, Raja bin Shivapa (defendant 2), employed another priest, Balachari by name (defendant 3), to officiate at the marriage ceremony of defendant 2 and paid the fees to defendant 3 to the exclusion of the plaintiff, the village Joshi. The plaintiff thus sued defendants 1, 2 and 3 for damages with an injunction against defendant 3 purporting to prohibit him from officiating in the home of the plaintiff's *yajmans*. The Bombay High Court in its decision handed down in 1879 awarded damages against the three defendants but did not grant the injunction for which the suit was brought for the following reason:

> We should not, as at present advised, be prepared to sanction any injunction which should have the effect of forcing upon any section of the community the services of a priest whom they are unwilling to recognize, and forbidding them to employ a priest whose ministrations they desire.
>
> (3 B. 232, at 233)

The *yajmans*' right to choose their priests thus began to be recognized by the Bombay High Court in the last decades of the nineteenth century, though the hereditary right of the village Joshi continued to be upheld. The judgement that *yajmans* who would wish to employ other priests than the village Joshi to perform ceremonies in their homes had to pay the same sum of the fees payable to the officiating priest to the village Joshi whose *yajmans* they were was a compromise between these two incompatible rights of village Joshis and *yajmans*.

The Beginning of the Non-Brahman Movement

In the 1870s, the so-called Non-Brahman Movement began to develop in Maharashtra, especially in the areas around Pune, under the leadership of Jotirao Phule (1827-90). Phule (literally meaning 'flowers'), who was a Mali (gardener) by caste, had been working tirelessly to free the Kunbi and other lower castes from the spiritual and material control of the Brahman Joshi since the 1850s. As the leading organ of the Non-Brahman Movement, the Satya Shodhak Samaj was established in 1873 by Phule. One of the most important tactics of the Satya Shodhak Samaj was the so-called Satya Shodhak-style marriage in which a priest selected from the members of the caste concerned was to perform ceremonies without employing the Brahman Joshi. It is doubtless that this Satya Shodhak-style marriage was incompatible with the hereditary right of the village Joshi to perform ceremonies in his *yajmans*' homes. Thus, disputes quite naturally began to occur between village Joshis and Satya Shodhaks.[9]

To the north of Pune, there is a village named Otur. The Satya Shodhak Samaj spread in this village during the 1880s. The leaders of this movement were members of the Patil family of this village. No wonder then that more and more conflicts between village Joshis and Satya Shodhaks began to arise in this village.

In 1888, Joshis of this village, Waman Jagannath Joshi and others, filed a suit against Balaji Kusaji Patil, one of their *yajmans*. The plaintiffs claimed that the defendant had not asked them to officiate at the marriage ceremonies of his daughters and consequently had not paid the fees to them, though they had been willing to offer their services, and that thus the defendant had violated the hereditary right of the village Joshi to perform ceremonies in their *yajmans*' homes. The plaintiffs thus sued for the recovery of the fees which should have been paid to them, whether they actually performed their duties or not. Opposing this, the defendant pleaded as follows:

> The marriages were performed without any prescribed ceremonies, and no priest, as such, was employed. There was no *ganeshpujan* [worship of Ganesha], the initial ceremony of the marriage. There was nothing beyond the placing of garlands on the necks of the bride and the bridegroom. There was no distribution of fees (*dakshana*): therefore the village *joshis* cannot claim any fees. There is a separate ritual of the *Sudras* of the defendant's caste. That ritual was not performed.
>
> (14 B. 167, at 168)

After hearing the statements of both parties and examining precedents, the Bombay High Court confirmed the following principle:

> But, as said in *Krishnumbhut* v. *Anant Gungadhurbhut* [4 B.S.D.A. 111, partly quoted above], 'if the ceremonies, whether optional or obligatory, have been performed, the person entitled by hereditary right to perform is entitled to his fees',— it cannot matter whether they are performed by another Brahman or by a person who calls himself a Kunbi priest, or any one else in the caste— there is equally, we think, an invasion of his privileges against which the village priest is entitled to be protected....
>
> (14 B. 167, at 169)

Following this line of judgement, the Bombay High Court decided to send down 'the following issue for a finding by the District Court: What ceremonies were performed on the occasions of the marriages, or either of them, and by whom?' (14 B. 167, at 170). The principle laid down by the court was that the 'plaintiffs were only entitled to recover in case a marriage was performed in any of the modes known to the Hindu law, or in the modes described by Mr. Mandlik with respect to castes other than the Brahmin caste, and that the marriages in disputes being not performed in any such way, they were not such marriages as they were entitled to recover fees for in virtue of any right acquired by grant or prescription' (ibid., at 169). The Bombay High Court thus sent down the above-mentioned issue to the lower court for investigation which had to be completed within two months. The District Court Judge, on the evidence on remand, 'stated his opinion that the ceremonial enumerated by the late V.N. Mandlik in his Hindu Law, as observed by lower castes, was not followed on these occasions'. Upon this, the Bombay High Court decreed in favour of the defendant.[10]

This decision of the Bombay High Court can well be said to have made a breach in the legal safeguard that had been protecting the hereditary right of the village Joshi. The village Joshi was disqualified by this decision to demand the fees as a matter of right, so long as a marriage was a Satya Shodhak-style marriage or non-Brahmanical marriage in general without performing any rituals prescribed in the Hindu laws for castes other than the Brahman castes. This was a step forward for the Satya Shodhak Samaj in particular and the Non-Brahman Movement in general.

On 7 February 1918, the Bombay High Court handed down a decision in a similar case over the hereditary right of the Joshi of the village Bhavdi, Khed District (42 B. 613; 20 Bom.L.R. 454). The plaintiff was Bala Genuji Navale, the village Joshi and the defendants were Balwant Laxman Ghatpande (defendant 1, a Maratha) and his friend Tatya Kondaji (defendant 2, a Kunbi). When the mother of defendant 1 died, he did not call in the plaintiff to conduct the ceremony prescribed for the tenth day after death as he was a member of the Satya Shodhak Samaj. Instead, he himself performed the ceremony with the help of defendant 2 who was also a Satya Shodhak. The plaintiff, however, sent his brother to the home of defendant 1 intending to make him perform the ceremony as a matter of course. But his brother was prevented from doing so and receiving the fees as well in the aforementioned circumstances. Upon this, the plaintiff filed a suit for damages against defendants 1 and 2. The defendants pleaded as follows. First, in case defendant 1 himself performed the ceremony without employing anyone else to do so, the village Joshi could not claim compensation for damages. Second, also in case the ceremony performed was such a non-Brahmanical one as ceremonial bathing and worship of a water vessel filled with water, the village Joshi could not claim compensation. In opposition to this, the plaintiff contested firstly that defendant 1 employed defendant 2 to perform the ceremony, so that the plaintiff was entitled to claim compensation. Secondly, though the defendants alleged that the ceremony actually performed was non-Brahmanical, it was in fact an imitation of a Brahmanical one, with the exception of no *mantras* being recited. The Bombay High Court decided in favour of the defendants taking cognizance of the following points:

> It is clearly proved that no Sankalp was made and defendant No. 1 simply made a formal show of the Dashpinda Kriya and bathed in the river and then bowed down and went away.... The reading, if at all by Kondaji [defendant 2], was the reading of the tenets of the [Satya Shodhak] Samaj and not any Mantra....
>
> [Thus, ...] it is a very different thing to say that though the villager may prefer another rite, and choose not to have the Brahmin ceremony, he is still under obligation to pay the Joshi, that is, to pay for not doing that which the villager deliberately wished to avoid.

This decision of the Bombay High Court is important in finally confirming that the villagers were not obliged to pay the fees to the village Joshi (the hereditary *vatandar* Joshi) if they did not perform Brahmanical rites. This was a victory for the Satya Shodhak Samaj and further for the Non-Brahman Movement in general over the Brahman Joshi. Thus, the next step or target to be achieved for the Non-Brahman Movement was the abolition of the village Joshi *vatan* itself.

Towards the Abolition of the Joshi *Vatan*

Introduction of the Joshi Bill

On 3 November 1925, a private bill commonly known as the Joshi bill was introduced in the Bombay Legislative Council by S.K. Bole. This bill was meant for amending 'the law relating the emoluments claimable by Watandar Hindu priests'. S.K. Bole, the mover of the bill, was a member of the Bombay Legislative Council representing labour circles and a member of Satya Shodhak Samaj as well. This bill was a short one having only three clauses.

1. Short title. This Act may be called the Invalidation of Hindu Ceremonial Emoluments Act, 192 .
2. Definitions. In this Act, 'Ceremonial emoluments' mean all perquisites, fees and any other dues claimable by any person for religious ceremonials, on account of his being a hereditary priest.
3. Right to claim ceremonial emoluments. No person shall be entitled to claim, as a matter of right, any ceremonial emoluments from any Hindu who does not call in the services of the person claiming those emoluments.

Thus, the substantial part of this bill was the third clause which was meant for invalidating the hereditary right of the village Joshi over his *yajmans*. S.K. Bole pointed out in the 'Statement of Objects and Reasons' of this bill that:

> The principle laid down in this Bill has been long the established law in all parts of British India except the Bombay Presidency, where it has been held that a watandar priest or Joshi can obtain a decree for his customary emoluments, though, as a matter of fact, his services for performing the ceremonies may not be requisitioned by a Hindu. This state of the law has caused considerable annoyances to non-Brahman Hindus in the Bombay Presidency. The priests who claim these emoluments, belong universally to the Brahman caste and non-Brahman Hindus resent their being forced by the law courts to pay for services which they neither desire nor utilise. This bill is intended to do away with the cause of this injustice to the non-Brahman Hindus and bring the law as administered by the Bombay High Court into line with the law laid down by the other High Courts.
>
> (B.L.C.D. XVII 1918)

S.K. Bole thus accused the Bombay High Court of its allowing to continue the hereditary right of the village Joshi. Referring to the aforementioned decision of the Bombay High Court concerning the hereditary right of Joshi of the village Bhavdi (42 B. 613), Bole criticized that the Bombay High Court 'has held that if a Hindu villager chooses to have a Brahmanical ceremony conducted, he must employ the village joshi or fee him as if he had employed him' (B.L.C.D. XVII 1502). As pointed out before, this decision of the Bombay High Court was favourable to the Satya Shodhak Samaj or the Non-Brahman Movement in general insofar as it held that the village Joshi could not claim the fees as compensation so long as the marriage ceremony was performed in the non-Brahmanical mode without employing anyone else as priest. Bole, however, criticized the reverse side of this decision, that is to say, the fact that the village Joshi could claim compensation, so far as any Brahmanical ceremonies were conducted employing either another Brahman or a priest of their own castes such as a Kunbi priest. Bole's bill was intended to make a break from this situation based on the principle that the village Joshi, who was not called in for performing the ceremony, could not claim the fees.

The Joshi bill introduced by S.K. Bole was read for the first time on 19 March 1926. S.T. Kambli from Dharwar District strongly supported this bill. As he was a Lingayat, he himself had personal experience of a dispute with Brahman Joshis. The main cause of disputes between Lingayats and Brahman Joshis was also the hereditary right of the village Joshi to officiate at the family rituals of Lingayats. In the Bombay Legislative Council, Kambli spoke as follows:

> Sir, the Lingayats had to spend money heavily in litigation and had to fight out their cases in the High Court which ultimately decided that the Brahman Joshi had no right to officiate at Lingayat marriages and that the said Joshi had consequently no right to demand fees or penalty from the Lingayats (B.L.C.D. XVII 1513).
> The decision of the Bombay High Court against the Joshi's claim so far as the Lingayat community is concerned is really the beginning of the end of the Joshi's claim (ibid. 1514).

This decision of the Bombay High Court referred to by Kambli was handed down on 13 August 1915. The plaintiffs were Venkatbhat Linganbhat Joshi and another, the 'hereditary Vatandar Joshis or Gramopadhyas of the village of Hallikeri', Dharwar District. Defendant 1, Rangappa Ningappa Immadi, had taken the 'Linga Diksha' (initiation of the Lingayat). Two marriages were performed at his place in the 'Panch Kalas' form, a Lingayat form of marriage. The Lingayat gurus (defendants 2 and 3) officiated at these marriages and received the customary fees. The Hindu form and Lingayat form of marriage characteristically differed in that the former began with the worship of Ganesha, while the latter began with the worship of Shiva. There were, however, certain ceremonies such as the 'fastening of Mangalsutra and Kankandhara' which were common to both forms. The plaintiffs therefore claimed that they were entitled to levy the customary fees so far as the ceremonies in common were concerned, although the marriages as a whole might have been performed in the Lingayat form. They thus sued for the recovery of Rs. 10-10-0 as their fees for the common ceremonies. Opposing this, the defendants pleaded that 'the Lingayats are not Brahmanical Hindoos and therefore they were not bound to employ a Brahman priest for their marriage ceremonies.... The ceremonies at marriage must be treated as one whole and cannot be split up.' The Bombay High Court took cognizance of the fact that 'the contest in this case resolves itself into this, whether the ceremonies observed by Lingayats in marriages are to be regarded as a whole ... or whether the ceremony can be split into parts' and consequently decided in favour of the defendants holding that if the ceremony actually performed was not a Hindu marriage as a whole the 'Joshis or Gramopadhyas' had no right to demand the fees (17 Bom.L.R. 950).

As indicated by Kambli, the Lingayats were by this decision of the Bombay High Court freed from the obligation to pay the fees to the village hereditary Joshi even though they did not employ his services. Kambli heartily supported the Joshi bill by reason of this bitter experience of his own community.

The Joshi bill was supported by the majority of the members of the Bombay Legislative Council but was finally decided to be referred to the Select Committee for technical amendment and further consideration. The Select Committee added two new clauses to the original bill, one of which was a purely technical amendment for prescribing the date of the enforcement of the law. The other clause was the substantial amendment, that is, Clause 5 of the amended bill which provided the procedure to free the village Joshi from obligation to serve the villagers, as the counterpart of the provision to free the villagers from obligation to pay the fees to the village Joshi (Clause 4 of the amended bill). This clause prescribed firstly that a village Joshi who held no *inam* land or received no cash allowance as remuneration for his services to the village should be deemed to be relieved of his obligation to perform ceremonies or provide a substitute to officiate at ceremonies in the village, and secondly that a village Joshi who held *inam* lands or received a cash allowance as remuneration for his service to the village should be relieved of his obligation to perform ceremonies or provide a substitute to officiate at ceremonies in the village, if he should agree to pay full revenue assessment on his *inam* lands or forego his cash allowance.

This new bill amended by the Select Committee thus included a totally new problem of the transference of *inam* lands of *vatandar* Joshis to the so-called Raiyatwari land (the fully assessed land), an administrative procedure technically known as 'resumption'.[11] This problem of resumption had been the heatedly discussed problem in the Bombay Legislative Council as it may have adversely affected all of the *inam* lands enjoyed by various strata of the Indian people. The amended Joshi bill brought this hotly debated problem of the resumption again into focus.

Debates over the Amended Joshi Bill

The debates over the amended Joshi bill continued from 28 July to 3 August 1926 in the Bombay Legislative Council. While Brahman members of the Legislative Council were quite naturally opposed to this bill, a section of non-Brahman members also stood in opposition to it fearing that all the other hereditary rights including even that of Maratha *sardars* might be abolished in future, if indeed the hereditary right of the village Joshi were to be abolished.

The opponents of the Joshi bill argued against it on the ground of the declarations of Queen Victoria and her successors, and more concretely on the basis of several decisions of the Bombay High Court which confirmed the hereditary right of the priest.

V.A. Surve from Ratnagiri District spoke as follows:

> In 1858 the late Queen Victoria made a public declaration promising that the Government in India would not interfere in religious matters of the Indian people. After that, His Majesty the late Edward VII repeated the promise at the time of his accession to the throne. After that, His Majesty King George V reiterated the promise given by Queen Victoria and Edward VII. This was done on two occasions. The position now is that the Government are supporting legislation which will interfere with the religion of the people. That is really a very surprising matter. The promise given by Their Majesties Queen Victoria and her successors have been carried out by the Government up to now, but there is no knowing, from their present attitude on this bill, that they will carry them out in the future.
>
> (B.L.C.D. XVIII 227)

The declaration of Queen Victoria referred to here by Surve was made on 1 November 1858, when the so-called Sepoy Mutiny was finally suppressed and India became a Crown Colony, to soothe the injured sentiments of the Indian people. It promised to 'abstain from all interference with the religious belief or worship of any of our subjects' and that 'due regard be paid to the ancient rights, usages, and customs of India'. Thus, it was quite natural that the opponents of the Joshi bill made the declaration of Queen Victoria the basis of their argument against the bill. This declaration, however, did not specify the concrete rights to be protected since it merely laid down the general principles of British colonial rule. The opponents of the Joshi bill therefore drew specifically on several decisions of the Bombay High Court that they regarded as materialization of the principles of British colonial rule manifested by Queen Victoria.

Amongst such decisions of the Bombay High Court was the one handed down by the well-known Indian judge N. Chandavarkar (1855-1923) to which was often referred by the opponents of the Joshi bill to support their case. N. Chandavarkar, after serving out his term as the Bombay High Court Judge, was nominated to the office of the President of the Bombay Legislative Council reformed by the Government of India Act of 1919 and remained in office until his death in 1923. He was thus a leading figure in the Bombay Presidency, especially in the judicial and legislative fields. Though he was regarded as a social reformer, his stance was such a moderate one that he opposed the legislative or administrative interference with social practises and privileges of the Indian people. Thus, the opponents of the Joshi bill counted on the decision of Chandavarkar for support of their argument against it.

The judgement of Chandavarkar which was well known for having confirmed the hereditary right of the priest and was often referred to in the Bombay Legislative Council as such was the decision handed down on 10 August 1911 concerning the Kachhia Kunbi caste group of Surat (36 B. 94). The plaintiff of this suit was a Brahman, Ghelabhai Gavrishankar by name, who claimed to have the hereditary right as 'kul gur' (*kul guru*, family priest) of 'Surat kasbe tad' (the group of residents in Surat) of the Kachhia Kunbi. Defendant 1, one of the plaintiff's *yajmans*, employed, however, other Brahmans to officiate at the marriage ceremonies of his sons and daughters and paid them the fees. The plaintiff therefore sued for the recovery of damages against defendant 1 and the Brahmans who actually performed the ceremonies. In this case, Chandavarkar decided in favour of the plaintiff, the hereditary priest, reversing the decision of the lower court. He wrote in the judgement as follows:

> To the enlightened sentiment of the present day it does seem unfair and oppressive that a man should be compelled by law to religious ministration from another person who is not of his choice, and that simply because that has been the course of the relations of the families of both for generations on the grounds of hereditary rights. But if a Hindu wishes to remain a Hindu and have the benefit of his religion he must take its burden also, when that burden is annexed to the benefit by Hindu law on the grounds of custom.

In fact, the hereditary right that was confirmed by this decision of Chandavarkar was not that of the village Joshi, but of the so-called Nyat Gour (*jñat guru* or *jat guru*, caste priest) who had the hereditary right to perform ceremonies in homes of a certain caste group, in this case, 'Surat kasbe tad' of the Kachhia Kunbi.[12] In spite of this, the opponents of the Joshi bill often referred to this decision of Chandavarkar for support of their argument on the ground that there was no difference between the village Joshi and Nyat Gour insofar as they hereditarily performed religious ceremonies in their respective *yajmans*' homes.[13]

In spite of the tenacious opposition of the Brahman members, the Joshi bill enjoyed the support of the majority of members of Bombay Legislative Council as all of the nominated members (nominated official members 20, nominated non-official members 5, in all 25 at this time; the total number was 111) in addition to most of the non-Brahman members were in favour of this bill. Therefore, the Brahman members accused the non-Brahman members especially Satya Shodhaks and the government of allegedly conspiring against Brahmans in enforcing the Joshi bill as follows:

> P.G. Joshi: We further know that the honourable mover of this bill is a member of the Satya Shodhak Samaj, and we also know that the Honourable Minister of Education, who has supported this bill, is also a leader of that Samaj. (An honourable member: What is that?) It is relevant in this sense, because we know that one of the tenets of the Satya Shodhak Samaj is that they should not call in the services of the Brahmin priests, and this tenet has been recognised judicially in 42, Bombay [42 B. 613], which has been quoted by the leader of the Swaraj Party.

B.V. Jadhav: The honourable member is misrepresenting the tenets of the Satya Shodhak Samaj.
P.G. Joshi: Without the intervention of the priest—that is the tenet. Therefore, Sir, the members of the Satya Shodhak Samaj do their best to see that the services of the Brahman priests are not requisitioned by the members of their community. (An honourable member: What harm is there?) There is no harm, and therefore I consider this bill as part of the propaganda of the Satya Shodhak Samaj, of which the honourable mover is a member. You are aware, Sir, that the members of the Satya Shodhak Samaj consider the Brahmins as 'Deshache Dushman', that is enemies of the country, and therefore, as they honestly believe in it, it is quite proper and natural that a member of the Satya Shodhak Samaj should introduce this bill in this House, to run down the Brahmins, to exterminate the Brahmins as early as possible.

(B.L.C.D. XVIII 320-21)

Another opponent of the Joshi bill (N.R. Gunjal) alleged further that this bill 'has been looked upon with distinct disfavour by all Hindus who follow the Sanatan Dharma, and these Hindus form nearly 96 per cent of the Hindu population, whereas the remainder 4 per cent who have been more or less Christianised Awaidik Nastik Hindoos, and followers of Jotiba Phule and who call themselves Satya Shodhaks, have engineered this bill' (B.L.C.D. XVIII 391).

Thus, the Brahman members accused those members who were in favour of the Joshi bill of conspiring with the government pointing out that 'the non-Brahmin party is consistently supporting Government in whatever they do' (B.L.C.D. XVIII 316). The Brahman members declared their values or viewpoint as the 'Sanatan Dharma' in contrast with that of 'the non-Brahmin party' which they criticized to be the Christianized, non-Vedic atheism. This idea of the traditional values of India expressed here by the Brahman members, that is to say, 'Sanatan Dharma' (*sanatana dharma*, orthodoxy, *sanatana* meaning 'eternal') was a cultural response to the 'reformists' (*sudharnavadis*) influenced by the European values, though the term *sanatana dharma* itself was an invention of the nineteenth century.

What excited the sentiments of the Brahman members still more was the aforementioned fact that all of the 25 nominated members supported this bill. Even the nominated members had a certain degree of freedom of voting when the bill in question was not an official bill but a private one. Though the Joshi bill was a private one, the Bombay government had previously decided to support it, so that the nominated members were implicitly obliged to uphold it as well. This was the reason why the opponents of the bill repeatedly demanded that the government grant freedom of action to the nominated members with regard to this bill. But the Bombay government never yielded to their request as this bill fell in line with the government policy of re-categorizing and abolishing unnecessary hereditary offices (*vatans*) which had been pursued since the middle of the nineteenth century.

In the clause by clause reading of this bill, the opponents moved amendments after amendment. One of them was moved proposing to add the following sentence to Clause 4 (Clause 3 of the original bill introduced by Bole): 'Such Hindu however for the purpose of being permanently relieved of his customary obligation to call in the Watandar Priest shall be liable to pay the Priest Re. 1 instead of such ceremonial emoluments as consolidated damages' (B.L.C.D. XVIII 395). This motion of seeking compensation for Joshis directly from the *yajmans* was lost by 17 for to 40 against (ibid. 399).

Clause 5 of the amended Joshi bill which provided the so-called resumption of *inam* lands of Joshis (transference of their *inam* lands to Raiyatwari lands to be taxed by the full revenue assessment) especially offended the Brahman members as well as other members who had vested interest in the *inam* land. As mentioned before, Act XI of 1852, Schedule B, 8 prescribed continuing permanently the *inam* lands of Joshis, with which Clause 5 of the Joshi bill was, without doubt, at variance. Paying no heed to this legal discrepancy, the Bombay government had made up its mind to enforce the resumption of *inam* lands of the village Joshi. Thus, several motions of amendment to this Clause 5 were moved by the opponents 'in order that the hereditary joshi may not be deprived of his land or emoluments, which were guaranteed to him by Act XI of 1852' (B.L.C.D. XVIII 453).

After withdrawal of these motions, the new motion 'that clause 5 be deleted' was finally put to a vote but was lost by 32 for to 46 against (ibid. 534). All the nominated members stood in opposition to this amendment in line with the intention of the Bombay government.

Thus all motions of amendment to this bill were either withdrawn or voted down but the motion for adding one new clause (Clause 6) to the bill was supported by the government. It read as follows:

Nothing in this Act shall affect the rights of a hereditary Hindu priest

> or an alienee from such priest to the *inam* lands or cash allowance attached to his office for the performance of any service pertaining to it, except to the extent specified herein.

The purport of this clause was to prevent the district officials or the like from forcing the hereditary Joshis to forgo *inam* lands or emoluments, under the plea that a single villager rejected the services of the village Joshi. One Brahman member (C.M. Saptarshi) expressed his apprehension by saying that 'there are more and more non-Brahmins belonging to the Satyashodhak party who are being taken as mamlatdars and deputy collectors' and 'a Satyashodhak deputy collector or mamlatdar will take it into his hand to commute all Joshi watan and compel the Joshis in his jurisdiction to give their consent to be relieved of their office' (ibid. 316). Taking these apprehensions of Brahman members into consideration, the Bombay government gave assent to this motion purporting to add Clause 6 to this bill.

The Invalidation of Hindu Ceremonial Emoluments Act (Bombay Act XI of 1926) thus enacted included substantial new provisions such as the resumption of *inam* lands of Joshis that were lacking in the original bill of S.K. Bole. This was a reflection of the Bombay government's policy to rearrange or abolish the hereditary offices (*vatans*) which now became unnecessary for the administration.

In spite of this intention on the side of the government, the Invalidation of Hindu Ceremonial Emoluments Act was, without doubt, a monumental success for the Satya Shodhak Samaj or the Non-Brahman Movement of Maharashtra. It eventually turned out to be rather a bitter success for lower castes, especially for untouchable castes like the Mahar, however, since it only led to the political strengthening of the Marathas in the 1930s.

Conclusion

The Vatan system thus comprised the threefold relationship. One was the official relationship between *vatandars* and the state. The second was the holistic relationship between *vatandars* and the village community. And the third was the dyadic relationship between respective *vatandars* and their *yajmans*. In the case of the Joshi-Kulkarni, he had the official relationship with the state as the Kulkarni who worked as a tax functionary of the state. Under British colonial rule, this function of the Kulkarni was, at last, abolished in the 1910s through the administrative procedure called commutation. The Joshi-Kulkarni held the holistic relationship with the village community as the village accountant and the village priest who officiated at the community rituals. The government took no interest in this non-official aspect of the Joshi-Kulkarni leaving it as it had been under former governments.

The dyadic relationship between the Joshi as *gharopadhya* and his *yajmans* as well was, without doubt, a non-official or private relationship in which the government was not to be involved. In the 1920s, however, pressure from non-Brahman members of the Bombay Legislative Council, which was extended and empowered to a certain degree by the Government of India Act of 1919, pushed the government towards the enactment of the Invalidation of Hindu Ceremonial Emoluments Act. This Act did not abolish the Joshi's role as *gharopadhya* at one stroke. It liberated, however, villagers (*yajmans*) from the obligation to employ or otherwise compensate the Joshi as *gharopadhya* by disqualifying the Joshi for demanding the fees regardless of whether he actually performed ceremonies for them or not.

In the longer run, this process must have been in line with the general move of Indian society 'from a state of status to a state of contract' as indicated by R.P. Paranjpye (Bombay University) in the Bombay Legislative Council (B.L.C.D. XVII 1505). In the case of the Joshi-Kulkarni, however, this process involved many factors such as the colonial rulers' concern with administrative efficiency and financial benefit on the one side and the Non-Brahman Movement, the conflicts between the orthodox and the reformists and others on the side of Indian society. Thus, the problem of priesthood, which would have remained otherwise a purely private problem, became a heatedly discussed subject in colonial India, especially in the Bombay Presidency.

Notes

1 In the case of untouchable castes, priests of their own castes used to officiate at family ceremonies as it was a long-standing custom that Brahman Joshis were not obliged to officiate at family ceremonies of the untouchables. As regards disputes centring around this problem between the Mahars and the Brahman Joshis of Paudkhor District, see Chapter 6 of this volume.

2 This Act, the Limitation Act of 1859, is not an Act of the Bombay government but that of the Government of India. This is the case with Act XI of 1852 (An Act for the Adjudication of Titles to Certain Estates Claimed to be Wholly or Partially Rent-free in the Presidency of Bombay)

to which will be referred below. By the Charter Act of 1833, the Bombay and Madras governments were deprived of the independent power to promulgate regulations. The legislative power was thus concentrated in the hands of the Central government whose law was thereafter designated as the Act. The independent legislative power of the Bombay and Madras governments was recovered by the Legislative Councils Act of 1861.

3 As to the commutation of the hereditary district offices (*vatans*) of Deshmukh and Deshpande, cf. *Papers Relating to the Settlement of the Hereditary District Officers' Watan in the Deccan and Gujarat*, Selections from Bombay Government Records CLXXIV, 1865. See further, Chapter 7 of this volume.

4 The land revenue leviable by reduced rates on *inam* lands was technically known as *judi*. The *judi* levied on *inam* lands of Kulkarnis, however, does not seem to be much reduced below the full revenue assessment. The statistics for the seven districts of the Central Division and some other districts, in all 11,752 villages, placed on the Council table by the Bombay government show that the total revenue assessment on all of the Kulkarnis' *inam* lands in 1913 was Rs. 3,27,070, whereas the total amount of *judi* actually levied on such lands was Rs. 2,69,928. This meant that *judi* on the Kulkarnis' *inam* lands was around 80 per cent of the full revenue assessment (B.L.C.D. LI 377). Thus, the commutation of *inam* lands of Kulkarnis, in fact, did not result in a great loss to the Bombay government.

5 In reply to the question in the Bombay Legislative Council on 'the number of kulkarnis who have given their consent to the commutation of their watans and of those who have refused it in the several districts in the Central Division', the goverment submitted the following table:

Table 1: Commutation of Kulkarni Vatan

Name of District	Total number of representative watandars who have so far agreed to commutation of their right of service	Number of representative watandars whose consent is yet to be obtained
East Khandesh	2,273	257
West Khandesh	1,001	7
Nasik	1,907	777
Ahmednagar	3,211	418
Poona	2,588	388
Satara	2,300	1,351
Sholapur	519	1,704
Source: P.C.G.B. LII 980		

This table confirms that the forcible commutation of the Kulkarni *vatan* had progressed much more in the northern than in the southern districts by this time.

6 The term 'domestic Opadhya' must be an English translation of *gharopadhya*. If the statement of the defendant is reliable, it would seem that

the *gharopadhya* of the defendant's family was a Brahman other than the village Joshi.

7 In another part of the judgement, the plaintiff's family was said to be 'hereditary Garoopadhyas, Gramoopadhyas, and Joshees of Mouje Amberree' (11 B.S.D.A. 111, at 113). 'Gramoopadhya' (*grāma-upādhyā, grāmopādyā*) is a term occasionally met with in medieval Marathi documents, though the relationship between the village Joshi and *gramopadhya* is not sufficiently clear.

8 See, *Hurgobind Surma* v. *Browaneepersaud Shah, Decisions of the Sudder Dewanny Adawlut, recorded in English, in conformity to Act XII of 1843*, Vol. VI, 1850, pp. 296 ff. See also 11 B.S.D.A. 111 at 114-15. Cf. Aiyar 1918: 57-58.

9 O'Hanlon briefly referred to conflicts between Brahmans and Satya Shodhaks over rituals drawing on several periodicals such as the *Din Bandhu* and *Din Mitra*. See O'Hanlon 1985: 301-2. As to J. Phule and the Satya Shodhak Samaj, see further Omvedt 1976: 98-123; Kavlekar 1979: 35-51; Gore 1989: 18-41; Phadke 1991.

10 This decision of the Bombay High Court is not published in the official casebooks, that is, *Indian Law Reports, Bombay Series*. Its conclusion, however, is quoted in 17 Bom.L.R. 950, at 954.

11 See Chapter 7 of this volume for the concept of 'resumption' in contrast with the concept of 'commutation' discussed above.

12 In the towns, especially of coastal Gujarat, there did not exist an office corresponding to that of the village Joshi who was the *gharopadhya* of villagers as well. Each caste group in a town had respective Nyat Gour (*jñāt guru* or *jāt guru*, caste priest) sent from the specific Brahman caste who conducted rituals in the homes of the members of the caste group as their 'kul gur' (*kul guru*). Thus, there was the hereditary and holistic relationship between the Brahman *guru* caste who sent Nyat Gours and the *yajman* caste who accepted them as Nyat Gours. This means that the communal structure of the towns in coastal Gujarat considerably differed from that of the village community in the medieval Deccan. See Chapter 4 of this volume for further details.

13 There seems to have existed a tendency to refer rather easily to the name of Chandavarkar for one's own support. For example, R.P. Paranjpye (Bombay University) spoke in the Bombay Legislative Council as follows:

> I remember quite well that about ten years ago a judgment was pronounced by the late Justice Sir Narayan Chandavarkar, in which a similar case arose. The village barber was not called for some ceremonial function: some other barber from outside was called. The village barber therefore did not get his proper dues and he brought a suit for the recovery of those dues. The case came to the High Court,

and the High Court pronounced a judgment in favour of the barber, that the barber must receive his due even though he had not performed those ceremonies (B.L.C.D. XVII 1505).

This suit over the barber's *vatan* (22 Bom.L.R. 410), however, was in fact not judged by Chandavarkar.

III

Rituals, Ideologies and Identities

9

Kingship, State and Local Society in the Seventeenth-to-Nineteenth Century Deccan with Special Reference to Ritual Functions

Introduction

Of late, the anthropological study of kingship in India, and a few other countries having been under the cultural influence of India, such as Sri Lanka and Nepal, is attracting more attention than the more commonly accepted historical study of kingship. It seems rather peculiar that anthropology as a discipline aiming at understanding modern society in the light of 'other cultures' is taking such an interest in kingship which has hitherto been studied principally in a historical context. Thus, anthropological studies of kingship have been inviting considerable attention by historians, though many of them, including the present writer, are more or less critical of this approach.

There are two principal problematic aspects of anthropological studies of kingship in India.

One is the problem inherent in the essentialist approach to 'Hindu' (hereafter, simply Hindu, though with reservations) kingship which has resulted in the search for ritual Hindu kings in the marginal areas and remoter hills and forests under Muslim or British political overlordship, and even in independent India. In this approach, the so-called auspiciousness-inauspiciousness ideology pivoting around the Hindu kings (as has been discussed, for example, in Inden 1985), as opposed to the pureness-impureness ideology being regulated by the Brahmans (Dumont 1980), is expected to play the central role in regulating such societal systems as the caste system. Thus, Muslim kings who could not perform Hindu rituals are to be ignored even though they were the bearers of central kingship in medieval India, and, as such, functioned as maintainers of the caste system as was formerly suggested by J.H. Hutton and will be discussed later in this chapter.[1]

Second is the problem of the endless downward diffusion of the concept of Hindu kingship from the king down to local chiefs, dominant castes, village heads and even to peasants, washermen and barbers under Muslim and British overlordship where Hindu kings of substantial standing were disappearing. After the virtual disappearance of Hindu kings worthy of the name, *yajmānas* (*jajmans*) at the village level have been observed in place of the king in anthropological studies of kingship in India (for example, Quigley 1993: 70, 129, 130, 155 and elsewhere). This downward diffusion of the concept of kingship seems to have made the very idea of kingship itself hollow and meaningless. Even Dirks' concept of 'sharing of the king's sovereignty' by local chiefs through the bestowal of the 'substance of kingship' to them (Dirks 1987: 86) can not counter the same tendency of downward diffusion of the concept of kingship.

Thus, the focus of this chapter is, firstly, to examine the actual functions of the king in any given society in Indian history without being constrained by the presupposition of the Hindu ritual king. The most difficult theoretical problem pertaining to kingship is the distinction and relationship between the state and kingship. If kingship is merely seen as one part of the state machinery as the impersonal apparatus of physical power of compulsion, it would be useless to discuss purposefully the problem of kingship in Indian history. The problem, therefore, is how to grasp the specific, supposedly ritual, function of kingship and, in a sense, how it outgrew the state machinery. In other words, the problem to be investigated is the personal function of kingship and its inherent limitation in the historical context of the development of kingship in Indian history.[2]

The second problem to be examined in this chapter is the actual relationship between the king/state and the local society such as the village and caste, and whether or not kingship or statecraft permeated down to the bottom of the local society, or conversely, whether or not the local society enjoyed a kind of local autonomy. This problem of relationship between kingship/statecraft and society in Indian history necessarily involves the problem of the role of local dignitaries like Brahmans functioning as Dharmadhikaris and Joshis in the local society.

This chapter aims to approach these problems by examining kingship, state and local society in the Maratha kingdom (1674-1818) against the background of the classical kingship theory of India, and in the outlook for social changes under the Bombay government as well. Medieval Marathi documents ranging from the state-level (state papers such as Royal Orders), down to the local-level (papers such as those preserved in the families of Kulkarni and Dharmadhikari), which are quite rich in quality as well as quantity, are expected to throw ample light on every side of the state apparatus and kingship down to the local social system.

Rājadaṇḍa, *Pariṣaddaṇḍa* and *Jātidaṇḍa*: Kingship Theory in Classical Law Books

The classical law books of India prescribed the protection of the subject as the first duty of the king (*rājadharma*). According to the *Manusmṛti*,[3] the Lord (*prabhū*) created the king in order to protect (*rakṣā*) the common people from the inevitable fear (*bhaya*) of chaos (*vidruta*) caused by the absence of a king (*arājaka*) (VII-3). The king, however, without the necessary means to achieve this purpose could not provide his people with the protection they required. Therefore, the Lord created punishment (*daṇḍa*) and gave it to the king (VII-14). Through the subsequent fear of the punishment to be inflicted by the king (*rājadaṇḍa*), people abided by their own required duties (*svadharma*) and could thus enjoy their lives (VII-15). In principle then, the concept of punishment governed people so as to protect them (VII-18).

Referring to the *Manusmṛti*, the seven constituent parts of the state (*saptāṅga*) were the king (*svāmi*), minister, capital, realm, treasury, army and ally (IX-294), so that the king was regarded as the first but still one of the constituent parts of the state. In spite of this, the *Manusmṛti* laid down the protection of the subject as the first duty of the king rather than that of the state as a whole comprising its seven constituent parts, including the king. Therefore the distinction between the impersonal state apparatus with the king at its head, and kingship with the personal authority embodied in the person of the king, was not sufficiently clarified in the *Manusmṛti*. As a result, the king was regarded as representing the entire apparatus of the state in its duty to protect the subject, with punishment by the state as well thereby being known as *rājadaṇḍa* (the punishment of the king).

Even in the classical law books, however, the role of protection of the common people was not meant to be concentrated in or monopolized by the king. Two other institutions were laid down in the classical law books as guardians of society complementary to kingship. One was *pariṣad* or the 'assembly of learned men' who prescribed penances (*pariṣaddaṇḍa* or *daivadaṇḍa*) to be undergone by grave sinners (Kane: IV 72). This means that crimes to be punished by the king were, at the same time, sins to be purified and removed through penances prescribed by *pariṣad*, though it was not clearly laid down whether all of the criminals were to be penanced. *Pariṣad* thus worked as a guarantor of social order by the imposition of ethical or moral obligation on the criminal as the sinner in laying down various penances for respective sins. In the *Manusmṛti*, rules providing penances for each sin occupied a conspicuous portion (XI-43-259).

The second institution meant to be complementary to kingship in providing safety to the people was the community (*jāti*) and the penalties imposed by it (*jātidaṇḍa*) (Kane: IV 76). The representative form of *jātidaṇḍa* was excommunication. Community members who violated the rules laid down by the community were excommunicated through performance of a ritual known as *ghaṭasphoṭa* (the breaking of a water vessel, *Manusmṛti*: XI-181,182). The excommunicated were designated as *patita* and any association (*saṃsarga*, *Manusmṛti*: XI-180) with community members, such as conversation (*sambhāṣaṇa*) and the sitting-together (*sahāsana*) with members of the community, were outlawed and further excluded from the inheritance (*Manusmṛti*: XI-183, 184). This means that the community (*jāti*) itself was equipped with the function to maintain order within itself.

Thus, the classical law books of India prescribed the protection of the subject as the first duty of the king, providing *pariṣaddaṇḍa* and *jātidaṇḍa* as a guarantor of social order complementary to the punishment by the king (*rājadaṇḍa*). This triad of *rājadaṇḍa*, *pariṣaddaṇḍa* and *jātidaṇḍa* with historical changes in meaning and designation constitutes the main point of the next section.

Kingship and Social Order in the Maratha Kingdom

Rājadaṇḍa and Brāhmadaṇḍa

In the seventeenth-eighteenth century Maratha kingdom, there existed concepts resembling *rājadaṇḍa* and *pariṣaddaṇḍa* as described in the classical law books. The concept of *rājadaṇḍa* in the medieval Maratha kingdom was, however, considerably different from that of *rājadaṇḍa* as outlined in the classical law books, while the word *pariṣaddaṇḍa* was substituted by the word *brāhmadaṇḍa* in the Maratha kingdom. The following case of a murder committed by a Brahman helps to clarify the meaning of *rājadaṇḍa* and *brāhmadaṇḍa* in the Maratha kingdom:

> Sadasiv Ganesh Kelkar appealed to the Hozur [a Persian word denoting the king: in the case of the Maratha kingdom of the eighteenth century, however, the word Hozur indicated Peshva] as follows: 'I was arrested under the suspicion of murdering the wife of Gunaji Ganesh Tiwalekar of the village Vanivade and imprisoned in the Vandan Fort for 10 years. I was recently discharged from imprisonment but was not purified through the performance of *prāyaścitta* [the purification ceremony]. So, I humbly petition the Hozur for ordering me to undergo *prāyaścitta* levying *rājadaṇḍa* in accordance with my means of livelihood and thus for releasing me from the sin [*doṣa*].' In response to his petition, Sadasiv Ganesh Kelkar was made to undergo *prāyaścitta* and was purified as prescribed by the assembly of Brahmans after levying *rājadaṇḍa* and *brāhmadaṇḍa* from him. This deed is issued as proof.
>
> (S.S.R.P.D. VIII 892. 1792-93)

In this case, the following three *daṇḍas* were inflicted upon the culprit: (1) imprisonment (within a fortress jail), (2) *rājadaṇḍa* paid to the king who sanctioned the performance of *prāyaścitta*, and (3) *brāhmadaṇḍa* paid to the Brahmans who prescribed the method of *prāyaścitta* and actually performed it. Of the three *daṇḍas*, (1) imprisonment was punishment determined by the state seen as an impersonal apparatus of power resembling that of punishment of modern states today. This *daṇḍa* (*sarkārdaṇḍa*) of imprisonment thus had no particular relationship to kingship. On the contrary, (2) *rājadaṇḍa* was closely connected to the personal authority of the king. This culprit appealed to the Hozur (Peshva) to sanction the performance of *prāyaścitta* to purify his sin after his release from jail. For a culprit who committed a grave crime (sin) such as murder, it was not sufficient to be punished by the state alone in order to be readmitted into society or a caste (*jāti*). He had to undergo the purification ceremony known as *prāyaścitta* after serving out his term of imprisonment to remove the sin from his body.

This document denotes that the authority to sanction the performance of *prāyaścitta* was embodied in the person of the king. Thus, this authority of the king is seen as a personal function of the king rather than as the impersonal function of the state as the power apparatus. *Rājadaṇḍa* in the Maratha kingdom can be understood as the reward paid to the king as a token of gratitude for his favour of sanctioning *prāyaścitta.* Thus, the meaning of *rājadaṇḍa* in the Maratha kingdom differed considerably from that of *rājadaṇḍa* prescribed in the classical law books. The historical development which brought about the change in the meaning of *rājadaṇḍa* would have been the establishment of the impersonal state apparatus (power structure), resulting in kingship itself having strengthened its personal aspect of ritual authority.

In contrast to *rājadaṇḍa* as a fine (reward) payable to the king, *brāhmadaṇḍa* was a reward paid to Brahmans who prescribed the method of *prāyaścitta* and actually performed it. There is no specific account of the 'assembly of Brahmans' in the document but it might have been the assembly of Brahmans engaged by the government. It is difficult to ascertain whether this 'assembly of Brahmans' was of the same character as *pariṣad* noted in the classical law books, though it can be regarded as the medieval variety of *pariṣad. Brāhmadaṇḍa*, likewise, can be deemed as the medieval successor of *pariṣaddaṇḍa.*

The next case referring to *rājadaṇḍa* and *brāhmadaṇḍa* in the Maratha kingdom is a suicide case. In the *Manusmṛti*, the rule regulating suicide is described in Chapter V, that is, the chapter concerning purification (pollution) as follows:

> The ceremony of water [*udakakriyā*] shall not be performed on those who have been born in vain [who neglect the prescribed], on those born in consequence of an illegal mixture of *jāti*, on those who are ascetics, and on those who have ruined themselves [who have committed suicide].
>
> (V-88)

This means suicide was regarded as an act which brought about pollution rather than as a crime (sin) which should be punished by the state and purified by *prāyaścitta* as well. In contrast to this, suicide was a kind of crime (sin) in the medieval Deccan.

In the suicide case of a daughter-in-law of a Brahman, Rangbhat Dekne, the father-in-law appealed to the Hozur as follows:

> My daughter-in-law, Tama, tried to take her six-year-old son to a river for *sparśasnāna* [the ablution of contact] on the night of the lunar eclipse in the month of Bhadrapad. I advised her not to take the boy for ablution as he was ill at that time. Becoming angry at this she went to the river alone and tried to commit suicide when women of my family stopped her and brought her back home. They continued to

> watch her at home but she managed to steal out of the house and went to the river for *mokṣasnāna* [the ablution of emancipation]. Since then we know nothing about her. She must have committed suicide as we could not find her though we searched after her for six months. Thus, we want to perform her funeral ceremony so as to enable us to perform *māṅgalya* [festive ceremonies like marriage]. I humbly appeal for your sanction to do this.

In response to this petition, the following deed was issued:

> Your daughter-in-law committed suicide. You have already been purified, however, by being made to undergo *prāyaścitta* in accordance with Shastra and paid *brāhmadaṇḍa*. Therefore, do the business of Brahman as before and live happily. In connection with this, *rājadaṇḍa* of Rs. 100 has been levied.
>
> (S.S.R.P.D. VII 592. 1765-66)

This document denotes that suicide was a kind of crime (sin) in the Maratha kingdom, which was transmittable to the family members of a suicide victim, so that they were obliged to undergo *prāyaścitta* to purify the sin transmitted onto them. For this, however, *rājadaṇḍa* and *brāhmadaṇḍa* had to be paid to the Hozur and Brahmans respectively.

Thus, the concepts of *rājadaṇḍa* and *pariṣaddaṇḍa* in the classical law books continued to exist and actually functioned in the medieval Maratha kingdom though their meanings and designations had changed in respective ways.

Caste Penalty and Governmental Punishment

There is no mention in the aforecited two documents of something similar to the counterpart of *jātidaṇḍa* in the classical law books. In the Maratha kingdom, however, the culprit and his family or kindred were excommunicated from their caste (*jāti*) and had to follow the prescribed procedure for being readmitted into the caste. This penalty of expulsion from the caste or, in the case of readmission, the payment of necessary expenses for a readmission ceremony was, in fact, *jātidaṇḍa* in the medieval Deccan, though the word *jātidaṇḍa* does not seem to be in common use in medieval Marathi documents. (As a rare example in a form of *dñātidaṇḍa*, see S.S.R.P.D. VIII 1128.)

Jātidaṇḍa in its original meaning must have been the expulsion from the caste, as the ceremony of *ghaṭasphoṭa* in the classical law books denotes. The following is one of the actual excommunication cases in the Maratha kingdom. Moraji, of the Bhoi caste (palanquin bearers), was suspected of murdering Karoji of the same caste by using *bhūta* (a malignant spirit). The caste meeting of Bhois of Pune District was thus convened and the suspicion of Moraji was subsequently affirmed. Therefore, the caste meeting decided to excommunicate him after breaking out his two foreteeth and also making him drink the water drawn from a well of Chambhars to disable his capacity to use *bhūta.* Against this decision of the caste meeting, Moraji threatened to attack the caste members by joining Ramoshis (a hill tribe) and Mangs in case he actually be excommunicated. Anxious caste members appealed to the government for help, in response to which the government imprisoned Moraji in a jail in the Kahaj Fort and decided in accordance with the decision of the caste to break out his two foreteeth and to make him drink the water of Chambhars' well (S.S.R.P.D. VIII 929. 1775-76).

In this case, the government was asked to excercise its power of physical compulsion against the caste member who refused to obey the decision of the caste meeting, and actually inflicted the punishment on him according to the decision of the caste meeting. This punishment thus can be regarded as governmental punishment as well as caste punishment executed by the state on behalf of the caste.

It is thus true that the caste in the medieval Deccan could excommunicate a caste member who violated the caste rule, but permanent expulsion from the caste was rather rare. In most cases, the excommunicated were readmitted into the caste by the prescribed procedure. The procedure of readmission to the caste seems to differ according to circumstances, particularly whether the excommunicated was a Brahman or a non-Brahman. It would be proper, therefore, to examine the cases of a Brahman first.

In the medieval Deccan, as was the case with ancient India, Brahmans were, in principle, prohibited from drinking liquor and eating the meat of animals. Therefore, Brahmans who took to drinking liquor and eating meat were excommunicated as *patitas*. In one case, a Brahman, Bhikaji Keshav, accused another Brahman, Ragho Lavate, of being a law-breaker (*adharmī*) and a drinker (*madya prāśanī*) to the Acharya Svami (the spiritual guide of Brahmans). Ragho was accordingly excluded from the commensal seat (*paṅkti*). Ragho complained of this treatment to a government official who conversely blamed him as follows:

I and many other persons have been advising you not to drink liquor, saying such an act will lead to the eating of animal meat [*prāṇamāsa*].

Ragho, however, turned a deaf ear to his warning and caused trouble again. So, the official decided to make him undergo *prāyaścitta* asking Brahman communities (*brāhmaṇa-samdāya*) to prescribe the method to purify the sin of Ragho (S.P.D. XXXXIII 159).

In another case of a similar nature, a Brahman, Baraji Dhonddeo, began to live with a dancer (*kaḷvantīṇa*) and took to drinking liquor (*surāpāna*) and eating meat (*māsabhakṣaṇa*). He was thus regarded as *patita*, and all of his kindred were also excluded from the commensal seat. Knowing this, the Hozur convened the assembly of Brahmans (*brāhmasabhā*) where it was decided to make them undergo *prāyaścitta*. They were accordingly sent to a holy place on the Ganga (Godavari) River after having completed the first half part of *prāyaścitta* (S.P.D. XXXXIII 29).[4]

These cases denote that even Brahmans who violated such an important rule for the Brahmans as the prohibition of drinking liquor and eating meat could be readmitted provided they underwent *prāyaścitta*. In the case of Brahmans, however, the caste network was much wider than that of the ordinary castes so that assemblies of Brahmans in many places had to be convened to prescribe the method of *prāyaścitta*.

There is no particular mention of *jātidaṇḍa* in the above-cited two documents. This could be attributed to the circumstances that *jātidaṇḍa* in the case of Brahmans in the medieval Deccan was nothing other than *brāhmadaṇḍa* though the character of the document, as an official report from an official to the government, might exclude the possible mention of *jātidaṇḍa*.

Jātidaṇḍa appears clearly in the case of non-Brahman castes such as the Kunbi (a peasant caste). In the medieval rural Deccan, peasants used to breed many cows, bullocks and other cattle so that the careless killing of cows (*gohatyā*) and other cattle was often unavoidable. In one case, a Kunbi, Vithuji Valekar, beat his cow one day while milking her in order to discipline her for teasing him (*nāṭhāḷpaṇa*) and unintentionally killed her. He became so frightened thinking he may suffer the curse (*abhiśrāpa* from a Sanskrit word, *abhiśāpa*) of cow killing and be made to fall into hell (*naraka*) that he came to Pune to ask an official of the government (*sarkār*) to punish him in a proper manner so as to remove the sin of cow killing from him. The following order was accordingly issued to the headman of his village:

> This peasant is very poor and does not have means to pay the government fine [*sarkārdaṇḍa*]. Trying to levy a fine by selling his bulls and cattle [*baela-ḍhora*], the government lands under his cultivation would fall out of cultivation. The fine was thus exempted taking into consideration his poverty and honesty and the cultivation of goverment lands. This deed was issued to certify it. You should send him to a holy place on the Krishna River to ask the favour of releasing him from the sin of cow killing before *devabrāhmaṇa* [God and Brahmans]. After his return to the village, you should make him hold the commensal meeting [*jāti jevaṇa*] and then readmit him into the caste body [*jāti gota*].
>
> (Oturkar 191)[5]

This document denotes that for a grave crime (sin), such as cow killing, inflicted on the criminal was not only the levying of a government fine but also the performance of *prāyaścitta* in a holy place and the holding of the commensal meeting of the caste by inviting all members of the caste. In this case, though, the government fine was exempted and there was no mention of *rājadaṇḍa* and *brāhmadaṇḍa* in connection with *prāyaścitta*. Thus, the holding of the commensal meeting of the caste (defraying its expenses) as a necessary procedure for readmission to the caste can be regarded as the equivalent to *jātidaṇḍa* in the medieval Deccan.[6]

Local Autonomy in the Medieval Deccan

Ritual Role of Dharmadhikari

In the Maratha kingdom, as mentioned earlier, the following three *daṇḍas* were combined to maintain social order and control crimes (sins): (1) governmental punishment, (2) *prāyaścitta* (the ceremony for penance) and (3) caste penalty. Ethical or moral offenses not constituting criminal or penal crimes were, however, generally handled without government's intervention. In other words, the local society in the medieval Deccan was equipped with its own institution of dispensing justice in such cases, at the centre of which there was the office of Dharmadhikari (*dharma+adhikārī*; the officer of *dharma*).

The office of Dharmadhikari was not an office of the state. It was a patrimony (*vṛtti* in Sanskrit and *mirās* or *vatan* from Persian) of specific Brahman families being inherited from generation to generation. There seem to have been two different types of Dharmadhikari. One was the

Dharmadhikari of the district (*parganā*). In one case of a dispute between the Mahars and Brahman Joshis of Paudkhor District as to whether the Joshis of a district could be requested to officiate as the priest at a marriage ceremony of the Mahars, the Brahman Joshi family of the district claimed to possess the *vṛttis* of Joshi, Upadya and Dharmadhikari of the district (S.S.R.P.D. VIII 1132). In another case, a dispute broke out between the Brahmans and Prabhus of Cheul District with regard to the marriage custom of the Prabhus, when the then Peshva, Bajirav, issued an order in favour of the Brahmans to the Dharmadhikari and to the other Brahmans of the district (A.S.S. VI 66). These documents denote that there must have been a Dharmadhikari office in each district, but their function is difficult to ascertain in detail.

The other type of Dharmadhikari office was the one that could be inherited within a Brahman family of a holy place. Though many Brahmans lived together in holy places, all of them did not hold the office of Dharmadhikari. Rather this office seems to have been inherited by a particular Brahman family but it is not certain whether the office existed in every holy place or only in specific sites.

The Dharmadhikari played the role of maintaining social order in the local society through the performance of such rituals as *prāyaścitta*. In connection with this function, two peculiar kinds of documents, *doṣa-patra* (the statement of sin) and *śuddhi-patra* (the certificate of purification), were handed down in the family of Dharmadhikari. The following description draws on *doṣa-patras* and *śuddhi-patras* being preserved in the family of Dharmadhikari of Nasik.

In one case, Gangaji, a son of Ranoji Jadhav formerly living in Nasik, submitted the following *doṣa-patra* to the Dharmadhikari of Nasik:

> My father ran mad and began to eat with persons of other castes so that our caste excommunicated my father and myself. We went to the village Gavade and lived there for two years, at which time my father died still in madness. I have repented of this and decided to get *prāyaścitta* performed on my father's bones as well as on myself, and then to perform my father's funeral on the Ganga [Godavari] River so that I may be released from the sin [*doṣa*] and discharge the obligation to my father, and be freed from exclusion from the commensal and marital relationship of the caste. With this in mind, I have presented myself before you and stated my sin. So please perform *prāyaścitta* on me and remove the sin which rests on me.
>
> (A.S.S. I 194. 1795)

In this case, the son of a man (his caste seems to be that of the Maratha as judged from the family name of Jadhav), who committed the crime (sin) of violating the commensal rule of his caste, tried to regain admission into the caste after his father's death by being allowed to undergo the purification ceremony (*prāyaścitta*). For this, he went directly to the Dharmadhikari of Nasik and submitted the *doṣa-patra* without appealing to the Hozur to sanction the ceremony. Thus, this procedure of removing the sin, as it were, side-stepped the king. This could be attributable to the circumstances that his father's crime was merely one of an ethical or moral character, that of eating with persons of other castes, and not one of a criminal or penal nature against which governmental punishment was mandatory.[7]

However, in the aforecited case of a Brahman who lived and dined with a dancer, resulting in his excommunication, the Hozur intervened, ordering him to undergo *prāyaścitta.* What seems to have differentiated these two cases was that the accused party in the former case was a Brahman, whereas that in the latter was a non-Brahman (probably a Maratha), though the Brahman in the former case might be regarded as committing the very graver sin of eating meat and drinking liquor.

In the case of crime (sin) of physical contact with an untouchable (*sparśāsparśa*), the offender could also be readmitted to his caste by merely undergoing *prāyaścitta* as prescribed by the Dharmadhikari.[8]

In one case, Vithu, the son of a barber, Mayaji of Nasik, submitted the following *doṣa-patra* to the Dharmadhikari of Nasik:

> When I was sitting on the Ganga [Godavari] River waiting for a customer, a man of Budhalakar [an Ati-Shudra caste of skin vessel makers] approached and asked me to cut his hair. I did not inquire into his caste, and he, as well, did not inform me that he was a Budhalakar. So, I wetted his head and began to cut his hair, when one of the members of my caste happened to come along and said to me: 'He is a Budhalakar. Why do you cut his hair? You should not cut his hair!' Thus, I [stopped and] returned home. Some days after, I went for the commensality to the house of a member of my caste where some members accused me of the *doṣa* of making contact with a Budhalakar's head. So, I walked out of the commensality while it was still going on. I have, on these grounds, come to you. The *doṣa* of touching a Budhalakar's head is on my body, from which I must be released.
>
> (A.S.S. I 193. 1795)

This barber, by committing the crime (sin) of *sparśa* (physical contact) with an untouchable through unknowingly cutting a Budhalakar's hair, was subsequently excluded from the commensal seat of his caste. The barber therefore directly asked the Dharmadhikari of Nasik to purify him by performing *prāyaścitta* without having to appeal to the Hozur for the sanction.

Accepting the *doṣa-patra*, the Dharmadhikari prescribed the method of *prāyaścitta* and performed it, as proof of which he issued the *śuddhi-patra* (the certificate of purification) to the party concerned. The following case illustrates the actual procedure of issuing the *śuddhi-patra*. The mother of Hari Jadhav and Ramachandra Jadhav, two brothers, committed suicide as a result of a quarrel with a maidservant (*kuṇbīṇa*) by throwing herself into a well. The sin of suicide being regarded as transmitted to the family members and relatives of the suicide victim, the brothers were excommunicated by their caste. One year passed in this state, after which they performed the funeral rites of their mother. Soon thereafter, they presented themselves before the Dharmadhikari of Nasik to submit the *doṣa-patra* and asked him to order them to undergo *prāyaścitta*. Brahmans of Nasik then assembled together to prescribe the adequate method of *prāyaścitta* to remove the sin from them, and actually performed the ceremony at the confluence of Aruna. Thus, the brothers were made fit for the commensality (*paṅktipāvana*) of the caste after paying the necessary expenses of the ceremony. The *śuddhi-patra* to prove this was issued, the main part of which reads as follows:

> *Prāyaścitta* having been performed, you are now fit for the commensality of the caste. There remains no sin on you. Everybody should communicate with you as before in every location and in every country. You, two brothers, are now pure. Nobody should have doubt about this in every location and in every country. As proof of this, this *śuddhi-patra* is issued.
>
> (A.S.S. I 203. 1806)

In this suicide case, the sons directly asked the Dharmadhikari of Nasik to make them undergo *prāyaścitta* without appealing to the Hozur to sanction it, while in the previously-cited case of the suicide of Tama, the father-in-law asked for the sanction from the Hozur. The procedural difference between these two cases can likewise be attributable to the circumstances that the former was a Brahman case while the latter was a non-Brahman case. (The caste of the brothers seems to be Maratha judging from their family name of Jadhav.) Though the circumstances of the latter case lead us to believe there was no doubt that the criminal (sinful) act was a suicide, the suicide case of Tama is less clear and might somehow contribute to the procedural difference noted.

In the case of the crime (sin) of *saṃsarga* (association, intercourse) with the untouchables also, there was a delicate problem as to whether the sin could be removed solely by the Dharmadhikari or required the intervention of the Hozur.[9]

In one case, Balajipant and others, members of the Joshi and Kulkarni family of the village Pokhali, Parner District, came to Nasik and submitted the following statement to the Brahmans there:

> We committed the *doṣa* [sin] of *saṃsarga* with a woman of Chandala, the skinners [*carmakī Cāṇḍāḷī*]. Therefore we have presented the *doṣa-patra* to the Dharmadhikari of Nasik. We humbly ask all of you to purify all of the members of our family.

Accordingly, *prāyaścitta* was performed and the Dharmadhikari of Nasik issued the following *śuddhi-patra*:

> All of the Brahmans assembled together at the confluence of Aruna and decided the method of *prāyaścitta* in accordance with Shastra taking into consideration their means of livelihood and then ordered them to undergo *prāyaścitta*. The prescribed ceremony of *prāyaścitta* was duly performed before all of the Brahmans so that they might become fit for the commensal seat [of the Brahmans].
>
> (A.S.S. I 200. 1756)

There is no mention of the circumstances in which *saṃsarga* occurred to the members of this family with a 'woman of Chandala, the skinners' (the classical name of Chandala in this document must be the Brahmanical expression of the Chambhar caste, as there did not exist a caste called Chandala in the medieval Deccan), though it was not rare that an untouchable woman was employed unnoticed at the home of a Brahman even as a maidservant.[10]

In this case also, there was no appeal to the king to sanction the performance of *prāyaścitta*, even though this was a Brahman case. In some other cases of the *doṣa* (sin) of *saṃsarga* with the untouchables, however, the king intervened in the procedure of purification of the sin.

The following is one such case. A maidservant (*baṭīka*) of the Prabhu caste, working at the home of the Mamledar of Sivner District, Balaji Mahadeo, was discovered to have committed adultery with a man of the *antyaja* (Ati-Shudras). She was therefore regarded as being as degraded and polluted as the untouchables. Thus, the members of the family of the Mamledar living with her were regarded as having committed the same crime (sin) of *saṃsarga* with an untouchable. They, the Mamledar, his mother, wife, sons, wives of sons and a nephew, thus had to undergo *prāyaścitta* called *prājāpatya*. In practisc, however, one *prājāpatya* was commuted for Rs. 2, and the money thus collected by the government was distributed among Brahmans of various places (S.S.R.P.D. VIII 1125. 1781-82). In spite of the fact that the parties of both of the above-cited cases were Brahmans, the procedure of purification differed considerably in relation to the Hozur. The exact cause of this procedural difference is difficult to ascertain but it might partly be attributable to the circumstances that the party in the latter case was a high official of the government like the Mamledar of a district.

The procedure of the purification ceremony of a sin thus differed considerably even in cases of ethical or moral crimes (sins) without any criminal or penal nature depending on the difference of *varṇa* of the accused party, specifically Brahman or non-Brahman, as well as the difference of the political status of the party. This means that the three constituent parts of the machinery for dispensing justice and maintaining social order, namely, (1) governmental punishment, (2) the purification ceremony of the sin and (3) the caste penalty, worked together in very delicate ways in the medieval Deccan. In other words, there was no uniform and concrete judicial procedure for dispensing social justice disregarding circumstances such as the difference of *varṇa* and political status.

The king (Peshva) played his own role in this flexible machinery of maintaining social order, since the king possessed the personal authority somewhat outreaching its part or role within the power apparatus of the state. *Rājadaṇḍa* in the Maratha kingdom was a representation of this personal authority of Hindu kings in the medieval Deccan. Maratha kings (Peshvas) thus played an ideological role in regulating social order through its ritual function.

This ritual function was, however, not the monopoly of the king, as in the local society the Dharmadhikari could discharge the same ritual function through prescribing and performing the purification ceremony without the sanction of the king. What guaranteed this independent ritual function of the Dharmadhikari was the authority bestowed on him by the structure of the local society itself which can be characterized as the Vatan system. The Vatan system constituted the basic framework of local society in the medieval Deccan in which the full-fledged members of local society held respective *vatans*. The *vatan*-holders (*vatandārs*) included local district officers like Deshmukh and Deshpande as well as such village establishment as Patil, Kulkarni and *bārā balute* (12 sorts of village servants) which comprised the Lohar (ironsmith), Sutar (carpenter), Kumbhar (potter), Nhavi (barber), Parit (washerman) and some untouchables like the Mahar and Mang. The patrimonial rights of *vatandārs* were so deeply rooted in the local society that the states in the medieval Deccan utilized the Vatan system as the substitute for the state's local administration system. The independent authority of the Dharmadhikari (the Dharmadhikari was also one of *vatandārs*) was therefore solidly sustained by this Vatan system.[11]

Division of Labour in Village Rituals

Various rituals and festivals similar in name at least to those held in the power centre by the king were also performed in villages of the medieval Deccan. On these occasions, all villagers played their respective roles assigned to them by the village system of the division of labour, that is, the Vatan system as mentioned previously. This means that the division of labour in a village of the medieval Deccan included not only the division of productive or material labour but also the division of spiritual or ritual labour. Thus, the village in the medieval Deccan was a kind of ritual community as well, in which each member had his own ritual part to play.

In the village of the medieval Deccan, there existed a body of village servants collectively known as the *bārā balute* as mentioned before. The services provided by the *bārā balute* to the village included ritual services seemingly with more relative importance in comparison with material services offered by them in the everyday life of the villagers. The following case of the Parit (washermen) serves as a good example of this. In a certificate (*dākhalepatra*) given to the Parits of Cheul District, their duties in relation to a marriage ceremony and some festivals such as Dasara, as well as the perquisites pertaining to each duty, are denoted as follows:

1. When Parits spread *pāighaḍyā* [the cloths that are spread from the place at which the bridegroom's party alight to the house of

the bride], they shall take four *lahārīs* [12 *āṇās*] with a meal.

2. When Parits overlay *maṇḍapa* [an open hall erected temporarily for a marriage ceremony] with cloths, they shall take four *lahārīs* with a meal.
3. When Parits give a robe and turban [cleansed by them] to the bridegroom at the marriage of the Shudra castes, they shall take two *lahārīs*.
4. When Parits sing a song on the occasion of a marriage of the Shudra castes, they shall take one *lahārī* with a meal.
5. When Parits wash the clothes of the bride and bridegroom, they shall take one *lahārī* from the bride and two *lahārīs* from the bridegroom.
6. On the occasion of Dasara, the *zamīndār* shall give a turban [cleansed by Parits] to the following persons: Deshmukh, Deshpande, ...
7. When Parits wave a burning lamp around the head of an idol on the occasion of Dasara and Navaratra, they shall take one *sajgaṇī* [two *pāīs*].

(S.C.S. X 4)

This document denotes that the Parit's services to the village were heavily inclined towards ritual services, even including the waving of a lamp on Dasara and Navaratra, and singing at the marriage of the Shudra castes. Their main duty of washing also was not limited to the washing of ordinary cloths or clothes. It further included, so to speak, the ritual washing of cloth and formal dress used in the marriage ceremony.

The ritual character of the labour (duty) of the *bārā balute* is discernible in the cases of village artisans as well. In the case of Kumbhar (potter), their main duty is assumed to be the production of earthen kitchen utensils to be distributed to the villagers. But the following duties of Kumbhar gathered from various articles of a very detailed document on the village rituals show that many of the Kumbhar's duties were also closely related to village rituals:

1. On the occasion of Akshayatritiya in the month of Vaishak, the Kumbhar shall give an earthen water vessel to every villager.
2. On Pola of cattle, the Kumbhar shall give an earthen bull to every villager.
3. On Nagapanchami in the month of Shravan, an earthen *nāga* [cobra] is to be installed in the village by the Kumbhar.

4. On Gauri in the month of Bhadrapad, the Kumbhar shall give an earthen Gauri to every villager.
5. On Ganapatichaturthi in the month of Bhadrapad, the Kumbhar shall give an earthen Ganapati to the Deshmukh, Deshpande, Patil, Chaugla and Hakim.
6. On Dasara in the month of Ashvin, the Kumbhar shall give a water vessel to the village god [*grāmadeva*] and to every villager.
7. On Holi in the month of Phalgun, the Kumbhar shall dance.

(A.S.S. III 127)

This list of the Kumbhar's ritual duties gives the impression that the ritual duty of supplying earthen idols of gods, bulls and other figures on festive occasions to the villagers was the essential part of their services to the village. Added to this ritual duty relative to his profession as a potter was the duty of dancing on the occasion of Holi which resembled the Parit's duty of singing at the marriage ceremony of Shudra castes.

As the following cases suggest, all members of the village played their own respective roles in village rituals. The articles concerning Dasara in the aforementioned document on various village rituals provide a good picture of the division of ritual labour at the village level in the medieval Deccan:

1. The Kumbhar shall give a water vessel to the village god [*grāmadeva*], and then to all of the villagers taking perquisites from them.
2. Instalment of the water vessel in front of the village god.
   (1) The Mokadam Patil shall perform *pūjā*.
   (2) The village Joshi shall take *dakṣinā*, the eatable offered to the idol, money and *supārī* cast in the water vessel when it shall be removed.

   The water vessel shall be brought to the house of the Patil where *śidhā* [undressed rice] and *dakṣiṇā* shall be offered to it.
3. Rules relative to the water vessel and Mokadam are as follows:
   (1) The Joshi shall proceed with the water vessel in hand.
   (2) All the villagers shall accompany him.
   (3) A goat shall be given [as a sacrifice] to the water vessel.
   (4) *Kaḍkaṇe* [a circular paper suspended over an idol] shall be put on the water vessel.

(5) A half-cut coconut shell shall be offered to the water vessel.

(6) The *vājantrī* shall perform music to whom the Patil shall give perquisites.

(A.S.S. III 127)

To these articles were added the list of perquisites which each participant to the festivals of Dasara and Navaratra would receive. On the left side of the list, there were names of village officials such as the Mokadam (Patil), Kulkarni, Joshi and Chaugla along with the *thala mirāsī* (*thalkarī mirāsdār*) who were the regular and full-fledged peasant members of the village community, more commonly known as the *vatandār* Kunbi, as compared to the *upārī* (a temporary-resident tenant). The right side of the list, on the other hand, included the Sonar, Nhavi, Tamboli and Gurav followed by some district officials, such as the Deshmukh.

Thus, in these articles concerning Dasara and Navaratra, almost all the villagers appeared in the list though roles of some important members of the *bārā balute* such as the Mahar and Mang were not clear in this document.

In the case of Holi in the same document, however, more members of the village including the Mahar took part in the festival:

1. The Koli shall prepare the festival site by sprinkling coloured powder over it.
2. *Viḍā* and *supārī* offered to *racavī* made by the Parit shall be taken by the Parit.
3. The Mali shall provide sugar cane and *eraṇḍa* [a castor-oil plant].
4. The Mahar shall bring the Holi fire. *Viḍā*, *naevedya* and a half-cut coconut shell offered to the fire shall be taken by the head of the Mahars.
5. The Mokadam Patil shall bring *poḷī* [a plain wheat cake] to tie it to the *eraṇḍa*.
6. The Joshi shall say a prayer. *Dakṣiṇā*, *naevedya*, *viḍā* and *supārī* shall be taken by the Joshi.
7. The next day, a half-cut coconut shell shall be broken in every home to be distributed to *phaḍkarī* [a music player], the children who danced and to the *bārā balute* who disguised themselves at the festival. What remains shall be distributed to the villagers.
8. *Naevedya* offered to the Holi fire by the village shall be given to the Koli, Kumbhar, Sutar, Nhavi, Parit, Chambhar and Mahar.

9. The Kumbhar shall dance.
10. The Sutar, Parit, Kumbhar, Nhavi and Gurav shall disguise themselves at the festival.
11. The Chambhar shall hold *divaṭī* [a torch or lamp].
12. Cloths used in the festival shall be taken by the Parit.
13. The Nhavi shall give *guḍguḍa* [a kernel of a coconut] to the disguisers [invited from outside].

(A.S.S. III 127)

The division of ritual labour at the village level discussed so far illustrates that the village in the later medieval Deccan was a kind of a ritual community which organized various rituals or festivals on the communal principle of the division of labour.[12] It is difficult to ascertain the influence of the king's rituals at the power centre on these village rituals, though the names of the rituals were almost identical.[13]

One of the other important rituals of the village was the one known as *śānti*. An epidemic such as cholera and smallpox, and any calamity like an earthquake was regarded as being caused by the anger of the *devī* (the goddess of soil). On these occasions therefore a ritual called *śānti*, where the untouchables such as the Mahar and Mang played the central role, was performed in the village to pacify the anger of the *devī*. In the village ritual of *śānti*, a bull decorated with flower garlands was made to walk around the village boundary with the Mahar and Mang walking before the bull throwing *peḍhā* (a sweetmeat) from a pot they carried outside the village boundary. Then, the bull was cut at the throat by the Mahar and Mang to be sacrificed to the *devī*. The blood shed from the throat of the bull was poured on the idol of the *devī*.[14] In this manner, the untouchables such as the Mahar and Mang played a very important role in the village ritual of *śānti*. Thus, it is also difficult to detect any trace of the king's ritual of *śānti* conducted to avert bad omens like the appearance of a comet and the eclipse through the medium of Brahmans in the village ritual of *śānti* performed by the untouchables.[15]

Kingship, State and Caste System

Religious Neutrality of the State

It was, by nature, the function of the caste meeting (*jāti pāñca*) to maintain order within the caste when arose problems or disputes among caste members. The caste, however, did not possess the compulsory power sufficient to enforce a decision of the caste meeting on a defiant member who refused to obey such a decision as the aforementioned case of the Bhoi caste demonstrates. In such cases, the state exercised its physical power of compulsion to punish such a caste member who disobeyed the decision of the caste. Thus, what guaranteed the effectiveness of caste penalty in the medieval Deccan was the actual physical power of the state.[16]

It was also the role of the states in the medieval Deccan to mediate when any disputes took place among various castes. In one case, a dispute regarding the animal on which a bridegroom was to ride in a marriage procession occurred in Khandesh between the Kumbhars as one party and the Kasars, Sutars and Lohars as the opposing party in the late 1770s. The Kasars and others accused the Kumbhars of violating the rule that prescribed the Kumbhars to make their bridegroom ride on a bull by actually making him ride on a horse in the marriage procession. This type of dispute often arose among various castes, as the animal on which a bridegroom of a caste rode indicated the rank of that caste. In this case, the caste whose bridegroom rode on a horse was assumed to be higher in caste ranking than the caste whose bridegroom rode on a bull. The government finally intervened and decided in favour of the Kumbhars (S.S.R.P.D. VIII 1123).[17]

A similar dispute cropped up between the Kasars and the Lingayat Vanis in Karad District. In the marriage procession of the Kasars, a man carrying a water vessel full of holy water (drawn from a holy river) would head the procession. The Vanis began to object, asserting that this type of marriage procession was a privilege of the castes belonging to the Kshatriya *varṇa.* This dispute was entrusted to the judgement of a state official who decided in favour of the Kasars on the ground that the Kasar was considered to belong to the Kshatriya of *somavaṃśa* referring to Shastras (S.S.R.P.D. VII 762. 1767-68).

It was thus the state as the apparatus of physical power of compulsion rather than the authority of kingship that played the role of maintaining social order embodied in the caste system (the order within each caste and between various castes). The state, in performing this function, exercised its public power paying no heed to the religion of the subjects as well as kings or the ruling class themselves. In other words, the distinction between the Muslim state and the Hindu state made, in essence, no difference in this function of the state in maintaining social order.

The religious 'neutrality' of the state in maintaining social order was clear in cases where disputes within, and between, Hindu castes were brought to the Muslim states, or where Hindu castes tried to make use of the Muslim state to their own advantage. A good example of this is the long-standing dispute among the Brahmans in Paithan, a holy place on the Godavari River.

A Brahman of Paithan, Narhari Ranalekar, was taken prisoner by the Afghans in the battle of Panipat in 1761 when the Marathas suffered a complete defeat at the hands of an Afghan troop, and was forcibly converted to Islam. After nearly 10-years' detention, Narhari Ranalekar was released and returned to the Deccan where the Brahmans of Paithan performed a ceremony to purify him. Other Brahmans, however, opposed his purification and appealed to the Hozur (Peshva) for a final decision. An assembly of *vaediks* and *paṇḍits* was thus convened by the Hozur to make a decision in accordance with Shastras. The outcome of the decision was that it was not proper to perform a purification ceremony on a man who had lived with the Muslims for more than 10 years. The Brahmans who purified him were therefore excommunicated (*bahiśkāra*) but many of them were then readmitted by undergoing *prāyaścitta*. Another 40 to 50 Brahmans, however, refused to undergo the penance and remained excommunicated.

At that time, Paithan was in a state of double-control or double-power shared by the Mughals (*Moglāī*, but in substance under the power of the Nizams of Hydarabad) and the Marathas (*Svarājya*), so that Mughal officials too were stationed there. The Brahmans who were excommunicated by the order of the Peshva appealed successfully to the Mughal officials in Paithan for support. They forced other Brahmans who had undergone *prāyaścitta* to accept them on their commensal seats (*paṅkti*), relying on the support of Mughal officials. Knowing this, the Hozur ordered district officials of the Maratha kingdom not to allow all of the Brahmans of Paithan to sit on the commensal seat with the Brahmans of other locations (S.P.D. XXXXIII 25. 1772).

This case shows that even Brahmans did not hesitate to make use of the power of the Muslim state if it proved to be advantageous for them in a dispute of religious character, such as reconversion from Islam.

Similar was the case with disputes between various castes. In the aforementioned case, the Mahars of Paudkhor District appealed to Aurangzeb, the then ruler of the northern Deccan, for a favourable decision in a dispute with the Brahman Joshis of the district. In the later seventeenth century, Aurangzeb camped in Aurangabad for the conquest of the entire Deccan and actually put a considerable part of the Deccan under his direct control. The dispute between the Mahars and the Brahman Joshis of Paudkhor District started around this same time. The Mahars, several thousand in number, flocked together from mountain forts where they were posted as *nāiks* and guards,[18] as well as from villages where they were *vatandārs* (holders of Mahar *vatan*), asserting that the Brahman Joshis should officiate at the marriage of the Mahars. They tried to press Aurangzeb to order the Brahman Joshis to comply with their request. Aurangzeb, however, decided that the Brahman Joshis were not obliged to officiate at the marriage of untouchables like the Mahar taking into consideration the long-standing custom of the locality (S.S.R.P.D. VIII 1132).

In this case, the Muslim king Aurangzeb played the role as arbitrator in the dispute between the Brahmans and the Mahars: Aurangzeb being a part of the power apparatus of the state, was in charge of maintaining social order even among Hindu castes, in which function his religious affiliation had no significance at all.

There were also the opposite cases of Muslim castes appealing to Hindu kings for arbitration in disputes among caste members. In one case, the *mhetar* (headman)[19] of the Atar (Muslim perfumers) petitioned the Hozur (Peshva) as follows:

> The *vatan* of the Atar *mhetar* of this district is mine. When a marriage or ceremony of circumsion is performed in a home of Atars, I can take perquisites in the form of a shawl and *pāna* [betel leaves] from the party requesting the ceremony. Buwaji, an Atar of Pune, however, rejected giving perquisites to me, thereby causing trouble. I humbly request you to summon him and order him to give perquisites to me.
>
> (S.S.R.P.D. I 300. 1745-46)

This petition from the headman of the Atar caste was sanctioned by the Hozur and an order of alleged purport was issued.

In this case, a Hindu king arbitrated in a dispute within a Muslim caste, as it was his duty to maintain order even within a Muslim caste living in his kingdom. Muslim castes did not feel it strange to appeal to a Hindu king to mediate in disputes among themselves, as the function of the king as an arbitrator of disputes among his subjects had no relationship whatsoever to the king's religion. The king in this function was merely a constituent part of the state without relevance to the ritual authority of the king, which extended somewhat beyond the state machinery. This means that what ultimately guaranteed the caste system was the state as the impersonal apparatus of the physical power of compulsion rather than the king equipped with his personified ritual authority.

Upward-movement of Castes and State: Maratha Kingdom and Bombay Government

As a corollary to the state's role in maintaining social order or social relations, the state in the medieval Deccan played the role of restraining the social upward-movement of castes by means of introducing Brahmanical practises which would have shaken the social order embodied in the caste system. (The concept of Sanskritization is not used here.) One of the castes who had been trying hard to move upward in the social ranking of castes in the medieval Deccan was the Prabhu. The Prabhu in western India consist of two sub-castes, that is to say, the Chandraseniya Kayastha Prabhu and the Pathare Prabhu. Both of these sub-castes showed a strong tendency of upward-movement regardless of the opposition of the Brahman and oppression by the state.

In 1736, the then Peshva, Bajirao, issued the following notice on the status of the Pathare (Patane) Prabhus to *paṇḍits*, Dharmadhikaris, *paurāṇiks*, Joshis, Upadyas and all Brahmans of Astagar and Revadanda Districts of Cheul Province:

> Pathare Prabhus residing in Cheul-Revadanda and Mumbai Province traditionally have followed the marriage practises prevalent among lower castes, such as the Shudra castes and mixed castes [*saṃkarajāti*]. It is known now that some Brahmans secretly perform *vedokta* rituals in the home of Pathare Prabhus for the sake of material gain and last year a Brahman, Vishvanath Joshi Rairkar, came to Mumbai and gave a *śāstrārtha* [declaring the Pathare Prabhu as Kshatriya]. In the month of Shravan, Brahmans [*paṇḍits*] assembled in Pune from Varanasi, Paithan, Shringeri in Karnataka and some other sacred places. Taking advantage of this opportunity, a meeting of *paṇḍits* was convened to inquire into the state of affairs by summoning Vishvanath Joshi Rairkar, and it was decided on the grounds of all of the *nibandhas* that the Pathare Prabhu were not Kshatriya but simply a *saṃkara* caste. Accordingly, Vishvanath wrote a letter addressed to all of you purporting that he had not given the *śāstrārtha* declaring the Pathare Prabhu as Kshatriya after a full investigation, and that now he officially acknowledged that the Pathare Prabhu are not Kshatriya, so that the Pathare Prabhu have no right to have *vedokta* rituals performed in their home. His

> letter of this intent was sent to you all. The Brahmans who secretly performed *vedokta* rituals were made to undergo *prāyaścitta* after taking *daṇḍa* in the form of money. Brahmans who now reside in the countryside or beyond the sea are to come here and undergo *prāyaścitta*. Until then, they are put out of the caste [*dñātibāhya*] and can not sit on the commensal seat [*apaṅkta*]. Furthermore, all of the *paṇḍits* assembled in Pune wrote a letter to you all, the gist of which was that any Brahman who performed *vedokta* rituals in the Pathare Prabhu's home could not sit on the commensal seat and would be punished. Keep this strongly in mind and perform the rituals meant for the Shudra castes in the Pathare Prabhu's home as you have been doing according to tradition.
>
> (A.S.S. VI 66)

Thus, the Pathare Prabhu had been endeavouring to obtain the status of Kshatriya as early as the first half of the eighteenth century by having *vedokta* rituals, forbidden to the Shudra castes, performed in their home by Brahmans. On this occasion, however, it was decided that the Pathare Prabhu was a *saṃkarajāti* (a mixed *jāti* assumed to be formed through the marriage of different *varṇas*) by the assembly of Brahmans from Varanasi and other sacred places.

But the Pathare Prabhus were not dispirited by this. In 1743, a man of Pathare Prabhu was excommunicated for the reason of his marriage with a widow. The Pathare Prabhu had been trying to move up the social ranking of castes by adopting the practise of prohibiting widow remarriage which had been the privileged practise allowed only to the Brahman. Brahmans, thus offended by the behaviour of the Pathare Prabhu, appealed to the Peshva stating that the remarriage of a widow was an established practise of the Pathare Prabhu. Accordingly, the then Peshva, Balaji Bajirao, issued an order to the Pathare Prabhu not to prevent the remarriage of a widow.[20]

In the last decades of the eighteenth century, the Prabhu further strengthened the social upward-movement of its caste in spite of repeated suppression by the government. In 1789, the following order was issued by the Peshva government to the district officials of Konkan, Khandesh and Gujarat:

> All of the Brahmans of the town Pen, Sakase District came to the Hozur and stated as follows: In the reign of the late Peshva, Narayanrao [1772-73], a settlement regarding the way of conduct

of the Prabhu was executed by the government. They must behave according to this settlement but they do not do so. They are behaving as they like abandoning their own *dharma* and secretly doing the business of the Brahman. So please command them in this regard and restrain them under control. In response to this appeal, an inquiry was conducted with the result that in the time of the late Peshva, an investigation regarding the conduct of the Prabhu was made and a settlement was reached. The Prabhu wrote the deed of pledge according to this settlement, the details of which were as follows:

1. We do not perform any ritual using the *mantras* of Veda.
2. We do not chant the *mantras* of Veda though we can do so.
3. We do not use the *piṇḍa* of rice.
4. We perform rituals like *devapūjā* by chanting the *mantras* of Purana: We do not offer food to Brahmans in our home.
5. We do not worship *śāligrāma* [a black stone found in the Gandak River and worshiped as sacred to Vishnu].
6. We worship in a temple where the Shudra worship.
7. We use the word *daṇḍvata* as a salute to the Brahman as well as among ourselves.
8. We do not engage *vaedik* Brahmans, *ācārīs*, *pāṇkyas* [water carriers], Shagirda Brahmans and Brahman women in our home.
9. If a widow wants to remarry on her own free will, we do not prevent it.

The Prabhu wrote the above nine articles, but they secretly continued to do the business of the Brahman in their home. Therefore, the dispute between Brahmans of Pen and Prabhus worsened and all of the business of the Prabhu was suspended. The Prabhu should behave as was formerly settled but they do not do so and behave as they like. This is improper for them. What is proper is the former settlement. The Hozur thus issued an order of the above substance to Prabhus residing in Pune. Therefore, force Prabhus to behave according to the former settlement in every district. If any Prabhu behaves otherwise, punish him and take a fine.

(S.S.R.P.D VIII 1144)

As this document demonstrates, the Prabhu dared even to do the business of the Brahman by chanting the *mantras* of Veda. Further it is clear from the last article of this document that they did not abandon their attempt to introduce the Brahmanical practise of prohibiting widow remarriage.

This type of dispute known as *grāmaṇya* still continued to occur, and in 1796, the order of the Peshva, numbering more than 300 but having the same substance, was issued to the Brahmans of various districts purporting that the Brahmans should perform rituals in the home of Prabhus according to the former practise (S.S.R.P.D. V 235).

In the Maratha kingdom the social upward-movement by means of introducing Brahmanical practises was thus opposed by the Brahman and oppressed by the state. Under British colonial rule, however, the Bombay government rejected any interference in this type of dispute, so that many castes, conspicuously the Prabhu and Sonar, began to adopt, without restraint, Brahmanical practises such as the prohibition of widow remarriage and the abandonment of drinking liquor and eating meat (Wagle 1980; Wagle 1987).

This change in the govenment policy under British colonial rule in regard to the caste system contributed in great measure to allowing Brahmanical practises, and subsequently pureness-impureness ideology, to become prevalent among various castes. The following extract from Baba Padmanji's autobiography, *Aruṇodaya* (Mumbai, 1879), serves to prove this tendency.

Baba Padmanji was born a Kasar (a caste of braziers commonly regarded as Shudra) in Belgaum in 1831, and was later baptized in the London Missionary Society's church in Belgaum.[21] The following extract depicts his experience when he was a small boy in the 1830s:

> My family is not Brahman but used to observe firmly *sovaḷā*. Needless to say, no one took a meal without performing ablution. We were to wear clothes of *sovaḷā* such as *mugtā*, *pītambara*, *dhābalī* and so forth when we performed *sandyā* and *devapūjā* or took a meal. No Shudra servants could enter our *devakhalī* [a chamber of gods] and kitchen. We received water from the hand of Shudra only after they had purification bathing. We used to draw water for the *devapūjā* ourselves from a well. When a Parit delivered washed clothes, we touched them after sprinkling drops of water on them. We did not touch new leather footwear without brushing them first with a bundle of dried grass. After bathing we did not touch a Hajam [a barber]. When we touched a Mahar in the bazar, we had to perform *sa-celasnāna* [ablution in one's garments]. I remember I did so several times. I took great care that the shadow of Mahars should not fall on my body.
>
> (Padmanji 1879: 7-8)

Thus the family of Baba Padmanji, though a Kasar of Shudra *varṇa*, used to observe the very troublesome rituals resembling those of the Brahmans. In relation to this, the word *sovaḷā* as opposed to the word *ovaḷā* was often used. The word *sovaḷā* was used in other parts of *Aruṇodaya* as well:

> In front of our house were two houses of the Sonar. We were obliged to bring water from a well of one of the two houses of the Sonar as the water of our well was brackish.... We could not get water from the well of the Brahmans. Even if possible, we men of Shudra castes had to carry a drawing rope from our house as Brahmans never allowed us and our servants to touch their drawing rope. If we touched it, they did not use it until having poured water on it. Their *sovaḷā* was like this.... Women of the Brahman took great care not to touch us. On a rare occasion when women of the Brahman visited our home, we had to offer them special stools to sit on. They never sat on our carpet. Their *sovaḷā* was so.
>
> (Padmanji 1879: 3-4)

Sovaḷā is a word derived from the Sanskrit word '*sa-maṅgala*' while *ovaḷā* is from '*a-maṅgala*', the original meanings of which must be auspiciouness-inauspiciousness. These dichotomous words of *sovaḷā-ovaḷā* were rarely used in medieval Marathi documents. Thus, the words *sovaḷā-ovaḷā* seem to have come into extensive use only in the nineteenth century with the change of meaning from auspiciousness-inauspiciousness to purity-impurity. *Sovaḷā-ovaḷā* can therefore be understood to be a popular expression of the normative or Brahmanical ideology of pureness-impureness which was becoming more and more prevalent among various castes under the rule of the Bombay government as a result of its non-interference policy to the social upward-movement by means of introducing Brahmanical practises. Thus, it can be assumed to be British colonial rule that ultimately brought about the social reality where the pureness-impureness ideology dominates in social relations.

Conclusion

As a result of the discussion presented above, the two problems posed in the Introduction can be addressed as follows.

Firstly, as far as the king's function as a part of the state machinery for maintaining social order is concerned, the king's role was 'secular', or impersonal, having no relevance to the religion of the king himself. There was no difference in this regard between the Mughals and the Marathas in the medieval Deccan. Kings (Peshvas) of the Maratha kingdom, however, did have the characteristic of a ritual king in sanctioning the performance of *prāyaścitta* for removing the sin from grave sinners like murderers and cow killers by imposing *rājadaṇḍa* on them. This ritual function of the Maratha kings (Peshvas) could not be shared by the Mughal kings.

The Maratha kings (Peshvas) using such ritual authority played an ideological role in maintaining social order. This role, however, was not the monopoly of the king, as the Dharmadhikari played a similar role in the local society independent of the authority of the king. The king could not deny or intervene in this ritual authority of the Dharmadhikari which was sustained by the structure of the local society, that is, the Vatan system itself.

Secondly, the autonomous feature of local society is to be noticed in ritual functions as well. The king's rituals in the power centre did not permeate down to the village rituals which were organized on the communal principle of the village division of labour (the Vatan system). The village ritual of *śānti*, performed by untouchables like the Mahar and the Mang, had nothing to do with the king's ritual of *śānti* performed by Brahmans. Taking into consideration the fact that these village rituals were not influenced by the king's rituals at the centre, it can not be affirmed that kingship ideologically permeated down to the village level through, for example, the bestowal of gifts such as emblems, titles, honours and land (Dirks 1987: 93) in the medieval Deccan, though in the Maratha kingdom, the Patil, as an example, was bestowed, supposedly once a year, with *sirpāv* (turban) and *pāna* (betel leaf) being given from the *dīvāṇ* (the government, not the king) (S.S.R.P.D. I 289).

Thirdly, as regards the autonomous character of the caste community, it is certain that the Maratha government occasionally intervened in the procedure of excommunication from and restoration to the caste, but there were many cases also in which this procedure was completed without interference by the government. Governmental intervention in this procedure seems to have been limited to the cases of Brahmans and high government officials. In this sense, the essentiality of the autonomous character of the caste can not be denied though it had become somehow difficult for castes to maintain their order totally independent of the state power apparatus.

Fourthly, the social upward-movement of a caste set free under the rule of the Bombay government accompanied by the gradual dying out of the so-called Hindu kings has made the purity-impurity ideology popularly expressed as *sovaḷā-ovaḷā* more and more prevalent among many castes, most of which are of Shudra *varṇa* such as the Kasar. To trace minutely this process of spreading *sovaḷā-ovaḷā* ideology among various strata of Indian society is a subject yet to be pursued energetically. However, this process can be assumed to bring about the social reality that lies at the base of the Dumontian understanding of the caste system. In this sense, overemphasis of the role of ritual kingship and the auspiciousness-inauspiciousness ideology in modern India will surely lead to misunderstanding of the social changes that took place under British colonial rule and continue to do so in independent India.

Notes

1 In his classical work on the caste system, *Caste in India*, J.H. Hutton points out:

> So clearly has the principle that the secular power is the final arbiter of caste been accepted in the past, that the Mughal rulers of Bengal and their British successors have in turn found themselves in the position of judges of such matters.... In Bengal the Mughal governors retained the right to sanction readmission to caste, and O'Malley quotes ... a case in which a Nawab of Bengal refused to restore a Brahman family that had been put out of caste. He goes on to quote Verelst (*View of the English Government in Bengal* [1772], p. 238) on the instructions drafted in 1769 for British officers in charge of the revenue administration there: 'When any man has naturally forfeited his cast (*sic*), you are to observe that he cannot be restored to it without the sanction of Government: which was a political supremacy reserved to themselves by the Mahomedans' (Hutton1961: 96).

The exact title of the book written by Verelst (Harry Verelst, the Governor of Bengal from 1767 to 1769) is *A View of the Rise, Progress, and Present State of the English Government in Bengal* (London, 1772) and the page of reference given by Hutton (p. 238) is the page of the Appendix of Verelst's book.

2 D. Quigley criticized Hutton in reference to the passage quoted in note 1 above saying: 'Hutton's characterization of traditional Indian kings as "secular" must, however, be challenged.... The secularization of the Hindu king is the converse of the assumption that "Brahmans are the highest

caste" and it is not only Dumont's theory of caste which depends on this assumption' (1993: 149). Quigley's criticism of Hutton, however, merely reveals the fact that Quigley's concept of the state and king is not clear enough. In the page cited, Hutton deals only with the king as a part of the impersonal machinery of physical compulsion of the state. He seems to be saying that as far as this function of the king in maintaining the caste system is concerned, the religion of the king or ruling class made no difference whatsoever. In other words, the king as a part of the state compulsory machinery was 'secular' in this function. As opposed to this, Hindu kings' personal authority in ritual function was not 'secular'. Quigley does not pay due attention to this double character of the king.

3 I have consulted the English translation of the *Manusmṛti* by G. Bühler in *The Sacred Books of the East* as well as the excellent Japanese translation by Prof. N. Watase throughout while also referring to the *Manusmṛti* in its original text. The number of chapters and clauses in the *Manusmṛti* referred to in this chapter are those of the original text edited by G. Jha.

4 In another case of a similar nature, a Brahman who went mad and began to eat Shudra's food (*śūdranna*), including meat, was sent to Trimbak to be purified (S.P.D. XXXXIII 113).

5 The date assigned to this document, that is, 1823, by the editor seems to be incorrect. Pune had been under British (East India Company) colonial rule since 1818, so that there could have been no other *sarkār* than the British in 1823, while the *sarkār* in this document cannot be the Company Sarkar.

6 In the case of non-Brahman castes, however, the purification ceremony (*prāyaścitta*) could be omitted, as the commensal meeting of the caste itself was regarded as the purification ceremony. In one example, a son of Sayaji, a Mali of Sasvad District, committed adultery (*bad amal*) with a Tamboli woman. The family members were thus excommunicated by the caste but they were readmitted as having been purified merely by holding the commensal meeting for two days at their home (Oturkar 167. 1748).

7 In a similar case, a Kasar began to live and dine with a maidservant (*kuṇbīṇa*) so that he and his brothers were excommunicated. In this case as well, the brothers directly asked the Dharmadhikari of Nasik to make them undergo *prāyaścitta* (A.S.S. I 190. 1791).

8 With reference to *sparśa* with the untouchables, see Chapter 6 of this volume.

9 With reference to *saṃsarga* with the untouchables, see Chapter 6 of this volume.

10 In one case, a maidservant of a Joshi, Anand Gopal, was discovered to be a woman of Chambhar, so that his family and guests were ordered to undergo *prāyaścitta* (S.P.D. XXXXIII 92. 1795).

11 With reference to the Vatan system, see Chapter 1 of this volume.

12 One of the most difficult problems pertaining to the village system of the

division of labour is the role of women. In the aforementioned document on village rituals as well, the mention of the role of women is rather sporadic. In one article related to festivals in the month of Margsirsh, women of the Parit, Mahar and Mang were assigned the role of waving a lamp around the head of an idol. In the case of Nagapanchami, the Nhavi played the role of calling for women (*bāikā*) to the worship of *nāga* installed on an anthill. These are the only items relating to the role of women, with some other ambiguous mention elsewhere to women of the Parit. Women in the medieval Deccan must have played various roles in the village rituals, but it is still difficult to ascertain women's role in detail.

13 In anthropological studies on kingship, the centrality of the king in organizing and maintaining social relations down to the village level is emphasized too often. N.B. Dirks notes as follows:

> A.M. Hocart pointed out the myriad interconnections which linked the constituent parts of the village community together and which in turn linked the village to the state.... The relation of the village to the state was based on the development of kingship, which played an important role in organizing the complex of ritual and social services. One of the fundamental requirements of Indic kingship was that the king be a munificent provider of fertile lands for Brahmans...; for festival such as Dasara which renewed the sovereignty of the king and regenerated the kingdom, and which together with temples were central to the constitution and maintenance of the social collectives of localities, villages, castes and subcastes;....
>
> (Dirks 1987: 121)

It might be possible in the case of 'little kingdom' or 'little chiefdom' that the king or chief himself was the organizer or maintainer of the whole social relations under his rule but this could not be the case with the ordinary kingdom, not to mention such great kingdoms as the Mughals and the Marathas. In regard to 'little kingdom', see Tanabe 1999.

14 With reference to *śānti*, see Chapter 6 of this volume.

15 Inden stresses the role of the king in performing the ritual of *śānti* in ancient and medieval India when a bad omen appeared (1985: 35-36). It is noteworthy, however, that in the medieval Deccan, the performers of *śānti* in the local society were the untouchables such as the Mahar and the Mang who could not be regarded as enjoying a share of the king's authority in performing the *śānti* at the highest level of the state.

16 The late Prof. H. Fukazawa greatly contributed in documenting this point by utilizing medieval Marathi source (1991: 199-244).

This fact, however, does not mean that the caste system was a status system established by the state (so to say, the state status system). The caste system was essentially a type of social order or social ranking produced from within society itself (so to say, the social status system). The caste system, however, had become unsustainable simply by the society itself in the time of the Maratha kingdom so that it needed the support of the state.

17 Similar disputes occurred even among untouchable castes as shown in the dispute between the Mahars and the Mangs of Parner District. See Chapter 6 of this volume.

18 The Mahar has been casually called an untouchable caste but at least as late as the eighteenth century a considerable portion of Mahars were still a kind of hillmen and some of them possessed the *vatan* of *nāik* (head of guards) of hill forts. See Chapter 6 of this volume.

19 Caste groups of each district in the Deccan had a headman called *mhetar* who was in charge of maintaining order within his own caste by convening the caste meeting when any problem arose within the caste. See Chapters 4 and 6 of this volume.

20 *Dñanodaya*, 1846-11-2. This document, however, can not be found in any authentic compilation of medieval Marathi documents.

21 As to the life history of Baba Padmanji, see Karhadkar 1979; Kotani 1999d.

10

Doṣa (sin)–*Prāyaścitta* (penance): The Predominating Ideology in the Later Medieval Deccan

Introduction

Two dichotomous concepts of pureness-impureness (*śuddha-aśuddha*, assumed to be Brahmanical ideology: cf. Dumont 1980) and auspiciousness-inauspiciousness (*maṅgala-amaṅgala*, assumed to be kingship's ideology: cf. Inden 1985) have often been emphasized as the pivotal ideology functioning in Indian culture throughout history. This positioning has been held regardless of whether these two are considered to have been incompatible with each other or permutable depending on the prevailing circumstances. Thus far as indicated through my empirical studies on the state and local society in the later medieval Deccan, however, the predominating ideology in medieval India seems to have been rather the *doṣa* (sin)-*prāyaścitta* (penance) ideology than the pureness-impureness ideology which has found expression in the pollution-purification rituals, not to mention the auspiciousness-inauspiciousness ideology that was merely implied in the state ritual of *śānti* performed through the medium of Brahmans.

The concept of sin (*doṣa*), however, was so closely related to the concept of pollution in Indian culture that difficult problems arise when we attempt to group them into two distinct categories. The difficulty in handling sin and pollution is caused mainly by the fact that both of them were required to be purified if they were to have been removed. That the very same term of *śuddhi* (purification) has been applied to both sin and pollution tends to obscure the distinction between these two. The difference in the socio-cultural context of sin and pollution, however, is revealed in the method of purification. In the case of sin (*doṣa*), various purification ceremonies collectively known as *prāyaścitta* had to be performed to remove the sinner from his sin. Conversely, pollution caused by physical contact (*sparśa*) with an untouchable, for example, was commonly held to be purified by ablution (*snāna*). This means that in spite of the very same term of *śuddhi* being applied both to sin and pollution, these two concepts had essentially different origins and functions.[1]

Compared with the ideas of sin and pollution prescribed in classical law books such as the *Manusmṛti*, [2] a salient feature of the medieval idea of sin and pollution seems to have been the predominance of the idea of sin over that of pollution. In other words, the sin (*doṣa*)-penance (*prāyaścitta*) ideology carried more weight than the pollution-purification ideology in maintaining order and stability. Thus, the development of the sin-penance ideology in history constitutes one of the crucial themes in the study of medieval India.

In medieval India, as was the case with ancient India, the one and the same act which was prescribed as a crime to be punished by the state as well as the local society, was, at the same time, a sin required to be purified or removed by the ceremony of *prāyaścitta*. As such, the word *doṣa* denoted both crime and sin. That is to say, the actual or material act constituting a crime was also regarded as an ideological act constituting a sin. Thus, the *doṣa* (sin)-*prāyaścitta* (penance) concept functioned as the ideological cloak to cover the material relationship of *doṣa* (crime)-*daṇḍa* (punishment) sustained by the physical power of compulsion exercised by the state as well as the communal control exerted by the local society.

This chapter aims to clarify the medieval concept of sin-penance which played the pivotal role in ideologically helping maintain the state order and societal stability with special reference to the medieval Deccan. I will mainly draw on medieval Marathi documents pertaining to the seventeenth-eighteenth-century Maratha kingdom (1674-1818) as it is difficult to find informative documents of earlier periods in this regard.

Saṃsarga Doṣa

Of various *doṣas*, the most interesting and important in the historical context of the development of the sin-penance ideology is *saṃsarga doṣa* that was assumed to result from an association or intercourse with one who had been excommunicated for reasons of committing a crime or violating a community rule. The idea of *saṃsarga doṣa* appeared first in the classical law books of India. The *Manusmṛti*, for example, enumerates the following five 'mortal sins' (*mahāpātaka*): killing a Brāhmaṇa, drinking *surā*, stealing gold (of a Brāhmaṇa), entering the bed of a *guru*'s wife, and associating (*saṃsarga*) with such offenders (XI-53). The last category of *mahāpātaka*, that is, association with grave criminals of the four former categories, thus, constitutes the principal case of *saṃsarga doṣa* in the *Manusmṛti*. However, association with every sort of criminal who was excommunicated from society for reasons of crimes or violation of communal rules was also regarded as *saṃsarga doṣa*. Those so excommunicated were designated as *patita* and association with *patitas* in general incurred *saṃsarga doṣa* on the associator (XI-180).

In the case of the *Manusmṛti*, however, the idea of *saṃsarga doṣa* with the discriminated, such as the Chandala (*Caṇḍāla*), was not yet highly developed with only such an obscure provision as follows: 'A Brāhmaṇa who unintentionally approaches a woman of *Caṇḍāla* or very low class, who eats [the food of such persons] and accepts [present from them], becomes a *patita*...' (XI-173).

The idea of *saṃsarga doṣa* seems to have developed considerably in medieval law books (commentaries on classical law books). In this regard, P.V. Kane points out:

> In spite of this medieval writers gradually extended the scope of *saṃsarga* in a spirit of exclusiveness and over-emphasis on ideas of ceremonial purity. For example, the Smṛtyarthasāra (p. 112) remarks that he who associates with the person that associates with a *mahāpātakin* has to undergo half the expiation that the first associator has to undergo. But that work does not go beyond this. The Mit[ākṣarā] (on Yāj[ñavalkya] III. 261) appears to hold that the associator even though he does not become patita is liable to undergo expiation and that even the 4th and 5th associators in a series are liable to undergo expiation though it is lesser and lesser.... Āpastamba-smṛti (III. 1-32) states: 'if a cāṇḍāla stays in the house of any one of the four castes without being known, the latter on coming to know of the fact should undergo expiation, which is Cāndrāyaṇa or Parāka for a member of the first three varṇas and Prājāpatya for a śūdra. Those who partook of cooked food in that man's house should undergo Kṛcchra; one should prescribe one half of Kṛcchra for those who took cooked food in the house of the 2nd associator and for those who partook of cooked food in the house of these last one-fourth of Kṛcchra is prescribed'. So besides the original associator three more

in succession were held to be liable for *prāyaścitta*.

(Kane: IV 27-28)

Thus, in medieval law books, *saṃsarga doṣa* is assumed to be transmittable to one who associated with the original associator, and further from the second associator down to the third and fourth associators with diminishing degrees of sinfulness. This seems to imply that the idea of *saṃsarga doṣa* had developed to a high degree in medieval India, though it is not certain whether or not this idea of transmission of *saṃsarga doṣa* reflects the actual reality in medieval states and societies in India.

Based upon this preliminary survey of the idea of *saṃsarga doṣa* in classical and medieval law books, it would be appropriate to examine the case of *saṃsarga doṣa* in the Maratha kingdom, particularly since various cases of *saṃsarga doṣa* appear in medieval Marathi documents.

In one case, a Brahman, Mahadeo Bhat Joshi, of the village Kadjalganv, Sevganv District, appealed to the Hozur (Peshva as the *de facto* king) as follows:

> My wife killed one of our Brahman relatives, Vitthal Joshi. Therefore I myself and all of my relatives were excommunicated. My wife executed her wicked act without informing me. Hozur, please do all of us the favour of sanctioning us to undergo *prāyaścitta* in accordance with our *doṣa*.

In response to this appeal, an order was issued to all of the Brahmans of the *kasbe* Sevganv to perform the ceremony of *prāyaścitta* on Mahadeo Bhat Joshi and his relatives in accordance with the nature of their *saṃsarga doṣa* (S.P.D. XXXXIII 151). In this case, *saṃsarga doṣa* resulted to the husband and relatives for reasons of their social association (*saṃsarga*) with the criminal wife. Social association thus included not only cohabitation with the criminal but also remote familial relationships. The *doṣa* of the murderer was assumed to be transmitted to the family members and relatives through *saṃsarga*. Thus, the husband and relatives had to undergo *prāyaścitta*, if they were to be readmitted to their caste.

In another case, Nibaji Kulkarni of the village Shahrtakli, Nevasa District, was accused of having committed *saṃsarga doṣa* by contracting a matrimonial relation with a Brahman of the 'Paithan Party'. Specifically here is meant a group of Brahmans excommunicated by reason of their performance of *prāyaścitta* on the Brahman who had been taken prisoner by the Afghans in the battle of Panipat in 1761 and forcibly converted to Islam, but returned home after 10-years' detention. The following order was issued by the Peshva govenment to district officials in this regard:

> Send the aforementioned Kulkarni with his family to Paithan and make them undergo *prāyaścitta* of *saṃsarga doṣa*, with Chimaji Naik Bhakare as a witness. If he would not undergo *prāyaścitta* to be purified, confiscate his Kulkarni *vatan* of the aforementioned village, and pass the proceeds of the said *vatan* to the government account, while sending his person to the government office.
>
> (S.S.R.P.D. VIII 1133. 1785-86)

In this case, *saṃsarga doṣa* was caused by association (matrimonial relation) with the man who had been excommunicated by the order of Peshva, resembling somewhat *saṃsarga doṣa* with a *patita* in classical law books.

Another case of *saṃsarga doṣa* with a criminal concerned the female slave who committed the crime (sin) of prohibited association. Ranoji Dhumal, the Patil of the village Sonke, Vai Province, had purchased a female slave (*baṭīka*) who had subsequently served in his home for four years. Thereafter it became known that this female slave had practised *annavyavahāra* (commensal relation) with a woman convert to Islam (*bāṭgī musalmān*, literally meaning a 'polluted Muslim woman'). Thus, the Patil was ordered to undergo *prāyaścitta* to purify his *saṃsarga doṣa* which accrued from having lived together in the same house with this female slave who had violated the commensal rule (S.S.R.P.D. I 399. 1752-53).

Thus, *saṃsarga doṣa* with criminals (sinners) occurred very often from various causes in the medieval Deccan, though the idea of transmission of *saṃsarga doṣa* to the second, third and even fourth associators as prescribed in medieval law books can not be found in medieval Marathi documents. This might mean that the idea of chain-transmission of *saṃsarga doṣa* in medieval law books was rather a Brahmanical ideal than an actual occurrence in medieval India.

On the other hand, the idea of *saṃsarga doṣa* with the discriminated developed considerably more in the medieval Deccan than as prescribed in classical law books such as the *Manusmṛti*. There are many cases of this sort appearing in medieval Marathi documents.

In one such case, Bajirao Moreshvar and his family had stayed in the home of Anandrao Gopal for four months, at which time it turned out that a maidservant (or a female slave, *kuṇbīṇa*) of Bajirao Moreshvar was a woman of the Chambhar caste. Thus, members of both families were assumed to have unknowingly committed *saṃsarga doṣa* with an untouchable woman through having lived in the same house such that they had to undergo *prāyaścitta.* In this case, *prāyaścitta* had to be performed on the house and the land on which the house stood as well to purify them from *saṃsarga doṣa* with the untouchable woman (S.P.D. XXXXIII 92. 1795). Yet in another similar case, a female slave (*baṭīka*) of Baraji Mahadeo, the Mamledar of Shivner District, a Prabhu by caste, was proved to have committed adultery with a man of *antyaja* (the untouchable), as a result of which family members of the Mamledar had to undergo '*prāyaścitta* of *saṃsarga* with an adulteress as lowly as an untouchable' (*nīcābhigata-yoṣit-saṃsarga-prāyaścitta*) (S.S.R.P.D. VIII 1125. 1781-82).

Thus, in the medieval Deccan, the idea of *saṃsarga doṣa* with untouchables developed extensively. The social reality which brought about this development must have included two essential factors. First was the development of untouchability in medieval India in general. Second was the strengthening of the norm-oriented nature of society or norm-consciousness in the medieval Deccan where even physical contact (*sparśa*) with an untouchable was accusable rather in the context of *doṣa* (crime, sin) of association (*saṃsarga*) with a prohibited person than in the context of pollution caused by untouchability. This will be discussed in the next section.

In the above-mentioned cases, all the persons accused of committing *saṃsarga doṣa* appealed to the Hozur (Peshva) for sanction to undergo *prāyaścitta* to be purified in response to which the Hozur sanctioned it accepting *rājadaṇḍa* as a token of gratitude. This means that, in the case of the Maratha kingdom, the sin (*doṣa*)-penance (*prāyaścitta*) ideology was the state ideology embodied in kingship or king's person for the purpose of putting an ideological cloak over the state punishment (*sarkārdaṇḍa*) to be inflicted on the criminal. However, this function of sanctioning *prāyaścitta* was not the monopoly of the Hozur. In many cases, the Dharmadhikari (a hereditary officer of *dharma*) of sacred places exercised the same authority as the Hozur's in the local society completely independent of the Hozur or the state.

The procedure of sanctioning *prāyaścitta* by the Dharmadhikari involved the following: (1) the person accused of committing a crime (sin) should submit the '*doṣa patra*' (statement of sin) to the Dharmadhikari stating his sin asking him to prescribe the adequate ceremony of *prāyaścitta*, and (2) the Dharmadhikari should prescribe and actually perform the ceremony of *prāyaścitta* and thereafter issue the '*śuddhi patra*' (certificate of purification). In one such case, the Joshi and Kulkarni of the village Pokhali, Parner District, submitted the '*doṣa patra*' to the Dharmadhikari of Nasik in the northern Deccan stating that he and his family had committed *saṃsarga doṣa* with a 'woman of Chandala, the skinners (*carmakī Cāṇḍāḷī*)', requiring them to be purified by the proper *prāyaścitta* ceremony. *Prāyaścitta* prescribed by Brahmans of the sacred place being duly performed, the Dharmadhikari issued the '*śuddhi patra*' certifying that they had now become fit for the commensal seat (*paṅktipāvana*) of the caste (A.S.S. I 200. 1756). This case indicates that the sin-penance ideology exercised through the Dharmadhikari was the ideology of the local society by which *jātidaṇḍa* (caste penalty commonly in the form of excommunication) to be inflicted on the offender of caste rules was ideologically cloaked.[3]

Thus, the Maratha kingdom as well as the local society under it relied upon this same sin-penance ideology though quite independent of each other through respective functionaries.

Sparśa: Sin or Pollution?

Sparśa (physical contact) with a certain kind of man and woman was assumed to bring pollution on the contactee. The *Manusmṛti* V-84 prescribes as follows:

> When he has touched a *Caṇḍāla*, a menstruating woman, a *patita*, a woman within 10 days after childbirth, a corpse or one who has touched them, he becomes pure by bathing.

Thus, in the *Manusmṛti*, pollution caused by the physical contact (*sparśa*) with *patitas* (the excommunicated) and the discriminated such as the Chandala is prescribed to be purified by ablution (*snāna*). In other words, physical contact with these types of men and women does not constitute a sin required to be purified by *prāyaścitta* according to the *Manusmṛti*.

The circumstances, however, considerably differ in the case of the medieval Deccan where physical contact with untouchables was rather assumed to be a *doṣa* (crime, sin) which had to be removed through performance of *prāyaścitta* than the act which would cause pollution to the contactee. A very interesting and important case in this regard is the case of rape committed against an untouchable woman in which *doṣa* of rape and pollution caused by physical contact (*sparśa*) with this class of woman seemed to have been intermingled.

In one such case, Gangaji Jagthap, the Deshmukh of Sasvad District, and six other men (3 Kunbis, 1 Mali, 1 Sali and 1 Muslim) were accused of committing the rape of a girl of the Mahar caste, though it was later found to have been a false accusation. The delicate point pertaining to this case is whether the act of rape accused against the men should have been *doṣa* (sin, crime) or whether they should have been blamed for pollution caused by the physical contact (*sparśa*) with an untouchable girl through the act of rape. That the Deshmukh and other men (perhaps excepting the Muslim man) who were assumed to have committed rape were ordered by the Peshva government to undergo *prāyaścitta* after going on a pilgrimage to Varanasi and Rameshvar (Rameshvaram) rather than to be purified by ablution (Oturkar 155) denotes that the act of rape was regarded as *doṣa* in the medieval Deccan. In other words, the act of rape had to be accused against the perpetrators as *doṣa* as it constituted a violation of the law of the state (Maratha kingdom) which would have endangered the state order.

As this act was accused as a crime (*doṣa*), *saṃsarga doṣa* with criminals accrued not only on the relatives of the accused persons but also on all of the inhabitants of the *kasbe* Sasvad as well as the *kasbe* itself. Thus, the relatives of the accused persons were ordered to undergo *prāyaścitta* after being tonsured and observing a three-days fast. All the inhabitants of the *kasbe* Sasvad were obliged to observe a one-day fast for the sake of *prāyaścitta* and further the ceremony of *prāyaścitta* had to be performed on the *kasbe* Sasvad itself to purify the town from *saṃsarga doṣa* with the criminals (Oturkar 152. 1732).

Thus, of the two blamable aspects of rape, that is, *doṣa* and *sparśa*, the graver one for the state (Maratha kingdom) seems to have been the aspect of *doṣa* as a reflection of the predominance of the idea of *doṣa* over that of pollution (pureness) in the state ideology.

This was the case with the local society as well in the medieval Deccan. This can be supported by a case pertaining to a barber. One day, a particular barber residing in Nasik was asked to cut the hair of an unknown guest while awaiting customers on the Godavari River. The barber did not ask his caste and the guest too did not intimate it. When the barber began to cut his hair, however, one of the members of the same barber caste happened to come along and accused him of touching the head of a Budhalakar (an Ati-Shudra caste of skin vessel makers). Thus, having committed the physical contact (*sparśa*) with an untouchable through unknowingly cutting his hair, he was excluded from the commensal relation of his caste. The embarrassed barber submitted the *doṣa patra* (statement of sin) to the Dharmadhikari of Nasik and asked him to prescribe a suitable ceremony of *prāyaścitta* to purify him (A.S.S. I 193. 1795). In this case also, the physical contact (*sparśa*) with an untouchable was accused against the barber rather as *doṣa* (crime) against the rule of the local society (caste community) than as an act that would cause pollution.

These two cases indicate that physical contact with the untouchable had to be accused as a crime of violating the law of the state in the former case and as one violating the rule of local society in the latter case. It should be noted that the problem of pollution through physical contact with the untouchable did not arise in either of these cases. This means that discrimination against the untouchable in the medieval Deccan was maintained by people's abiding by the laws of the state and community rules through the fear of punishment (*sarkārdaṇḍa* and *jātidaṇḍa*) rather than by the fear of pollution.[4]

Suicide: Sin or Pollution?

The other type of case which involves the problem of whether an act constituted sin or pollution is that of suicide. The *Manusmṛti* V-88 contains such a provision pertaining to suicide as follows:

> The ceremony of water [*udakakriyā*] shall not be performed on those who have been born in vain [who neglect the prescribed], on those born in consequence of an illegal mixture of *jāti*, on those who are ascetics, and on those who have ruined themselves [who have committed suicide].

This provision follows those prescribing the method of purification of pollution such as that caused by a physical contact with a Chandala (V-84) such that suicide is deemed to be an act that brings about pollution according to the *Manusmṛti*.

As opposed to this, suicide was *doṣa* (sin) required to be removed by *prāyaścitta* in the medieval Deccan. The following cases testify to this. In one, Tama, a daughter-in-law of a Brahman, Rangbhat Dekne, was assumed to have committed suicide in a nearby river on account of a disagreement with her father-in-law. On the night of the lunar eclipse in the month of Bhadrapad, she wanted to take her six-year old son to the river for *sparśasnāna* but her father-in-law dissuaded her from doing so as the boy was ill at that time. Being offended by this act, she went to the river alone and tried to commit suicide, at which time other female members of the family prevented her from doing so and brought her back home. Some time later, however, she stole out of the house and went to the river for *mokṣasnāna.* She subsequently vanished and was assumed to have committed suicide though her corpse could not be found in spite of a search conducted for it over six months. Upon this, Rangbhat Dekne appealed to the Hozur (Peshva) to sanction the performance of her funeral ceremony to enable the family to celebrate such auspicious ceremonies (*māṅgalya*) as marriage. His appeal was accepted and he was ordered to undergo *prāyaścitta*, after paying *rājadaṇḍa* of Rs. 100 to the Hozur and *brāhmadaṇḍa* to the Brahmans who prescribed and actually performed *prāyaścitta* (S.S.R.P.D. VII 592. 1765-66). This case indicates that a suicide victim was deemed as a criminal (sinner), to whose family members *saṃsarga doṣa* was to accrue. Accordingly, the father-in-law of Tama, the suicide victim in this case, had to undergo *prāyaścitta* to be freed from *saṃsarga doṣa.*

In another case, a mother of two brothers, Hari Jadhav and Ramachandra Jadhav, committed suicide, having been prompted by a quarrel with a female slave (*kuṇbīṇa*). The two brothers were excommunicated by reason of *saṃsarga doṣa* with the suicide victim. One year thereafter, they submitted the *doṣa patra* (statement of sin) to the Dharmadhikari of Nasik and asked that a suitable ceremony of *prāyaścitta* to remove *saṃsarga doṣa* from their bodies be prescribed. *Prāyaścitta* being performed accordingly, the two brothers became fit for commensality of their caste (*paṅktipāvana*) and the *śuddhi patra* (certificate of purification) of this purport was issued by the Dharmadhikari (A.S.S. I 203. 1806). In this case also, suicide was regarded as a crime that was to result in *saṃsarga doṣa* to the family members of the suicide victim.

These two cases show that suicide was assumed to be a sin by the state (Maratha kingdom) as well as the local society in the medieval Deccan. That the problem of pollution being caused by the death of family members (*sutaka*) did not arise in either of these two cases should not be overlooked as it also indicates that the idea of *doṣa* (sin) predominated over the idea of pollution in the medieval Deccan.[5]

Thus, it is clear from these cases of suicide that the same ideology of *doṣa-prāyaścitta* played a pivotal role in the state apparatus of the Maratha kingdom as well as in the social organization of the local society in the medieval Deccan. This same sin-penance ideology of the state and local society functioned quite independent of each other but, at the same time, worked in mutual complementarity with each other in maintaining the state order and societal stability.

Śānti

This same independence and mutual complementarity in ideological functions between the state and the local society can be seen in the rite of *śānti* (propitiation rite) that is commonly assumed to be the expression of the auspiciousness (*maṅgala*)-inauspiciousness (*amaṅgala*) ideology though the terms *maṅgala-amaṅgala* rarely appear in medieval Marathi documents.

Śānti is the rite performed by the state as well as the local society to propitiate when extraordinary natural phenomena occurred. The state ritual of *śānti* was performed by Brahmans whereas that of the local society was performed by untouchables such as the Mahar and Mang. Thus, these two types of *śānti* must have been essentially different in nature as well as function.

The following passage outlines the procedure of the rite of *śānti* performed under the government order:

> Khandoji Kondve, the *sarnāik* [headman of *nāiks*] of the Narayangad Fort, petitioned the government for sanction to perform the rite of *śānti* as a bad star [*duṣṭa graha*] appeared on the zodiac. Accordingly, a government order was issued to Antaji Kathkar, the *havāldār*, and the *kārkun* to make them perform *śānti*, defraying Rs. 10 to 15 for expenses.
>
> (S.S.R.P.D. II 319. 1747-48)

The appearance of bad stars, eclipses, a comet and a meteor had been typical bad omens frequently referred to in the classical literature (Kane: V 719-814). On the occasion of a solar eclipse, for example, the Maratha (Peshva) government ordered Brahmans to perform certain rituals and granted *inām* lands to the Brahmans concerned (S.S.R.P.D. VII 679. 1762-63; S.S.R.P.D. VII 683. 1763-64).

An example of more local or non-classical bad omen can be seen in the following case. In Pandharpur, a lizard touched the image of Vithoba so that the rites of *mahārudra* and *śānti* had to be performed. For these rites, 1,000 Brahmans were gathered in Pandharpur and the government sanctioned the expenditure of Rs. 400 to feed those Brahmans (S.S.R.P.D.

VIII 1109. 1773-74). In this case, the physical contact of a lizard must have been assumed to be a bad omen.

The state ritual of *śānti* performed to avert bad omens which found expression in such extraordinary phenomena as an epidemic, thunderbolt or earthquake was particularly called *adbhutaśānti* (*adbhuta* means a wonder; cf. Kane: V 733-34). In one case, an epidemic disease spread throughout the Visapur Fort, affecting more than 100 persons, and mounted to a death toll of 25. Therefore, the *havāldār* of the fort, with consent of all of the fort personnel, petitioned the government to issue an order that the rite of *adbhutaśānti* should be performed. The government gave assent to it (S.S.R.P.D. II 326. 1753-54). Another example of *adbhutaśānti* was the case of the occurrence of a thunderbolt. On the Dasara day, the flagpole of the Mahuli Fort was struck and split by a thunderbolt. Thus, Brahmans were invited to recite 1,00,000 times the incantation for the planet Saturn (*śanicā japa*) for its propitiation. For this rite of *śānti*, the expenditure of Rs. 10 in addition to Rs. 100 to feed the Brahmans thus invited was sanctioned by the government (S.S.R.P.D. II 312. 1740-41).[6] This rite of *śānti* was also performed in the case of an earthquake. In one such case, the government order was issued to the district official of Kalyan-Bhivandi to summon learned Brahmans and make them perform *śānti* (S.S.R.P.D. II 325. 1751-52).

Without doubt, the Maratha (Peshva) government thus used to make Brahmans perform the rite of *śānti* to avert bad omens which otherwise might have shaken the state order and stability.

The rite of *śānti* performed in the local society, however, conspicuously differed from the state ritual of *śānti* conducted by Brahmans. The salient feature of the former *śānti* was that it was performed with the sacrifice of animals to propitiate the anger of *devī* (goddess of soil) expressed by an epidemic or extraordinary phenomena like an earthquake. Due to this characteristic of *śānti* of the local society, its performers were untouchables such as Mahars and Mangs. Brahmans therefore had no place in this local society *śānti*. The village rite of *śānti* was more routinely performed in the local society on festive occasions, specifically during Dasara. *Śānti* performed in the local society seems to have also been meant for throwing out evil spirits haunting the village outside the village boundary in addition to the propitiation of *devī*.

The relevant portions of a document pertaining to one such case of village *śānti* performed on the occasion of the Dasara read as follows:

1 A Mahar proceeds with a pot of *peḍhā* [sweetmeats] in hand and a

Mang follows him also with a pot of *peḍhā* in hand.

2 A buffalo decorated by turmeric and garland is to be made to walk around the village boundary.

Iraḍa [a bundle of trees] is carried at the head of the procession, followed by the Mahar and Mang with pots of *peḍhā* in hand and then the buffalo walking around the village boundary.

3 A *ratha* [float] made by the Sutar is decorated and drawn to the place of the Kumbhar. An idol of *devī* made from clay by the Kumbhar is put in the *ratha* and drawn to a temporary *maṇḍapa* in front of the temple of Hanuman to musical accompaniment. The idol of *devī* is installed in the *maṇḍapa* and the *ratha* is cleansed and put by the side of the idol.

4 The Mahar worships the buffalo which has come to the *maṇḍapa* after walking around the village boundary. The offering and leaves of betel placed before the idol [of *devī*] is to be taken by the Mahar and Mang.

5 The buffalo is taken before the idol and its neck is to be cut on a certain line by the Mahar and is then to be cut off by the Mang.

6 For three days the idol is worshipped. All the villagers, old and young, are to bring offerings to the idol.

7 On the fourth day, the idol is to be brought to the village boundary and thrown out of the village.

(M.I.S. XXII 215)

The *peḍhā* (sweetmeats) thrown out of the village boundary by the Mahar and Mang while walking around the boundary seems to have been assumed to entice evil spirits haunting the village out of the village boundary (cf. Whitehead 1916: 46-53). Thus, *śānti* in the local society had its own peculiar function which the state ritual of *śānti* did not share.

This document clearly shows also that this rite of *śānti* in the local society was the joint activity of the village as a ritual community in which all the villagers played their respective roles with the Mahar and Mang as its leading actors.

Thus, the rite of *śānti* in the local society considerably differed from the state ritual of *śānti* in nature as well as functionaries. This implies that the state ideology of bad omens or auspiciousnes-inauspiciousness finding expression in the Brahmanical rite of *śānti* did not permeate down to the local society where the rite of *śānti* had almost nothing to do with these Brahmanical concepts. In other words, the state and local society conducted the rite of *śānti* quite independently with respective ideas and functionaries but in mutual complementarity with the same intention of maintaining order and stability. This was also the case with the ritual performed on the occasion of an eclipse. With regard to the state, Brahmans performed certain rituals, while in the local society people went to a nearby river for ablution, as indicated in the above-cited suicide case of Tama.[7]

This point, however, stands in total contrast to what N.B. Dirks claims occurred in a south Indian 'little kingdom'. He maintains that the royal gift (kingly grants) to 'village officers, servants, and artisans were concerned with the maintenance of the structure of village ritual' and that 'village headmen could not conduct their ritual duties in village festivals without worshipping and prominently displaying the emblems that had been granted by kings' (Dirks 1987: 128, 130). In the case of the Maratha kingdom as well, the royal gift was bestowed, perhaps once a year, to Patils, Kulkarnis and caste headmen (*mhetars*). *Śirpāv* (turban) and *pāna* (betel leaf), for example, were to be bestowed to the Patil of the village Bhangaon, Karde District (S.S.R.P.D. I 289. 1730-31) and *śirpāv* to the Kulkarni of the village Khed, Junnar Province (S.C.S. I 283. 1740). In the case of caste headmen, *taśrīf* (investment of honorary dress) with *pāna* and/or *viḍā* was the usual form of the royal gift (a Kumbhar headman's case, S.C.S. I 34. 1650-51; another Kumbhar headman's case, S.C.S. I 27. 1642; a Mahar headman's case, S.C.S. VII 43. 1657). These royal gifts of the Maratha kingdom, however, seem to have played no roles in such village rituals as *śānti*, since they never appear in the documents pertaining to village rituals as indicated in the aforecited document on the village rite of *śānti*. What it means seems to be that the ritual relationship between the state and the local society differed considerably depending on the historical circumstances such as, for example, whether it was a 'little kingdom' or a 'great kingdom'.

Conclusion

From the discussion above, it can be concluded that the sin (*doṣa*)-penance (*prāyaścitta*) ideology predominated in the medieval Deccan over the ideology of pollution-purification, not to mention the ideology of auspiciousness-inauspiciousness. It played the pivotal role of ideologically sustaining the state order as well as societal stability, of which the material basis was the crime (*doṣa*)-punishment (*daṇḍa*) relationship with physical power of compulsion being exercised by the state (*sarkārdaṇḍa*) and communal control being exerted by the local society by means of caste penalty (*jātidaṇḍa*) respectively. Thus, the state as well as the local society in the medieval Deccan drew on this same sin-penance ideology quite independently through respective functionaries, but in mutual complementarity with each other, for maintaining order and stability.

This conclusion implies that the two dichotomous ideas of pureness-impureness and auspiciousness-inauspiciousness have been too often overemphasized as playing the central ideological role in Indian history.[8] These two dichotomous ideas, however, do not seem to have played strong ideological functions, at least in medieval India, as these ideas lacked such a physical power of compulsion as *sarkārdaṇḍa* and *jātidaṇḍa*, as in the case of the sin (*doṣa*)-penance (*prāyaścitta*) ideology. The *Manusmṛti* is quite categorical in this regard, stating that: 'The whole world is kept in order by punishment (*daṇḍa*), for a guiltless man is difficult to find; through fear of punishment the whole world yields the enjoyments' (VII-22). This realism of the *Manusmṛti* should always be born in mind while dealing with the ideology, rituals and symbolism.

Notes

1 The concept of pollution itself includes a variety of ideas of different origins and functions. For example, pollution caused by the death of family members and relatives was assumed to dissipate after the lapse of the prescribed time, during which period, however, the parties concerned were obliged to avoid social association with other persons (*Manusmṛti* V-57-61; cf. note 5 below), whereas pollution caused by physical contact with the dead body of a stranger had to be purified by ablution (*Manusmṛti* V-84). This means that even the concept of death-pollution includes two different ideas of different origins and functions. Thus, the essentialist approach to the concept of pollution, a good example of which is Mary Douglas, saying 'As we know it, dirt is essentially disorder' (Douglas 1984: 2), seems to be destined to fail to account for the entire range of this pollution concept.

2 The number of chapters and clauses in the *Manusmṛti* referred to in this chapter are those of the original Sanskrit text edited by G. Jha.

3 This 'autonomous' ritual authority of the Dharmadhikari was sustained by the structure of local society which can be conceptualized as the Vatan system. The office of Dharmadhikari was also one of these *vatans* to be hereditarily inherited by particular Brahman families in sacred places. Thus, the authority of the Dharmadhikari in exercising the sin-penance ideology independent of the state rested on the hereditary right conferred on him by the Vatan system. As to this Vatan system, see Chapter 1 of this

volume and further on the Dharmadhikari, see Chapter 9 of this volume. This ritual 'autonomy' of the local society in the medieval Deccan is the main theme of Chapter 9.

4 The so-called untouchables, such as the Mahar and Mang, however, were not merely discriminated beings in the medieval Deccan. They had a somewhat ambivalent existence in two senses. First, they played an indispensable and leading role in the village ritual of *śānti* (see the section on *śānti* in this chapter). Second, considerable portions of Mahars and Mangs were a sort of hill soldiers posted as *nāiks* (hereditary head of guards) of hill forts as well as *ṭhāṇas* (soldier-posts in plains) who had the *nāikī vatan* (Chapter 6 of this volume).

5 *Sutaka*, being the corrupted form of the Sanskrit word *sūtaka*, originally meant pollution caused by childbirth but also referred to pollution caused by the death of a family member. The act of avoiding social association with other persons due to these sorts of pollution was also known as *sutaka*. When a man or woman died a natural death, family members and relatives had to observe *sutaka* (dis-association). In one such case, Sakho Moreshvar and others, relatives of Khando Shamraj, the Kulkarni of Jezuri, were excommunicated from their caste by the government order on the grounds that they did not observe *sutaka* when Khando Shamraj's wife gave birth to a child and also when his brother's wife died (S.P.D. XXXXIII 11. 1771).

6 Propitiatory rituals for planets seem to be performed on various occasions. In one case, the Peshva government defrayed Rs. 286 or so for the performance of a ritual (*anuṣṭhāna*) to propitiate planets which included incantations of 1,00,000 times for the planet Saturn, 20,000 times for Jupiter, 20,000 times for Mars and another 20,000 times for Rahu (S.S.R.P.D. II 313, 1742-43).

7 Inden refers to these bad omens which were 'destructive of people of the countryside (*jana*), of the royal capital (*nagara*), and also of kings' (Inden 1985: 34), and says as follows:

> The kingdom constituted by the royal capital and the countryside was, in turn, hierarchically related to the king, the overlord of earth and people, their commander and protector. The king, an earthly realization of the Primordial Man (*puruṣa*), the Cosmic Overlord himself, was thought to include within his persona all of the constituent elements of his kingdom just as the Cosmic Man included the constituent elements of the universe in his [34].... Yet, because the king includes the people and country of his kingdom within his persona, every portent that appears in his kingdom, no matter who is directly affected, is also a catastrophe for the king. This is why the king, above all others, was concerned with omens in ancient and medieval India

[35].

Though this might have been the state ideology of kingship, village people (*jana*) in the medieval Deccan do not seem to have accepted this ideology of kingship as their own, as the village rite of *śānti* amply indicates.

8 It is noteworthy that the popular Marathi terms indicating pureness-impureness in the nineteenth and twentieth centuries have been *sovaḷā-ovaḷā* not *śuddha-aśuddha*. (See, for example, Padmanji 1879: 3-4, 7-8, 45.) *Sovaḷā-ovaḷā* are the corrupted form of Sanskrit terms, *samaṅgala-amaṅgala* (auspicious-inauspicious). How the terms *samaṅgala-amaṅgala* have changed their meanings to pureness-impureness in Marathi under British colonial rule is an interesting issue yet to be researched. See, further, Chapter 9 of this volume.

11

The Development of Hindu Identity Relative to British Colonial Rule

Introduction

Hindu identity or the collective consciousness of being Hindu has begun to sway politics in India in a very precarious manner. One important task for historians under such circumstances is to re-examine, or retrace, the historical process of the development of Hindu identity, which should be considered as having a rather recent origin though it might sound paradoxical (Frykenberg 1997; Thapar 1997). This chapter attempts to help further this task, specifically focusing on the circumstances which brought about the development of Hindu identity under British colonial rule. For source material this chapter draws on early administrative documents pertaining to the English East India Company and a collection of judicial decisions handed down by the Bombay Sadr Divani Adalat, the predecessor of the Bombay High Court, during the early part of the nineteenth century.

Hindu-Muslim Dichotomy in British Colonial Administration

In 1765 the then figurehead Mughal emperor granted the Divani (the office of Divan, Divan being the financial chief officer of the province) of the Mughal provinces of Bengal and Bihar to the East India Company as a result of his defeat at the battle of Baksar in 1764. The East India Company, however, did not immediately take direct charge of the Divani, appointing instead two Indian 'Naib Duans' (Nayeb Divan, deputy Divan) each to administer the provinces of Bengal and Bihar.

Direct rule came only in 1771, when the Court of Directors of the East India Company decided to 'stand forth as Duan' by abolishing the office of Naib Duan.[1] Subsequently in 1772, Warren Hastings was nominated as the Governor of Bengal and mandated to elaborate a plan for the direct rule in Bengal and Bihar by the Company. For this purpose, a Committee of Circuit was established, with Hastings as its president along with four other members of the Council of Bengal. 'A Plan for the Administration of Justice' drafted by the Committee of Circuit on 8 August 1772, and then approved by the Court of Directors, laid the foundation of the judicial system not only in the Bengal Presidency but also in the Madras and Bombay Presidencies. (This very important document will be discussed later.)

This embryonic period of British colonial rule played a crucial role in shaping a dichotomous image of India, that is, an India composed of Hindus and Muslims. At the onset of colonial rule, the British were actually faced with two sets of dichotomous images of India. One was the Gentoo-Moor dichotomy handed over to the British by the Portuguese. The Portuguese had found on the western coast of the Indian subcontinent people distinct from Muslims, who were known as Moors, and called these people Gentio meaning the infidel (gentile in English). From this Gentio the British came up with the corrupted form, Gentoo (Yule and Burnell 1886: 367-69) as the following document indicates:

> In the Answer from the President and Council to the Council of Revenue, they entirely assent to the Distinction proposed in the above Letter; declaring that all Cases of Inheritance, Marriage, or other Matters for which the Mahometan Law has made Provision, and likewise all Matters respecting Inheritance, and the particular Laws and Usages of the Casts of the Gentoos, should be decided by the established Magistrates, assisted by the proper Persons of the respective Religions, according to the Laws and Usages of each (Letter from the Council of Revenue at Moorshedabad to the President and Council, 1772). [2]

The other dichotomy was the Hindu-Musalman dichotomy in the Persian context. In this Persian dichotomy, the term 'Hindu' meant the whole of the non-Muslim inhabitants of the Indian subcontinent lumped together as the idol worshipper (*bot-parast*). For example, a passsage from the *Futūḥāt-i Fīrūz Shāhī* which is assumed to be the autobiography of Firuz Shah Tughluq (reigning 1351-88) reads as follows:

> Another blessing of God: The unclean and idolatrous Hindus of Marmak (*Hindū-yi Marmak va bot-parast*) had agreed to pay the *jizya* and their persons and property were accordingly protected. But some among them had begun to construct new temples (*bot-khāneh-yi jadīd*) within the city and in its environs. Under the *sharī'a* of the prophet Muhammad, peace be upon him, construction of new temples dedicated to idol worship is forbidden. By the grace of God, the Exalted and Almighty, I had these sinful structures pulled down, the leaders of the unbelievers who habitually led them astray were put to death and their followers rebuked or punished, until this evil was wholly eradicated.
>
> Another matter: In the village of Mulvah there was a pond called *kund* where Hindus had constructed a temple. On a certain day of the year, some of them came to this place, in imitation of each other, on horseback bearing arms, accompanied by their womenfolk and children in palanquins and carriages, to worship the idols (*bot-parastī*). The number gathered grew in thousands. So far so that shopkeepers transported there all kinds of valuable merchandise and set up a bazar to sell it. Then certain irreligious Muslims joined in this capacity out of desire for worldly gain. When that was brought to my attention, I decided, by the help and grace of God, to go there in person on the very day of the people's congregation, in order to root out an evil that could cause harm to the religion of Islam. I ordered the execution of the leaders who had seduced and misled the people, and other Hindus were deterred from continuing the practice by severe punishments (English translation, 26).

As this passage shows, the term 'Hindu' in medieval Persian works of India was a synonym for the 'idol worshipper' (*bot-parast*) which included adherents to every kind of religion in the Indian subcontinent other than Islam.

This Persian dichotomy was slightly transformed into the Hindoo-Mahometan (Mahomedan) dichotomy during the early phase of British colonial rule. The instructions of the then Governor of Bengal, Harry Verelst (in office from 1767 to 1769), and his Council in 1769 given to the newly nominated Supervisor (later re-denominated as Collector) of the district constitute an important document as an early example of the appearance of the clear-cut Hindoo-Mahometan dichotomy:

> The Instructions of the President and Council, communicated by

> the Resident at the Durbar [Richard Becher] to the Supervisors of the several Districts, after observing the Degree of Corruption to which the Courts of Judicature were degenerated, and particularly the mischievous Consequences of allowing arbitrary Fines, and the Compromise of Offences, direct the Supervisors "... that they endeavour to reform all the Corruptions which have encroached on the primitive Rights of the Mahommedans and Hindoos, particularly in respect of the arbitrary Impositions of Fines... ".[3]

During the latter half of the eighteenth and early nineteenth centuries, these two dichotomies were freely used interchangeably with no heed being paid to their etymological differences as the evidence of Harry Verelst before a committee of the House of Commons indicates:

> Harry Verelst, Esquire, further informed Your Committee, that the Gentoos are more attached to their Manners and Customs than any other People upon the Face of the Earth–That they would suffer Death rather than any Indignity to their Cast–That from every Knowledge he had of the Gentoos, he was persuaded, that the Mahomedans, who have usually carried their Conquests by the Edge of the Sword, on all former Occasions, when they arrived in Indostan, found it absolutely necessary to sheath the Sword, from a thorough Conviction, that they would deluge the Country with Blood before they could convert one Gentoo to their Laws and Religion; and that they therefore wisely became the Guardians and Protectors of the Hindoo Religion; and that he conceives the Country to have been preserved in that State to the Time he left it in the Year 1770– ... And being asked, Whether he had any Reason to alter his Opinion since the Publication of that Work, from subsequent Information? the Witness informed Your Committee, That he was far from having altered his Opinion, being now thoroughly convinced, that what he then wished to impress on the Minds of People, regarding the Impossibility of introducing the English Laws into Indostan, has been but too fatally realized–That the Hindoo Religion tends to keep its Followers in a State of Separation from Strangers; for it admits of no Converts, and consists of more than Ninety separate Sects or Casts, as they are called–That many of these are subdivided again; but that they may be all properly termed Hereditary Religions, as they are preserved distinct from each other, and each is governed by its own peculiar Laws–That these Laws are fundamentally taken from the Bede [Veda]; but that their Customs

> and Manners are also considered as Laws, and held as sacred as the Bede itself.[4]

Within these dichotomous frameworks, all Indian people other than Muslims were categorized together as the Gentoo or Hindoo, without any reference to the many differences in religious belief, world view and/or social practises among this latter group. As an example, a witness before a committee of the House of Commons, G. Harper, being asked: 'What was the proportion of Hindoos and Mahomedans in the Province of Oude?', answered that he 'could not precisely answer, but that the Mahomedans bear a very small Proportion to Gentoos'.[5]

It was only in the middle of the nineteenth century that the term Gentoo fell into disuse and the term Hindoo (or Hindu) remained as the only term denoting the non-Muslim inhabitants of the Indian subcontinent.

To the so-called Hindoo (Hindu) in this dichotomous framework, the early administrators of the English East India Company attributed the following three collective characteristic features which became stereotyped and fossilized during the course of the nineteenth century:

1. Laws regulating the life of the Hindus are contained in such classics as the 'Bede' (Veda) and the 'Shaster' (Shastra). These classical legal codes have been continuously handed down from antiquity to the present by Brahmans, who have been universally held in great esteem due to their knowledge of these laws. Warren Hastings, for example, was very categorical in this regard:

> Among the various plans which have been lately formed for the improvement of the British interests in the provinces of Bengal, the necessity of establishing a new form of judicature, and giving laws to a people who were supposed to be governed by no other principle of justice than the arbitrary wills or uninstructed judgments, of their temporary rulers, has been frequently suggested; and this opinion I fear has obtained the greater strength from some publications of considerable merit in which it is too positively asserted that written laws are totally unknown to the Hindoos, or original inhabitants of Hindostan. From whatever cause this notion has proceeded, nothing can be more foreign from truth. They have been in possession of laws, which have continued unchanged, from the remotest antiquity. The professors of these laws, who are

spread over the whole empire of Hindostan, speak the same language, which is unknown to the rest of the people, and receive public endowments and benefactions from every state and people, besides a degree of personal respect amounting almost to idolatry, in return for the benefits which are supposed to be derived from their studies. The consequence of these professors has suffered little diminution from the introduction of the Mahomedan goverment, which has generally left their privileges untouched, and suffered the people to remain in quiet possession of the institutes which time and religion had rendered familiar to their understandings and sacred to their affections. I presume, my lord, if this assertion can be proved, you will not deem it necessary that I should urge any argument in defence of their right to possess those benefits under a British and Christian administration which the bigotry of the Mahomedan goverment has never denied them.[6]

2. Lawsuits among the Hindus, therefore, can not be decided without the advice of Brahmans. The aforementioned instructions of the President and Council to the Supervisors of several districts (1769) further ordered that cases which might lead to excommunication from a caste, for example, were so fatal for the party concerned that they should not be decided without 'Sentence of the Bramin'. The relevant portion runs as follows:

> ... that all Persons claiming any judicial or religious Authority should be summoned to produce their Sunnods [*sanads*], and that Registers of these Sunnods be kept, in order to prevent any from exercising a judicial, because a lucrative, Function, who is not appointed by Government, if a Mahometan, or elected by his Cast, if a Hindoo;.... – that the Forfeiture of Cast should never be inflicted in any Case but by Sentence of the Bramin, in a regular Process, and upon clear Proof of the Offence; but that, as the Policy of the Mahometan Goverment had provided, that where a Hindoo has legally forfeited his Cast, he cannot be restored to it without the Sanction of the Government; that this Principle should be kept up, as a direct Assertion of the Subordination of the Hindoos, who are a very considerable Majority of the Subjects. (See note 5 below.)

This quotation in the Parliamentary Paper from the instructions is, however, not a verbal quotation. The original sentences of the instructions are more categorical as the following extract shows:

> The officers of justice and Kazies, who are established by the Mahomedan law, as also the Bramins, who administer justice among the Hindoos, in the every village, town, and quarter, should all be summoned to appear, produce their Sunnuds, or authority for acting, and register them.
>
> The register of Sunnuds is intended to deter any from exercising a judicial, because lucrative, function, who may not be legally appointed by government, if a Mahomedan, or fairly elected by his cast, if a Hindoo.
>
> The peculiar punishment of forfeiting casts, to which the Hindoos are liable, is often inflicted from private pique and personal resentment amongst themselves; and requires to be restrainted to those occasions only where there may be a regular process, and clear proofs of the offence before the Bramins, who are their natural judges. But when any man has naturally forfeited his cast, you are to observe that he cannot be restored to it, without the sanction of government; which was a political supremacy reserved to themselves by the Mahomedans, and which, as it publicly asserts the subordination of Hindoos, who are so considerable a majority of subjects, ought not to be laid down; though every indulgence and privilege of cast should be otherwise allowed them (Verelst 1772: Appendix 237-38).

Naib Duan (deputy Divan) of Bengal, Mahomed Reza Cawn, however, was very critical of allowing 'a Bramin to be called in to the Decision of any Matter of Inheritance, or other Dispute of Gentoo', on the grounds that 'the Bramins had never admitted to any such Jurisdiction...since the Establishment of the Mahometan Jurisdiction in Hindostan'.[7]

3. Among the Hindus, customs and manners were considered as laws and held as sacred as classical legal codes. Due to this strong attachment of the Hindus to their customs and manners, the introduction of foreign laws (English laws) must be peculiarly offensive to them, as Harry Verelst pointed out in his evidence before a committee cited above. Another point of evidence before the same committee runs as follows:

> Mr. Baber informed Your Committee, That the Gentoos are so

> prejudiced in favour of their own Customs and Manners, and of that Government under which they have been brought up, that they have no Idea of, much less a Wish for, any Alteration– That the Laws of England are quite opposite to their Manners, Customs, and Religion– That their Laws are so intimately connected with their Religion, that a Stranger cannot be easily acquainted with them–That to acquire sufficient Knowledge, a long Residence, and a close Application to the Study of their Laws, is absolutely necessary– That even then, the learned in Mahomedan and Hindoo Laws must, on many Occasions, be consulted– That the Connection of the Laws of that Country with its Religion, must render the Introduction of foreign Laws peculiarly offensive to its Inhabitants; and that, in order to introduce them, their Customs, Manners, and Religion, must be changed– That the Inhabitants would be much displeased to see the Power and Influence of the Zemindars destroyed, by the Equality which the Exercise of English Law Courts would produce.[8]

As a result of these stereotyped assumptions, it was proposed in 'A Plan for the Administration of Justice' drafted by the Committee of Circuit under the presidentship of Warren Hastings in 1772 as follows:

> That in all Suits [among the Hindus] regarding Inheritance, Marriage, Cast and other religious Usages or Institutions, the Laws ... of the Shaster [Shastra] ... shall be invariably adhered to: On all such Occasions ... Brahmins shall ... attend to expound the Law, and they shall sign the Report, and assist in passing the Decree.[9]

This proposal of the Committee of Circuit was approved by the Court of Directors of the East India Company, and Brahmans (Shastris, designated as Hindu Law Officers in English) were actually posted in all civil courts established by the East India Company not only in the Bengal Presidency but also in the Madras and Bombay Presidencies. This constituted a total revamping of the judicial system of India as the Naib Duan Mahomed Reza Cawn criticized, which was a result of prejudice in favour of the Brahman on the part of the early British colonial administrators.

Shaping of the Brahmanically Normed Hindu

The Shastris posted in the civil courts wrote their opinions on the point at issue in lawsuits in a specific style of literature known as Vyavastha which the British judges consulted in rendering decisions. At the same time, some of the important Shastras, such as the *Manusmṛti* as well as important commentaries on them, such as the *Mitākṣarā* on the *Yājñavalkyasmṛti* were translated into English for the sake of availing the British judges of the original law codes.

The actual function and role played by the court Shastris and Vyavasthas written by them as well as those translated Shastras that were actually administered in the judicial courts is a subject that should be examined with great care since it can be assumed that Brahmanical or textual norms of classical law books gradually infiltrated into Indian society through the application of those laws in the civil courts established by the British.

Here, this problem will be discussed by referring to decisions passed by the Bombay Sadr Divani Adalat between 1800 and 1820 while this court was situated in Surat on the Arabian Sea coast.

In the first compilation of reports on the decision handed down by the Bombay Sadr Divani Adalat, the compiler, H. Borradaile, pointed out three classical law books held in great esteem in this part of India. They were: (1) the *Mitākṣarā*, a commentary on the *Yājñavalkyasmṛti* composed in the Deccan around the twelfth century, (2) *Vyavahāramayūkha* written between 1615 and 1645 by Nilakantha and regarded as a work of the highest authority in Gujarat and North Konkan, and (3) *Manvarthamuktāvali*, a commentary on the *Manusmṛti* written by Kulluka between 1150 and 1300 (1 B.S.D.A. 14).[10]

While mentioning these classical law books, Borradaile expressed a sort of distrust for the Vyavasthas written by the Shastris on the grounds that 'scarcely one of the Vyuvusthas of the Shastrees, recorded in these reports, fairly quotes the very works of the authors to which it refers, and in very few instances is even the Chapter named'. Seeing 'no security against partiality or wilful misstatement' on the part of the Shastris, H. Borradaile was led to consult the original law books with the assistance of his own *paṇḍit*.[11] As a result of his strenuous efforts in comparing the opinions of the Shastris with the original legal texts, his compilation of reports on the decision was greatly augmented by detailed notes referring to the portion of the original sources on which the opinions of the Shastris seemed to depend.

This heavy reliance on classical laws of Shastras in preference to the opinions of the court Shastris thus observable with the British judges played an important role in shaping the clear-cut profile of the Brahmanically or textually normed Hindu. This process actually helped produce the somewhat homogenized Hindu from the divergent realities of the inhabitants in pre-colonial India. This is traceable in cases adjudicated by the Bombay Sadr Divani Adalat during the early part of the nineteenth century.

In those cases that concerned the favourite topics of the Shastras, such as marriage and inheritance, the laws of Shastras were literally applied. In one such case concerning a marriage contract, (the caste of the litigants is not mentioned in the report, though it seems to have been a Gujarati merchant caste judging from the names of the litigants), a 'Mungnee' (*māgṇī*, betrothal) lacking the consent of the daughter's father was held to be invalid. The Shastris of the court gave the opinion that 'by the Laws of the Shastr', 'while a father is alive and sound in mind, he is the proper authority to sanction a contract for the marriage of his children'. The compiler of reports, H. Borradaile, attributed this opinion to the *Mitākṣarā* (First Book, Vivah Prakarana) which reads: 'Let a virgin be given away by her Father, Paternal Grandfather, Brother, Paternal and Maternal Uncle, and Mother, in their proper order, the next who is unblemished, in default of the one above him' (1 B.S.D.A. 14). In one case of inheritance which was contended between the widows of two brothers (their caste is Beesa Modia Vania), one leaving a son while the other none, the court Shastri stated that the only son was the son of both the brothers, so that he had the right to inherit the property of his deceased uncle in preference to his uncle's widow, so long as the family remained an undivided family. H. Borradaile grounded this opinion on the *Manusmṛti* which reads: 'If any brother, sprung from one [father], one have a son, Manu has declared them all to have male offspring through that son' [12](1 B.S.D.A. 154). In another case of inheritance, the family was held to be undivided on the grounds that 'according to the Mitakshura and Muyookh [*Vyavahāramayūkha*] the following acts must be performed separately to constitute a Division: first, Dressing of victuals; second, Religious ceremonies; third, The Shradh or annual funeral ceremonies; fourth, Houses, Lands &c. must be divided; fifth, Deeds of Partition should be executed'. In this case, the authority given by Borradaile was the *Yājñavalkyasmṛti* quoted in the chapter of Daya Vibhaga of the *Mitākṣarā* and *Vyavahāramayūkha* (1 B.S.D.A. 207).

The disability of a blind person of Beesa Vayada Vania caste to inherit was also literally upheld by the decision of the Bombay Sadr Divani Adalat based on the authority of the *Manusmṛti* (Chapter 9, Verse 202. In Bühler 1886, Verse 201) which prescribes: 'Eunuchs and outcastes, [persons] born blind or deaf, the insane, idiots and the dumb, as well as those deficient in any organ [of action or sensation], receive no share'[13] (1 B.S.D.A. 411).

In these cases, laws of Shastras were strictly followed with the result that there was a gradual spread of Brahmanical or textual norms of Shastras into various strata of Indian society, among whom Shastras were theretofore almost unknown.

Whenever there was a discrepancy between laws of Shastras and the customs of a particular caste, the courts were inclined to follow the former. In one such case of inheritance contended between a daughter of a deceased man and her stepmother of the Shrimali Brahman caste, the court 'resolved first to ascertain the laws of the Shastrees [Shastras?] on the point, and then to see how far the custom of the Cast differed from it'. The Shastris of the court gave the opinion that 'the wife or stepmother was sole Heiress during the term of her natural life' on the authority of the *Mitākṣarā* (leaf 55th, page 2nd). In rebuttal, the daughter claimed that there existed a caste custom contrary to the law of Shastras on this point. 'The Court considering the Rules of Cast proved to differ from the law, asked their Pundits [Shastris] whether the Hindoo Law or the custom of the Cast was to be upheld.' To this the Shastris answered that though both were equally valid, the 'disposition under the law, was in their opinion the best'. Accordingly the court decided in favour of the stepmother (1 B.S.D.A. 384).[14]

In another similar case concerning a breach of marriage contract, the father of a girl whose marriage had not been consummated, sought divorce of his daughter on the ground that her husband married another woman for the purpose of cohabitation. In this case, the court at first had found that the custom of the caste (Lewa Kunbi) did not agree with the law of Shastras. Through further examination, however, 'fresh evidence' of a caste custom agreeable to the law of Shastras was found. The court, accordingly, decided that the father of the girl 'had no right, either by the Laws of Shastr or Customs of his Cast, to demand a Divorce for his daughter' (1 B.S.D.A. 59).[15]

In the cases of such legal versus customary discrepancies, the courts either held rigidly for the prevalence of a particular custom among a caste or tried to bring the caste customs in question into line with the laws of

Shastras, such that these laws began to be adopted widely among various castes.

In yet another type of case involving a point at issue for which laws of Shastras lacked any prescription, a sort of pseudo-classical law was formulated through decisions of the civil courts. In one such case of adoption of an 'only son' of a Dasa Oswal Vania caste, the Shastris of the court 'allowed that the Law of exclusion of the only son from the privilege of adoption, related to Brahmans alone, and Plaintiff being a Shoodru, was not bound by it'. On this seemingly classical distinction between the twice-born and the once-born in the case of adoption of an 'only son', however, no authority of the *Mitākṣarā*, *Manusmṛti* and *Vyavahāramayūkha* could be found by the compiler, H. Borradaile (1 B.S.D.A. 75). Still, this type of make-believe distinction between the twice-born and the once-born began to prevail in the civil courts during the course of the nineteenth century, resulting in the formation of a pseudo-classical tradition of law.[16]

Through legalization of this pseudo-classical distinction between the twice-born and the once-born, the Brahmanical or textual norm with its own ideology of discrimination and unequal distribution of human value began to be shared among various strata of Indian society in an ever greater degree under British colonial rule than in pre-colonial India. Thus, British colonial rule was in a sense responsible for transfiguring the textual or bookish discriminatory system into social reality by making Shastras the basis of legal decisions.

The only cases in which arbitrary reliance on laws of Shastras cannot be found are those pertaining to caste rules on such matters as excommunication and commensality. In one case of excommunication from a caste, the appellants' prayer for the case being referred to the decision of the members of the same caste residing in other parts of Gujarat was complied with in the Bombay Sadr Divani Adalat under the express condition that their decision as to readmission to the caste should be final and binding on the parties in this suit (1 B.S.D.A. 35. cf. Chapters 4 and 5). In another case relating to the commensality rule of a caste, the Bombay Sadr Divani Adalat dismissed the suit, 'observing that according to the verbal opinion of their Shastrees the consent of the majority of a Cast, at least, if not of all the members, was necessary to make any act or Rule binding among them' (1 B.S.D.A. 108. cf. Chapters 4 and 5)

In these cases, the majority opinion of the caste members was upheld by the court without any reference to the laws of Shastras. This seems to have led to the renowned caste autonomy policy of the Bombay government, which was formulated by the so-called Elphinstone Code of 1827.[17]

It was in this way that a system of law based mainly on the laws of Shastras was gradually framed through the decisions of the civil courts established by the British in India. This legal system concerned the so-called family law pertaining to such matters as marriage, divorce, inheritance, adoption, maintenance and guardianship. This system of family law is commonly known as Hindu Law or Anglo-Hindu Law which was not statutory in nature, but was the customary law or case law formed by the decisions of the civil courts.

The formation of this legal system during the early phase of British colonial rule in turn led to the emergence of Brahmanically or textually normed Hindu, that is to say, the unified, standardized and homogenized 'Hindu' from the disintegrated, irregular and heterogeneous social realities in pre-colonial India. To this unified, standardized and homogeneous 'Hindu' corresponded the Brahmanical, textual and normative 'Hinduism' arising from the high esteem accorded to the Brahmans and Brahmanical learning by early British administrators in total disregard for the religious diversity and complexity that actually existed on the Indian subcontinent (Sontheimer 1991;King 1999: 98-708). The term *Hindu Dharma*, which is now in common use, must have been the pseudo-classical translation of this English word 'Hinduism', as there had been no word like *Hindu Dharma* in pre-colonial India (Rajvade Śake 1838:49-53).

Conclusion

Thus, the framework within which 'Hindu' has begun to function as the term to express self-identity or collective consciousness of being the Hindu was prepared in the early phase of British colonial rule. Once this framework began to work, people were compelled to confess themselves as the Hindu and act as the Hindu, only if they did not think themselves as Muslims or Christians, though they had never thought themselves in such a manner in the pre-colonial age. Put another way, the inhabitants of the Indian subcontinent were forced to adjust themselves to this dichotomous framework of Hindu-Muslim under British colonial rule. The term Hindu in this subjugated adjustment to the Hindu-Muslim dichotomy in turn was transformed by the last decades of the nineteenth century into the positive expression of self-identity of the people who did not think themselves Muslims or Christians.

Notes

1 This process is recorded in a document as follows:

> That the Court of Directors having, by their Letter to the President and Council at Fort William, dated the 28th of August 1771, signified their Determination "to stand forth as Duan, and by the Agency of the Company's Servants to take upon themselves the entire Care and Management of the Revenues"– and having therefore authorized and required the President and Council to divest Mahomed Reza Cawn, and every Person employed by him, or in Conjunction with him, or acting under his Influence, of any further Charge or Direction in the Business of the Collections–.... the President and Council took the said Orders into Consideration, and have removed Mahomed Reza Cawn from the Office of Naib Duan for the Province of Bengal, and Shitabroy from the same Office for the Province of Bahar; and issued, at the same Time, a Proclamation at Moorshedabad and at Patna, advertising the Removal of those Officers, and of the Abolition of the Office of Naib Duan of the Provinces; and they directed the Chief and Council of Revenue at Moorshedabad, and Chief and Council at Patna, to take Charge, for the present, of the Office of Duan of their respective Provinces, until a proper Plan could be settled for the Management of that important Business;... (Sixth Report from the Committee of Secrecy appointed to enquire into The State of The East India Company, 26 April 1773, in *The Reports from Committees of the House of Commons 1715-1801*, IV 299).

2 Seventh Report from the Committee of Secrecy appointed to enquire into The State of The East India Company, 6 May 1773, *The Reports from Committees of the House of Commons 1715-1801*, IV 329.

3 *The Reports from Committees of the House of Commons 1715-1801*, IV 326-27. The quotation from the instructions in this extract is not perfectly correct. The original sentence runs as follows:

> ... that it is your part to endeavour to reform all these corruptions which have encroached on the primitive rights of both the Mahomedans and Hindoos; particularly by abolishing the arbitrary imposition of fines, and recommending all in your power the more equitable method of arbitration.

4 Report from the Committee on Petitions relative to the Administration of

Justice in India, 8 May 1781, *The Reports from Committees of the House of Commons 1715-1801*, V 37.

5 Ibid. 41.

6 Warren Hastings's Letter to Lord Mansfield, Chief Justice of England, dated 21 March 1774, Gleig 1841: 399-400.

7 The relevant portion of the document runs as follows:

> The Council of Revenue, in a Letter to the President and Council, May 1772, inclosed a Remonstrance of the Naib Duan, respecting that Part of the Instructions in the Last Letter of the President and Council, which directed, that in Cases of the Inheritance of the Gentoos the Magistrates should be assisted by the Bramins of the Cast to which the Parties belong; in that Memorial, the Naib Duan strongly remonstrates against allowing a Bramin to be called in to the Decision of any Matter of Inheritance, or other Dispute of Gentoos. That since the Establishment of the Mahometan Dominion in Hindostan, the Bramins had never been admitted to any such Jurisdiction: That to order a Magistrate of the Faith to decide in Conjunction with a Bramin would be repugnant to the Rules of the Faith, and an Innovation peculiarly improper in a Country under the Dominion of a Mussulman Emperor: That where the Matter in Dispute can be decided by a Reference to Bramins, no Interruption had ever been given to that Mode of Decision; But that, where they think fit to resort to the established Judicatures of the Country, they must submit to a Decision according to the Rules and Principles of that Law, by which alone these Courts are authorized to judge: That there would be the greatest Absurdity in such an Association of Judicature, because the Bramin would determine according to the Precepts and Usages of his Cast, and the Magistrates must decide according to those of the Mahometan Law: That in many Instances the Rules of the Gentoo and Mussulman Laws, even with respect to Inheritance and Succession, differ materially from each other (Letter from the Council of Revenue at Moorshedabad to the President and Council, May 1772, Seventh Report of the Committee of Secrecy appointed to enquire into The State of The East India Company, 6 May 1773, *The Reports from Committees of the House of Commons 1715-1801*, IV 329-30).

8 Report from the Committee on Petition relative to the Administration of Justice in India, 8 May 1781, *The Reports from Committees of the House of Commons 1715-1801*, V 38.

9 A Plan for the Administration of Justice extracted from the Proceedings

of the Committee of Circuit, 15 August 1772, Seventh Report from the Committee of Secrecy appointed to enquire into The State of The East India Company, 6 May 1773, *The Reports from Committees of the House of Commons 1715-1801*, IV 350.

10 Cf. Kane: III 878 and the Chronological Table.

11 The relevant portion in 1 B.S.D.A. 14 runs as follows:

> It will be observed that scarcely one of the Vyuvusthas of the Shastrees, recorded in these Reports, fairly quotes the very words of the authors to which it refers, and in very few instances is even the Chapter named. The Vyuvusthas appear therefore at first sight to be opinions on the case, worked up with the Shastree's own views of Equity and Custom, as well as Law, instead of a Quotation of the writings of Hindoo Law authorities bearing on the point at issue, the applicability of which the Judge of the Case is to be left to decide upon. He might be assisted by the remarks of the Shastree in his Vyuvustha upon these passages, but without such quotation, there is no security against partiality or wilful misstatement, while few would have leisure, if they possessed the means, for examining their correctness by a reference to the standard works on the subject in our own language. I was led by these circumstances to analize the Law opinions I met with, by referring, with the assistance of my own Pundit, to the authors upon whose works they are said to be framed....

12 Chapter 9, Verse 182. Translation by G. Bühler (*The Laws of Manu* in the *Sacred Books of the East*). The number of verses (clauses) referred to in this chapter are those of Bühler's.

13 Translation by Bühler.

14 One passage of this decision runs as follows:

> In opposition to this, the Appellant (the daughter) called six members of the Cast, who deposed that the Childless daughter alone, and not the second wife of a Sreemalee Brahmun deceased without male issue, would succeed to his Estate, that the wife retained her Pulla [*pallum̤*, dowry] and obtained a maintenance, and might live with her own father, but possessed no right to share. In proof of it they named three or four instances of daughters succeeding before the widow.
>
> The Court held that the evidence adduced in favor of the particular custom of the Cast had by no means established the position of Appellant that the Sreemalee Brahmuns entertained such a general usage in respect to the point at issue as would warrant the Court's

departure from the law of succession laid down in the Shastru, declaring the Widow to be the Heiress.

15 Members of the Lewa Kunbi in Bombay answered the questions put by the Bombay Sadr Divani Adalat as follows:

> (*Question*) Can a person, having already married a Wife under 11 years of age, but without mental or bodily defect, marry a second Wife, on the grounds of the small stature, and tender age of the first?
> (*Answer*) It is not the custom in our Cast to send a Girl of 11 years of age to her husband's house, and unless she has been sent there, her Husband cannot marry another.
> (*Question*) If he can, may the first Wife claim a divorce from her husband in consequence of the second marriage, or demand a dissolution of that second marriage?
> (*Answer*) If there be no bodily defect in the first Wife, but the husband in consequence of some quarrel between their relations, marry another, he may allow the first Wife to divorce, and he should repay the expenses incurred by her.

Members of the same caste in Kaira and Moondah, however, gave different answers to these same questions. This was recognized by the Bombay Sadr Divani Adalat as the 'fresh evidence' to disprove the prevalence of the alleged caste custom.

16 Among these pseudo-classical laws might be included the adoption cases of a son of one's sister or one's daughter. In these cases, the fundamental line of decisions was that among the twice-born castes, the adoption of one's sister's son or one's daughter's son was not permitted, while among the once-born castes it was permissible. See the following decisions of the Bombay High Court: 4 B.H.C.R. (A.C.J.) 130 , 8 B.H.C.R. (A.C.J.) 67, 12 B.H.C.R. (A.C.J.) 364, 3 B. 273, 6 B. 524 and 19 B. 428. In 12 B.H.C.R. (A.C.J.) 364, as an example, it was stated that the 'adoption of a sister's son, though not permitted to the three superior classes, is declared to be "the most proper for Sudras" ', citing merely *Vyavahāramayūkha* (ch. iv, sec. v, 11, 36) as its authority. On the laws of adoption in the classical law books (Shastras) in general, see Derrett 1977: 25-83 et al.

17 As to the caste autonomy policy of the Bombay government, see Chapter 5.

12

The Transformation of People's Self-Identity under British Colonial Rule with Special Reference to Western India

Introduction

In the pre-colonial age the people of the Indian subcontinent held several self-identities, that is, the collective consciousness of constituting 'ourselves' as opposed to 'others'. Conspicuous among these were the regional or ethno-regional identity, religio-cultural identity, the political identity, each of which presupposed the existence of respective 'others', that is to say, regional (ethno-regional) 'others', religio-cultural 'others', and political 'others'.

In the latter half of the eighteenth and early part of the nineteenth centuries when the British had been expanding their colonial territories, the people of the Indian subcontinent encountered another type of 'others', that is, the British. They attempted to accommodate the British within the pre-existing framework of distinguishing 'others' from themselves. The British were, however, the unexperienced 'others' who exhibited characteristics outreaching the pre-existing framework of their 'ourselves-others' consciousness. As a result of this, the framework itself had to be transformed to a considerable degree so as to incorporate the British within it. This must have brought about some unexpected turn in the self-identity of the people and would have influenced the subsequent course of the socio-political history of India.

This chapter addresses this question with special reference to late seventeenth-to-early twentieth century western India or, more precisely, Maharashtra, where the Maratha kingdom and the Bombay government ruled in turn, drawing mainly on medieval and modern Marathi documents.

Manifold Construction of Self-Identity in Pre-colonial Western India

Regional or Ethno-regional Self-Identity

Historically, the collective consciousness of constituting 'ourselves' has become most acute when the very existence of this collectivity was jeopardized. For the Maratha state (1674-1818) the most crucial period was that from 1689 when Sambhaji, the second king, was captured and killed by the Mughals to 1707 when Aurangzeb, the sixth Mughal emperor, died and Shahu, the son of Sambhaji, was released from captivity in the Mughal camp and returned to Maharashtra to be enthroned as the Maratha king. In this critical period for the Marathas, Rajaram, the stepbrother of Sambhaji and the third king, dispatched a large number of written appeals and deeds of assurance to the Maratha leaders remaining in Maharashtra from his refuge in Jinji (Senji) in faraway south India. As an example, he sent a written appeal to Jedhe Deshmukh of Bhor in 1690 that runs as follows:

> This is *Mahārāṣṭrarājya*. You have been enduring a stomachache [*poṭṭiḍīka*, meaning hardship] for the interest of this kingdom.... You should collect armed forces, remain vigilant and do every service to the king [*svāmīkārya*] you find necessary.... Aurangzeb has made the people of Maharashtra [*Mahārāṣṭraloka*] Muslims. Netoji Raje ... and some Brahmans were also polluted [converted, in Marathi '*bāṭvile*'].
>
> (M.I.S. XV 282)

This consciousness of *Mahārāṣṭrarājya* (the kingdom of Maharashtra) or *Mahārāṣṭraloka* (people of Maharashtra) was ever strengthened when the Maratha state was forced to face the menace of the Mughals invading from north India. They called the Mughals then *tāmra* or *tāmbra* (more properly *tāmra mukhī*) indicating persons or monkeys whose faces (*mukha*) were as red as burnished copper (*tāmra*). To the people of Maharashtra the Mughals must have looked as strange a people as red-faced monkeys. In opposition to these *tāmra* or *tāmbra*, they identified themselves with *Mahārāṣṭraloka* and their kingdom *Mahārāṣṭrarājya*. Rajaram's deed of assurance granted to Nagoji Mane Deshmukh of Mhesvad exemplifies this reading:

> You had formerly taken sides with the *tāmbra* [Aurangzeb]. You,

> however, reconsidered that this kingdom [*svāmīceṃ rājya*] was the land of gods [*devatābhūmi*] which must not be troubled by the *tāmbra*, and that *Mahārāṣṭradharma* [spirit of Maharashtra] should be preserved and this kingdom should prosper. With this intention in mind,... you proceeded to the king's palace in Chandi [Jinji], Karnataka.
>
> (S.G.R.A.O. Sanads and Letters V 9)

Rajaram's *vṛtti-patra* bestowing the *vṛtti* (*vatan*) of Sardeshmukh to Amritrao Nimbalkar Deshmukh of Phaltan runs in the same vein as follows:

> The *tāmbra* Aurangzeb invaded the South (*dakṣṇa*) and occupied Vijapur and Bhagnagar. Hearing this, the king [Rajaram] sought refuge in Karnataka. Since then, you had been serving the *tāmbra* [Aurangzeb]. [You, however, reconsidered that:] 'This kingdom [*svāmīceṃ rājya*] was the land of gods and Brahmans [*devabrāhmaṇaṃcī bhūmi*] which should prosper, and that *Mahārāṣṭradharma* should be preserved.' ... When the *tāmbra* advanced to Chandi [Jinji] and predominated in the region, you proceeded from your country [*deśa*] to Chandi with one brother to fight against the *tāmbra* and defeated them.
>
> (S.G.R.A.O. Sanads and Letters V 11)

This identity represented by such terms as *Mahārāṣṭrarājya*, *Mahārāṣṭraloka* and *Mahārāṣṭradharma* can be defined, without doubt, as the regional identity in so far as the term *Mahārāṣṭra* indicated.[1] Further in another document such terms as *Mahraṭarājya* (kingdom of the Marathas) and *Mahraṭaloka* (Maratha people) were employed in place of *Mahārāṣṭrarājya* and *Mahārāṣṭraloka* respectively (M.I.S. XV 347). This means that the people of Maharashtra, at least those of the ruling class, identified themselves and the people of Maharashtra in general as the Maratha meaning the Maharashtrians.[2]

Taking into consideration the term *tāmra* (*tāmbra*) in use here for denoting their opponents, however, this self-identity seems to be better interpreted as an ethno-regional one. The term *tāmra* (*tāmbra*) reflected their sense of physical or ethnic difference from the Mughals who looked too reddish (perhaps by reason of their fair-complexion) for them. Their regional identity being thus closely interrelated with their sense of ethnic foreignness of the outlanders, this self-identity as opposed to *tāmra* or *tāmbra* could be defined as the ethno-regional self-identity.[3] Further, the term *Mahārāṣṭradharma* seemed to express a sort of ethno-regional spirituality or ethos distinguishable from those of the outlanders though the concrete substance of this term is yet to be ascertained.

Religio-cultural Self-Identity

Such expressions as *devatābhūmi* (land of gods) and *devabrāhmaṇaṃcī bhūmi* (land of gods and Brahmans) found in the aforecited deeds of Rajaram denote that medieval Maharashtrians or Marathas held religio-cultural self-identification with their land (*bhūmi*) as a 'holy land'. This identity seems to have placed the Muslim on its opposite side though not categorically so indicated in the above-cited documents. Based on this identity, conversion to Islam was held to be an unholy act. This is exemplified by the following expression in Rajaram's letter to Jedhe Deshmukh cited above: 'Netoji Raje... and some Brahmans were also polluted (converted, *bāṭvile*).' Another deed of assurance granted also to Jedhe Deshmukh stated that Aurangzeb polluted (converted, *bāṭvile*) *Mahraṭaloka* (Maratha people) including some Brahmans (M.I.S. XV 347). The Marathi term *bāṭviṇeṃ* (verb) used here for indicating forcible conversion to Islam literally means 'to pollute or defile someone'. This means that for medieval Maharashtrians 'to be converted to Islam' was nothing less than 'to be polluted or defiled'. Thus, a convert to Islam was designated in the medieval Marathi documents as *bāṭgā* (the polluted) in the case of the male gender and *bāṭgī* (the polluted) of the female gender. Such social associations with *bāṭgā* or *bāṭgī* as matrimony (*lagnavyavahāra*) and commensality (*annavyavahāra*) were deemed to constitute a grave *doṣa* (crime/sin). The following case of *prāyaścitta* (purification ritual of *doṣa*) amply testifies to this.

Ranoji Patil, the headman of the village Sonke in Vai District, purchased a female slave (*baṭīka*). She lived in his home for four years at which time it turned out that she had had a commensal relationship (*annavyavahāra*) with a female convert to Islam (*bāṭgī musalmān*) before she was purchased by Ranoji. Thus, Ranoji Patil was ordered by the government to undergo *prāyaścitta* (penance) to purify his *doṣa* (crime/sin) accrued to him from social association (*saṃsarga*) with a criminal (sinner), that is, the female slave (S.S.R.P.D. I 399. 1753-54). This means that by living together with a person who had committed the crime (sin) of breaking the commensal rule by taking a meal with a convert to Islam, the crime (sin) of the criminal (sinner) was deemed to have been transmitted to other persons of the home in which the criminal (sinner) lived.

While the terms *bāṭgā* and *bāṭgī* indicated converts to Islam in general, the term (verb) in medieval Marathi documents unmistakably denoting forcible conversion to Islam was *bhraṣṭa karṇeṃ* (v.t.; in the case of v.i., *bhraṣṭa hoṇeṃ*). This verb *bhraṣṭa karṇeṃ* meant 'to make someone morally degraded or fallen from the norm (*dharma*)'. In one case, a Putaji Wadghar was taken prisoner by the Mughals in Surat, south Gujarat. He was then forcibly converted to Islam by the Mughals (*Mogalāneṃ yās bhraṣṭa kelā*). He was released after six years' detention in the Mughal camp. On his return home, it was decided by the government that he could be purified (*śuddha*) according to the provision of Shastra (classical law books) as he had been forcibly made fallen (from the norm), namely, converted to Islam, and not of his own free will (S.S.R.P.D. I 373. 1721-22).[4]

Thus, there existed in medieval Maharashtra such an idea that voluntary conversion to Islam was simply an act of polluting oneself of one's own free will while forcible conversion to Islam constituted an Islamic conduct of making a non-Muslim morally degraded or fallen from his own norm. Placing the Muslim or Islam with the opposing implication, the concept of *devatābhūmi* (land of gods) or *devabrāhmaṇaṃcī bhūmi* (land of gods and Brahmans) functioned as a religio-cultural identity for medieval Maharashtrians that implied the pure and divinely normed land.

Political Self-Identity

The term representing the political self-identity of the people in medieval Maharashtra was *Svarājya* (land under their own rule) as opposed to *Moglāī* (land under Mughal rule). These dichotomous terms seem to have come in common use from around the 1710s. This is attested to by the notification of the Maratha government addressed to the Deshmukh and Deshpande of Dahiganv District. It runs as follows:

> Sidoji Mane Deshmukh was in possession of the *ṭhāṇas* [soldier station] of Atpadi and Mhasvad then situated in *Moglāī*. When the *Pātshāh* [Mughal emperor] invested the [Maratha] king [*svāmī*] with *Svarājya*, Sidoji Mane pledged allegiance to the *svāmī* and surrendered the *ṭhāṇas* including that of Atpadi to the *svāmī*.
>
> (S.C.S. V 863. 1718)

The terms *Svarājya* and *Moglāī* thus indicated, in its simplest meaning, the territorial division between the Mughal empire and the Maratha kingdom. This is exemplified by many other passages of medieval Marathi documents such as follows:

> The *jāgīr* village of the Harishchandra Fort was situated in *Moglāī* when the fort was under *Moglāī*. Now, the aforementioned fort has come under *Svarājya*.
>
> (S.S.R.P.D. VIII 32. 1747-48)

These dichotomous terms of *Svarājya-Moglāī*, however, contained by implication a sort of cultural or ethical meaning as well. In other words, *Svarājya-Moglāī* reflected the values of the people in medieval Maharashtra. The prolonged dispute between the Mahars and the *vatandār* Joshis of Paundkhor District served as a good example of this. In 1784, the Mahars of this district appealed to the district official to order the Brahman Joshis to officiate at a marriage ceremony of the Mahars with which the district official complied taking a previous case into consideration. As the Joshis disobeyed his order for this purpose, he fined them. Against this the Joshis petitioned the government (Peshva government of the Maratha kingdom) for its intervention stating that it was not the custom for the Brahman Joshis to officiate at a marriage of the untouchables. After inquiring into the case, the Peshva government decided in favour of the Joshis and reprimanded the district official as follows:

> Once two to four thousand Mahars serving in hill forts as guards and in villages as village servants assembled together and created a clamour claiming that the Joshis should officiate at a marriage of Mahars. They made a representation of this purpose to Aurangzeb [who was ruling this part of the country at that time]. Aurangzeb accordingly decided that it was not mandatory for the Joshis to officiate at a marriage of the Mahars taking the long-standing custom into consideration. This custom has since then continued to this day.... Even under the *Moglāī* administration a new custom [of making the Joshis officiate at a marriage of the untouchables] had not been introduced by replacing the long-standing one, such that it is improper under *Svarājya* to insist on enforcing the new custom.
>
> (S.S.R.P.D. VIII 1132. 1785-86)

This document indicates that the political self-identity of the people in medieval Maharashtra represented by the term *Svarājya* as opposed to *Moglāī* included by implication the idea that *Svarājya* should be more tradition-abiding or, put another way, ethically higher than *Moglāī*. Thus, the term *Svarājya* gave expression to the values cherished by the people of medieval Maharashtra.

The British as Unexperienced 'Others'

Accommodating the British in the Pre-existing Framework of Self-Identity

As a result of the third Anglo-Maratha War in 1818, most of western India was placed under the administration of the East India Company (Company Sarkar) constituting the Bombay Presidency. This means that the opportunity for the common people to encounter British people was greatly enhanced. The people then attempted to accommodate the British within the pre-existing framework of distinguishing 'others' from themselves. The Marathi terms serving this purpose were *tāmra mukhī* (the red-faced) and *bāṭyā* (the polluted) corresponding to *tāmbra* (*tāmra*) and *bāṭgā*/*bāṭgī* which used to be applied to the northern invaders (the Mughals) and converts to Islam respectively in pre-colonial Maharashtra.[5]

This is exemplified by many passages in various Marathi periodicals and books published in the nineteenth century. To wit, in a letter from a reader to the editor of the *Dñanodaya* (The Dawn of Knowledge), a Christian periodical then published from Bombay, the writer observed as follows:

> Brahmans are claiming that as the present being the *Kali Yuga* [the iron age], the *tāmra mukhī* [the red-faced, meaning the British] who have come here across the oceans occupied this country, and that the authority of the Brahman has entirely ceased to exist for that reason. They are now worrying that they will lose even the means of livelihood.
>
> (*Dñanodaya* 1 May 1849. 168)

Thus, the people attempted to incorporate the British within exactly the same framework that they had used for distinguishing the northern invaders (the Mughals) from themselves in earlier times. Again for them, the British looked too reddish and as ethnically different from themselves as the Mughals.[6]

In the same vein, a convert to Christianity was designated as *bāṭyā* (the polluted), a term derived from the Marathi verb *bāṭṇeṃ* (to become polluted), in the nineteenth century Bombay Presidency, precisely as a convert to Islam had been termed *bāṭgā* or *bāṭgī* in pre-colonial Maharashtra. This is convincingly attested to by passages from Baba Padmanji's autobiography, *Aruṇodaya* (The Dawn). Baba Padmanji was born a Kasar (brazier caste) in Belgaum in the southern Deccan in 1831, but later in 1854 he was baptized in the London Missionary Society's church in Belgaum. His autobiography minutely recorded his passage to Christianity.

In 1849, he was admitted to a school managed by the Scottish Free Church in Bombay (formally called the General Assembly's Institution). As to what he had experienced in his first few days in this school, he wrote:

> Mr. Govind Narayan decided to admit me into the second class of the School Division. The master of this class was a Brahman. The boy who had introduced me to this school was in the first class. Again another boy of the Sutar caste who was living in the lane where my marriage had been celebrated was also in the first class. These two friends of mine insisted on my studying in their class. The master of the first class, however, was... Mr. Narayan Sheshadri. As he was a 'polluted' [converted, *bāṭlele*] Brahman, I felt it not proper to study under his guidance.
>
> (Padmanji 1879: 64)

Narayan Sheshadri was a well-known Brahman convert to Christianity who was baptized in Bombay in 1843 creating a clamorous happening involving entire communities in Bombay. His conversion triggered a prolonged dispute especially in the Brahman communities of Bombay which were divided into two parties. One party was, so to speak, the *sanātana dharma* (orthodoxy, *sanātana* meaning 'eternal') party that opposed the purification of Shripat Sheshadri, the younger brother of Narayan, who was assumed to have been polluted by living together with his brother, a Christian convert. The other party was the 'reformist' (*sudhārṇāvādī*) party that attempted to perform the purification ceremony (*prāyaścitta*) on Shripat (Navalkar 1893: 6-8; Valimbe 1962: 208-60; Wagle 1999: 130-56). It is thus little wonder that Baba Padmanji held an unfavourable opinion of Narayan Sheshadri. Still, however, it is rather amazing that such a boy as Baba Padmanji who willingly became admitted into a school managed by a Christian mission described a convert to Christianity as 'polluted' (*bāṭlele*).[7]

In another passage of his autobiography, he wrote as to what he had felt when he had been initiated into a secret society named the Paramhamsa Mandali (or Paramhamsa Sabha) in 1851 as follows:

> Through friendship with a friend [who was a member of the committee of the Paramhamsa Mandali] I was initiated into the Paramhamsa Mandali.... One day they [members of the Mandali] heatedly engaged me (and one of my friends of the same opinion) in debate against the caste system. When we admitted that the caste system was false, and said that we were prepared to destroy the caste system, they asked us if we were willing to destroy it before their eyes. We answered yes. While our discussion was still in progress, one of them quietly went out of the room and in no time returned with some biscuits [*biskuteṃ*] in hand. He placed the biscuits before us saying: 'Take this, if you think the caste system is false.' We answered: 'You take it first, then we will take it.' They accordingly ate biscuits, as a result of which it became mandatory for us to eat biscuits. It is difficult to say how embarrassed I got at that time. My body began to tremble and sweat flowed in streams. I felt that my mother would turn me out of the house, when I would return home. I was in a plight as if a mountain had fallen on me. I felt as if I had lost all members of my family and had been ousted from my caste only to wander out. I feared people would call me '*bāṭyā*' (the polluted) for I had never until then eaten a bread-biscuit [*pāvbiskuteṃ*]. My friend was also very bewildered but he ate one or two pieces of biscuit mustering up courage.... They then brought a glass filled with water and made us drink from the glass (*glās*).
>
> (Padmanji 1879: 94-95)

The Paramhamsa Mandali was a secret society active at that time in the Bombay Presidency, especially in Bombay, whose tenet was somewhat atheistic and radically anti-traditional (Priyolkar 1966). The reason why the members of the Mandali asked Baba Padmanji to eat biscuits as a proof of his seriousness in destroying the caste system was that at that time it was a taboo of the caste system to eat such eatables as biscuits since biscuits were 'polluted' European foods. So also was the case with a glass (*glās*). Drinking water from a glass, a 'polluted' European vessel, precisely amounted to eating biscuits so that it constituted the crime (sin) of violating the caste rule. Thus, in the initiation (*praveśak vidhi*) of the Paramhamsa Mandali, the candidates were made to eat a piece of bread or a biscuit and to drink water or milk from a glass as a pledge of defying the caste rule.[8] Baba Padmanji was deadly struck with horror of his being called '*bāṭyā*' (the polluted) as he was about to eat the biscuit and drink water from the glass. For him at that time such acts as eating a biscuit and drinking water from a glass seemed to amount even to conversion to Christianity.[9]

Thus, the people of the Bombay Presidency attempted to accommodate the British within the pre-existing framework of their self-identity by employing such terms as *tāmra mukhī* and *bāṭyā* exactly as they had once attempted to incorporate the northern invaders (the Mughals) and a convert to Islam within the framework of their self-identity using such terms as *tāmbra* (*tāmra*) and *bāṭgā*/*bāṭgī*.

The British as the 'Cow Slaughterer'

It turned out, however, that the British constituted an entity that outreached the pre-existing framework for distinguishing 'others' from themselves. This was exemplified by the aggressive stance of the Christian missionaries sent to India by Protestant organizations such as the London Missionary Society, Church Missionary Society and Scottish Missionary Society all of which were established in the 1790s being stimulated by a sort of missionary enthusiasm of the time.

The East India Company had prohibited Christian missionaries from entering its Indian territories fearing that their activities might offend the feeling of Indian people. The missionary enthusiasm then prevailing in Great Britain, however, moved the Parliament (House of Commons) to insert a clause in the Charter Act of 1813 that lifted the ban on missionary activity in India. From then onwards, many Protestant organizations sent their missionaries to various parts of India.[10]

In western India the Scottish Missionary Society's mission had been active since the 1820s. Well-known Scottish misssionaries such as John Wilson and Robert Nesbit travelled widely in various parts of western India to spread the Christian faith by preaching in spoken Marathi language and distributing the tracts written in simple Marathi. They used to record their activities in a sort of diary commonly known as the missionary journal that was to be sent to the headquarters in Edinburgh in Scotland. These missionary journals were of great use for the purpose of knowing the actual activities of Christian missionaries and the response of the people to them or to Christianity. The missionary journal of Robert Nesbit written while on a tour in the Deccan preaching in the areas around Pune in February-March 1834 (*Oriental Christian Spectator* V-5, 156-65) serves as a good example of this.

In his preaching he often stressed the miserable state of Indian people by placing it in marked contrast to the God-blessedness of the British that had been testified, he believed, by the very fact of their acquiring India as a colony. Put another way, he thought that British colonial rule itself served to prove the superiority of Christianity over Indian religions. He wrote in his aforementioned missionary journal:

> Kati [name of a village] evening of the 3rd and morning of the 4th February: The principal persons of this village were full of complaints against the English government, and objected murder and systematic spoliation as its great characteristics. After clearing away the question of the slaughter of cows and criminals, I asked them whether God had no reason for bringing upon them the poverty and distress under which they were suffering. To this they very readily replied that they were suffering for their sins and that the English were enjoying the fruit of merit [*puṇya*] which they had acquired in a former birth. I then told them that the only likely way of bettering their conditions was to repent of their sins and turn to the God whom they had forsaken. They acknowledged that the gods they now worshipped were not worth a rush—that they absolutely quailed before the Englishman, and could make no opposition to his encroaches and attacks. These confessions they made, not with shame and sorrow, but with anger and bitterness; and I fear that the announcement of the Gospel of grace and peace had but little, if any, towards soothing their mind and sweetening their disposition.[11]

Being forced to face this oppressive reasoning based on the very fact that British colonial rule had come to India, the people could do nothing other than admit with 'anger and bitterness' the merit (*puṇya*) acquired by the British in their former lives and the supremacy of Christianity. The last resort for them in this situation was to seek the morally degraded habits thought common in the way of life of the British. Nesbit's mention of 'the question of the slaughter of cows' in the passage cited above referred to this point. As the only fault they could discover in the lifestyle of the British was cow slaughtering and beaf eating, they clinged to this subject for refuting the aggressive reasoning of the Christian missionaries. Nesbit wrote down in the same missionary journal his embarrassing experience accrued from this subject as follows:

> Nimbgaum February 3: Owing to the practice of the English of killing and eating cows, the Hindus always regard them as murderers and cannibals. In the afternoon I was attacked on this subject, and was obliged to have recourse to the 'argumentum ad hominem'. 'Why do you daily kill thousands of grains of corn, seeing that, according to your doctrine, all life is one and the same? ... Why do you walk on the ground and kill millions of insects...?'... The practice of sacrifice still subsisting among Brahmans, as well as their practice of eating beaf, mutton and venison in the golden age [*Satya Yuga*], is then referred to; and the question is just whether the practices of the golden age or of the iron age [*Kali Yuga*] are best.... With Hindus this question should never be shirked, as it lies fretting in their mind, although never expressed, and has but to be remembered and referred to in order to nullify a host of arguments and still a conscience that would otherwise be ill at ease. 'The gentleman's reasoning is very powerful; and his exposure of sin carries with it the best painful conviction; but ... he kills cows and eats their flesh.'

To sidestep the charge of cow slaughtering and beaf eating against the British, Robert Nesbit thus had recourse, first, to the Upanishadic tenet of the oneness of *brahman* and *ātman* by which all beings, living creatures as well as vegetation, are deemed to be of one and the same element and, second, to the practice of cow sacrifice mentioned in the *Ṛg Veda*.[12] People, however, were never persuaded by this reasoning since cow slaughtering and beaf eating were the only vulnerable points of the British on which they could concentrate attacks. Thus, they repeated this charge against the British saying: 'The gentleman's reasoning is very powerful, and his exposure of sin carries with it the best painful conviction; but... he kills cows and eats their flesh.'[13]

People would readily bring up cow slaughtering by the British when something unusual occurred. In one case, there was a cholera epidemic in Ahmadnagar in 1844. As a consequence, people thought that as the British came to India and slaughtered cows to eat beaf, the gods had gotten angry and inflicted a cholera epidemic (*Dñanodaya* August 1844. 124). In another case, it was observed that a cow was bowing to the Sun in a confluence (*saṃgam*) of the Krishna River in 1852. The Brahmans gave the interpretation to this occurrence that as such a grave sin as cow slaughtering (*gohatyā*) had been committed under British colonial rule, the cow was praying to the god Narayana to bring British colonial rule to an end (*Dñanodaya* 15 May 1852. 159).

Thus, the unexperienced 'otherness' of Christianity or the British in general that outreached the pre-existing framework of the 'ourselves-others' consciousness of the people was counterbalanced by assigning the attribute of the cow slaughterer and beaf eater to the British in opposition to their self-identification as the cow protector (*go rakṣak*). These dichotomous identities of the cow protector-cow slaughterer thus became prominent only under British colonial rule. Accordingly the framework of people's self-identity was also extended to contain this emerging new self-identity of the cow protector as opposed to the cow slaughterer.

Concluding Remarks

The transformation of people's self-identity for incorporating the newly emerged self-identity of the cow protector as opposed to the cow slaughterer took another turn in the last few decades of the nineteenth century in a direction that would change Hindu-Muslim relations for the worse.[14] In the 1880s, the so-called cow protection movement began to gather momentum in western India concurrently with the cow protection movement promoted by the Arya Samaj in north India. In Bombay the Go Rakshak Mandali (Cow Protection Society) and Go Palan Upadeshak Mandali (Cow Breeding Instruction Society) were established in 1887 and 1893 respectively. In Pune the Go Rakshak Mandali was established by the Nathu brothers, the well-known orthodox militants, in 1888. These societies might have initially aimed at protecting cows from the British. Their main target, however, seems to have changed gradually from the British to the Muslim who sacrificed cows on the occasion of *'Īd al-aḍḥā* (sacrificial festival of Islam performed on 10-13 *Dhu al-Hijja*), commonly known as *Baqr Īd* (festival of cattle) in India. This was attested to by the communal riot which occurred for the first time in Bombay. On 11 August 1893 Hindus and Muslims of Bombay clashed against each other and in all 80 persons were killed and 530 injured. Some one month before this incident a similar clash occurred in Patan (Somnath) in Gujarat in which the Hindu temple there was damaged by Muslims. This incident may have sparked off the communal riot in Bombay. Thus, the communal conflict between the Hindu and the

Muslim began to loom large in the last few decades of the nineteenth century, due at least partly to the cow protection movement, the basic ideology of which was the polarizing identity of the cow protector as opposed to the cow slaughterer, by then mainly implying Muslims instead of the British.[15]

This rising of communal tension stimulated the formation of a new type of Hindu ideology. As mentioned ealier in relation to the conversion of Narayan Sheshadri, the Hindu community was divided into two parties, that is to say, the *sanātana dharma* (orthodox) party and the 'reformists' (*sudhārṇāvādī*), in the middle of the nineteenth century. The contestation between these two parties culminated in the controversy over the problem of widow remarriage. In 1865, the Punarvivah Uttejak Mandali (Remarriage Encouragement Society) was established by the 'reformists' in Bombay. The *sanātana dharma* party which had already founded the Hindu Dharma Sabha (Hindu Dharma Society) naturally harboured a violent ill will against this move by the 'reformists'. Moroba Kanhoba, the vice-president of the Punarvivah Uttejak Mandali and a Prabhu by caste, remarried a widow in 1870. His remarriage caused a violent tumult in Bombay in the aftermath of which he and his wife were found dead in a well in 1871. They might have been killed by the *sanātanas*, most probably those of the Prabhu caste who were more orthodox than the Brahmans.

Thus the *sanātana dharma* party had always been dominant over the 'reformists' during at least the nineteenth century. The ideology of the *sanātana dharma*, however, was too narrow to unite all people other than Muslims and Christians as Hindu in the sense that it always functioned to exclude some sections of Hindus who held different views from the *sanātana dharma* as well as believers of other religions of the same root such as the Jain, Sikh and Lingayat. Thus, the ideology of *sanātana dharma* was to be replaced by one that was inclusive enough to unite all these people under the banner of Hindu. The Hindutva ideology advocated by V.D. Savarkar in the 1920s was meant to meet this requirement of the age of communal tension. According to his concept of Hindutva, specifically, 'a common nation (Rashtra), a common race (Jati) and a common civilization (Sanskriti)', all Indians other than Christians and Muslims were Hindu (Savarkar 1989: 116). Thus, in the 1920s, people of divergent religions originated on Indian soil began to be lumped together as Hindu in opposition to Christian and Muslim by the Hindutva ideology.

Notes

1 These ideas of *Mahārāṣṭrarājya*, *Mahārāṣṭraloka* and *Mahārāṣṭradharma* must have been shared at least by the ruling class of the Marathas. In the statement (*karinā*) of the Jedhe Deshmukh family, this was professed as follows:

> The Muslim [*musalmān*] are faithless. They will cause us to perish on a false plea once their purpose be attained. This is *Mahārāṣṭrarājya*. All of us should command the armed forces courageously and in close attendance singleheartedly serve the king (*Śivacaritra Pradīp*, p. 43).

See S.C.S. V 767 for another mention of *Mahārāṣṭrarājya*. The term *Mahārāṣṭradharma* is found in *Śivadigvijaya* quoted in M.I.S. IV 113, S.S.R.P.D. I 379 (1734-35) and S.S.R.P.D. III 5 (1741-42) as well.

A. Wink commented on *Mahārāṣṭradharma* as follows: 'Still, this *mahārāṣṭradharma* never became anything else than a paroachial blend of elements of Hindu dharma that prevailed everywhere in India' (Wink 1986: 48). It is very questionable, however, whether such a term as 'Hindu dharma' can be used with regard to medieval India since this term seems to be a translation of the English term 'Hinduism' in the nineteenth century. As to the colonial construction of 'Hinduism', see Chapter 11 of this volume as well as Frykenberg 1997: 82-88, Thapar 1997: 54-56 and King 1999: 98-108.

2 In another document this was stated as follows: 'This kingdom is that of the Marathas and gods-Brahmans.' (*He rājya Marāṭhe, devabrāhmaṇaṃce*. S.G.R.A.O. Sanads and Letters V 26). Though the term Maratha is often deemed to indicate the caste of Maratha that had been separated from the Kunbi caste of ordinary peasants, the term Maratha in medieval Marathi documents seems to denote the people of Maharashtra in general.

3 See further M.I.S. XV 285, 288 and 356 in which the Mughals were designated as *tāmbra* or *tāmra*. The term *tāmbra* is referred to in such later documents as follows: S.S.R.P.D. I 39 (*Sāmprat tāmbraṇeṃ bahut balbal ārambhilī*. Now the *tāmbra* began to cause a lot of problems. 1727-28) and S.S.R.P.D. I 77 (*Rājśrī pantpradhān yāsi sāmīl houn tāmbrācā parābhav karṇeṃ mhaṇun ādñāpatra*. This is the king's order that you should join the Pantpradhan and defeat the *tāmbra*. 1750-51).

4 In another case, a Brahman, Narhari Ranalekar by name, was taken prisoner by the Afghans after the complete defeat of the Marathas in the battle of Panipat in 1761. They converted him to Islam (*bhraṣṭa kele*). After some 12 years' detention in Afghanistan, he was released. On his return home, however, a prolonged dispute as to whether or not he could

be purified (*śuddha*) by a purification ritual arose (S.P.D. XXXXIII 25. 1772).

5 Another Marathi term applied in common to the northern Mughal invaders in the medieval period as well as the British in the nineteenth century was '*yavana*', a term assumed to be derived from the term Ionian (Greek) comparable to Persian '*yauna*' ('*yūn*') or '*yūnān*' (Trautmann 1997: 44). See, as examples of the former application of the term, S.S.R.P.D. VIII 1129 (*Devadarśanās mātbar yetāt tyānjbarobar yavana yetāt.* When dignitaries visit [Pandharpur] for worshipping the god [Vithoba], *yavana* accompany them. 1783-84) and S.P.D. XXXXIII 25 (*Narhari Ranalekar yājla yavananīṃ Pānipathāntūn dharun neun bhraṣṭa kele. Yavana* captured and took away Narhari Ranalekar from Panipat to pollute [convert] him to Islam. 1772).

As an example of application of the term *yavana* to the British, the Brahman *paṇḍits* of Pune wrote as follows in a *śāstrārtha* with regard to the well-known *śuddhi* case of Shripat Sheshadri, the younger brother of Narayan Sheshadri (see below):

> The boy [Shripat] ate flesh of various kinds and lived together with *yavana* [missionaries] and drank liquor like wine and others (Jambhekar 1950: III 546).

The term *yavana*, however, was a generic term indicating the foreigners, especially those from countries west of the Indian subcontinent, so that the term *yavana* did not have such particular implication as that implied by the terms *tāmra mukhī* and *bāṭgā*/*bāṭgī* or *bāṭyā*.

6 Robert Nesbit, a Scottish missionary who will be referred to below, wrote in his missionary journal his experience while on a missionary tour in southern Konkan in 1840-41:

> Rutnagherry: There was a good deal of noise and confusion, while I proceeded with the instruction; the spirit of tumult at the close of them prevented the distribution of books; and when I rose to depart, the younger part of my audience raised a universal shout of mingled mirth and scorn. They followed me along the street hooting like monkeys, perhaps to indicate their belief that the English are only monkeys in disguise (quoted in Mitchell 1858: 388).

Thus, the 'belief that the English are only monkeys [*tāmra mukhī*] in disguise' seems to have been prevalent among the people.

7 The term *bāṭlelā* (*bāṭlele*) was applied not only to the Christian converts but also to those who held social association (*saṃsarga*) with the British

or Christians in general. With regard to Shripat Sheshadri's *śuddhi* case, the *Prabhakar*, a Marathi periodical, wrote:

> There existed at present two parties [*phaḷī*] in Bombay. One party claims that Shripat be readmitted to his caste in accordance with the provisions of Shastra. People of the opposite party refute that he should not be readmitted to his caste since there are no customs to this day to readmit the polluted [*bāṭlele*] (quoted in Jambhekar 1950: III 549).

Thus, Shripat was commonly deemed to be polluted (*bāṭlelā*) by living together with his Christianized brother and Christian missionaries, though he was not actually baptized. Likewise in the decision of *paṇḍits* of Pune regarding Shripat's *śuddhi* case, it was stated as follows:

> In Goa, some Brahmans were polluted [*bāṭlele*] through holding commensal relationship [*annodakavyavahāra, annodaka* literally meaning 'food and water'] with Christians [*Kiristaṃ*]. They were eventually not purified by undergoing the ceremony of *śuddhi*. Accordingly a boy who was polluted [*bāṭlelā*] through holding commensal relationship with *yavana* should not be purified. Thus, those who request to make him undergo *prāyaścitta* [purification ceremony] are sinful [*doṣī*] (Jambhekar 1950: III 560).

8 As to the actual procedure of initiation of the Paramhamsa Mandali, Baba Padmanji wrote:

> They read the rule of the Mandali to the candidate. If he gives assent to this they pour water down from the hollowed palms. After this being done they bring a glass [*pyālā*] filled with milk. The president and some members of the Mandali touch the glass with lip and then they made him drink milk from the glass. Thereafter they give him a piece of bread [*roṭī*] (or *pāv*) to eat (Padmanji 1879: 96).

9 Padmanji 1879: 96. In another passage of the *Aruṇodaya*, Baba Padmanji likewise wrote:

> When I was in the [primary] school [in Belgaum], Professor Bal Gangadhar Jambhekar twice visited our school for the inspection. The people respected him much. It was rumoured, however, by

> reason of his 'reformed' (*sudhārlelā*) thinking that he was inclined to Christianity, and that he ate bread and biscuits (*pāvbiskuteṃ*) and drank water from a glass (Padmanji 1879: 12).

Bal Gangadhar Jambhekar (1812-46) was the well-known social reformer of the Bombay Presidency who started the first Marathi periodical, the *Bombay Durpun*, in 1832. Cf. Jambhekar 1950.

10 As to the actual process of lifting the ban on missionary activity in India, see Neill 1985: 151-55.

11 He employed everywhere this same reasoning as exemplified by the following:

> Lasurna January 31 and February 1 morning:... In the morning, I spoke to a large assembly of the villagers, of the sins for which they were suffering so much distress now and for which, unless they repented, they would suffer still more in another state of being. When some of them pleaded for their idols, I told them that the English had once idols like the Hindus, but that they had destroyed them and now trusted only in that God who sent his son into the world to save sinners. I then asked them whether the English had been blessed or cursed for throwing away their idols; to which they most readily replied that they had been blessed abundantly.

See further Nesbit's missionary journal printed in Mitchell 1858: 351-94 for this same reasoning.

12 Robert Nesbit had resort to the same argument in a discussion with a Brahman while on a missionary tour in the Deccan in 1838-39:

> Apparently with the view of balancing my objections to Hinduism the Brahman referred to drew my attention to the slaughter of cows perpetrated among the English, and asked me what I made of that. I quoted a Sanskrit verse in which it is said that the slaughter of cows is forbidden in the iron age [*Kali Yuga*]. He at once admitted the soundness of the inference, that it had been practised in the ages preceeding [*Satya Yuga* and another two *Yugas*]. I then told him that the English followed, in the particular to which he referred, the practise of the golden age [*Satya Yuga*] and the manners of his ancestors (quoted in Mitchell 1858: 371-72).

13 Robert Nesbit attempted to justify himself, in the last resort, by refuting the charge of cow slaughter or animal killing in general as follows in a

discussion with a Brahman (Priest) who blamed him on that account:

> M[issionary]—You know that the destruction [of life] will take place; and, if it be a sin, you ought never to walk. Nay, you ought never to sit; for, even in sitting, you occasion it.... Your only plan is to surrender your lives: for life cannot be supported without destruction of life, and, if that destruction be in every case sinful, it is better to die than live. P[riest]—It well becomes you to speak in that way, who kill animals with shot! M—If they are killed for food, it is not wrong; for God has made and given them for that purpose. All life is not the same as you say it is. We act in consistency with our belief; you act contrary to yours (quoted in Mitchell 1858: 381).

John Wilson, the most well-known Scottish missionary in nineteenth-century western India, commonly known as Dr. Wilson, also refuted the charge of animal killing exactly as Nesbit did:

> Christians condemn the giving of unnecessary pain to animals. They perceive, however, that the souls of men and of animals are entirely different in their nature and destinies. Those of the former they consider intelligent, and morally responsible. Those of the latter they consider as non-intelligent, and not morally responsible. They find in some countries a deficiency of vegetable food for the sustenance of man. They find a permission in the Bible of the use of flesh [cf. Genesis IX-3]; and many of them receive with gratitude what God has given to them (Wilson 1832: 108-109).

The first debate between Brahman *paṇḍits* and Christian missionaries in Bombay was held from 21 to 24 May 1830 between Wilson and Mor Bhat Dandekar. Wilson published later his points of discussion in a book titled *An Exposure of Hindu Religion in Reply to Mora Bhatta Dandekara* (Bombay 1832) to which was prefixed a translation of Dandekar's tract, *Hindū Dharma Sthāpana* (Verification of the Hindu Religion). As to the life history of John Wilson, see Smith 1878. The missionary journal of Wilson was printed in *Oriental Christian Spectator* V-4, 5, 1834. Wilson's works on missionary activities in India include *Evangelisation of India*, Edinburgh, 1849 and *The Darkness and the Dawn in India* (with Narayan Sheshadri), Edinburgh, 1853.

14 Until the middle of the nineteenth century, at least, the relationship between the so-called Hindu and the Indian Muslim had never been so tense as it became in the last decades of the nineteenth century. It is

exemplified by the fact that many Hindus took part in the Islamic festival of Muharram. As one such example in western India, Baba Padmanji wrote as follows in his autobiography:

> During the festival of Muharram I used to wander about in the town [of Belgaum]. I spent much time in seeing men in the disguise of tiger dancing and jumping. I also watched *kustī* [Indian wrestling]. At night, I walked out to look at *tābūts* [model coffin meant for Husain, a grandson of Muhammad, who was killed at Karbala in 680]. On the occasion of the Muharram every year, my mother used to fulfil the vow made to one *pīr* [Islamic saint] or another. For this purpose, she disguised me and other children as *fakīr* [Muslim mendicant]. We accordingly dressed ourselves in *fakīr*'s clothes with *nāḍā* [coloured cord] around the neck and *jhoḷī* [beggar's bag] and *tabak* [beggar's plate] in hand to visit some homes for alms.... Brahmans of Belgaum did not disguise their children as *fakīr*. In Ahmadnagar, however, some Brahmans disguised themselves as *fakīr* in the Muharram for fulfilling the vow. People of Shudra castes everywhere disguised themselves as *fakīr*. Some of them even prepared *tābūts* (Padmanji 1879: 44).

In the *Mumbaīceṃ Varṇan*, as another example, G.N. Madganvkar wrote as follows on the Muharram celebrated in Bombay in the middle of the nineteenth century:

> It is true that the Muharram is an Islamic festival. One-third of the Hindu population in this city [Bombay], however, are a party to this festival.... Kamathi [Telugus] and even Hindus prepared here and there *tābūts*.... Our people give a [Hindu-like] name of Imamjayanti to this festival [after the name of Imam Husain].... Some Hindu people disguised their children as *fakīr* with *jhoḷī* [beggar's bag] at their armpits and made them beg alms [*fakīrī*] and offerings [*cirākhī*] at the doors crying 'Imam Husain!'(Madganvkar 1961: 335-36).

As to the Muharram in nineteenth-century Bombay, see further Masselos 1982.

15 In 1924 when Hindu-Muslim relations were ever more tense and strained in the aftermath of sudden suspension of the Civil Disobedience Movement, M.K. Gandhi wrote as follows in his review titled 'Hindu-Muslim Tension: Its Cause and Cure' (*Young India* VI-22. 29 May 1924):

> The first is cow slaughter. Though I regard cow protection as the central fact of Hinduism, central because it is common to classes as well as masses, I have never been able to understand the antipathy towards the Musalmans on that score. We say nothing about the slaughter that daily takes place on behalf of Englishmen. Our anger becomes red-hot when a Musalman slaughters a cow. All the riots that have taken place in the name of the cow have been an insane waste of effort. They have not saved a single cow, but they have on the contrary stiffened the backs of the Musalmans and resulted in more slaughter.

Gandhi was thus well aware that the main target of the cow protection movement had been by then completely changed from the British to the Indian Muslim. As to the actual process of the cow protection movement and its political implication, see Yang 1980; Pandey 1983; Robb 1986.

Appendix

Introduction to H. Fukazawa, *The Medieval Deccan: Peasants, Social Systems and States, Sixteenth to Eighteenth Centuries*

Hiroshi Fukazawa (1932-86) completed his Ph.D. in Economics at Lucknow University in 1960 under the guidance of the late Dr. V.B. Singh. The theme of his Ph.D. dissertation was the historical development of the cotton industry in India, a section of which, entitled 'The Cotton Mill Industry', was published in V.B. Singh, ed., *Economic History of India, 1857-1956*, Bombay, 1965.

While in Lucknow, Fukazawa became aware that a large number of documents pertaining to the pre-British Deccan were available in print in Marathi and Persian. He also observed that many more documents existed, in manuscript form, which were yet to be researched. These documents, especially those in Marathi, are of great value because, in other regions of India, historical records of medieval periods are rarely available in indigenous languages. For example, there are few documents in Hindi which deal with the medieval history of north India. Thus, one has to depend mostly on documents in Persian to attempt a reconstruction of medieval Indian society. However, since Persian was the language of the ruling class and not of the common people, these documents do not allow a full understanding of the social and cultural life of the people. In this regard, the documents in Marathi assume an added importance in that Marathi is the language of the people. It is to be expected, therefore, that these documents will give a more complete picture of the social and cultural life of the medieval Deccan.

Fukazawa subsequently decided to extend his research into Maratha history. After having completed his Ph.D. in 1960 he went to Pune, where he studied medieval Marathi and Persian at the Bhārat Itihās Saṃśodak Maṇḍal under the guidance of the late Dr. G.H. Khare. When I met Dr. Khare in Pune, he related to me precisely how hard a worker

Fukazawa had been and how he would save money to buy as many books as possible. Once he had become proficient in reading and understanding medieval Marathi and Persian and had collected numerous source books in these two languages, Fukazawa returned to Japan where he was appointed professor at Hitotsubashi University, Tokyo, the university from which he had graduated.

As a teacher of Indian economy and history, Fukazawa wrote many articles on the history of the medieval Deccan. These ranged from essays on the Adil Shahi dynasty to those on the last phase of the Peshva's rule. In 1972, he compiled several of his articles into a book entitled *Studies in the Social and Economic History of India.* These articles were written in Japanese. Some of them were translated into English and appeared in journals like the *Hitotsubashi Journal of Economics.* These articles drew the attention of Indian historians because of their unique approach and thorough documentation, and Fukazawa was invited to contribute articles to the *Cambridge Economic History of India* (1982-83).

The present anthology contains articles on various aspects of the medieval Deccan taken from Fukazawa's book *Studies in the Social and Economic History of India.* Six of these (articles 1 and 4-8) were translated by Fukazawa himself, and two others (articles 2 and 3) by Dr. S. Taniguchi, a former student of Fukazawa and now a professor at Hitotsubashi University.

Characteristics of Fukazawa's Approach

Fukazawa himself defined his approach as 'socio-economic rather than purely economic'. This socio-economic approach attaches greater importance to 'movements of men and formation of communities in relation to movements of goods and money, than to movements of goods and money themselves' (Fukazawa 1976).

The socio-economic approach has been one of the main trends of historical studies in post-war Japan. The economy is, no doubt, the base of every social structure. All human activities, cultural, social and political, have their basis in the economy, but, at the same time, the economy itself is a result of human activity in all fields. Mentality, or the mental activity of human beings, is closely related to the economy. In other words, the economy of a particular stage of development of society is the basis of the prevailing mentality. In turn, the mentality of a society is a reflection of the relationships between man and that society. Thus, the economy is in close correlation with the characteristics of social relationships in a given society. The socio-economic approach pays due regard to this aspect. This approach may thus be called a synthesis of the historical materialism of Karl Marx and the sociology of Max Weber.

Fukazawa was very cautious about relying completely on any particular theory, whether Marx's or Weber's. He did accept many of Weber's concepts though and was especially influenced by Weber's religious sociology; in fact, in 1983 he translated into Japanese 'Hinduismus und Buddhismus' from Weber's *Die Wirtschaftsethik der Weltreligionen.* Yet he did not completely adopt Weber's theory nor did he approach his work with any ready-made theories or models in mind. Fundamentally, his approach was marked by its empiricism. He collected as much material as he could, using this material to reconstruct the social and cultural life of the medieval Deccan.

Deshmukh and Local Society

In various parts of this anthology, especially in the first article, Fukazawa discusses the functions and rights of local hereditary officers, the most eminent among whom was the Deshmukh (or the Desai). He makes four specific points. First, the prototype of the Deshmukh existed even before the commencement of Muslim rule in the Deccan and can be traced back to the Rashtrakuta period. Second, the local administrative divisions, such as *pargaṇā*, *samt* or *ṭappā*, were originally local units over which the Deshmukh had control. Third, the Deshmukh's office and rights were considered as *vatan* or *mirās*, which meant hereditary property or patrimony. Fourth, the Deshmukh tended to become the feudal lord when the central power declined and state control over him slackened.

These points are vital for an understanding of the historical process, that is, the various stages of societal development in the medieval Deccan. Whether or not the concept of feudalism is applicable to Indian history is a question which has been much discussed recently. Fukazawa recognized a tendency towards feudalization in the development of the Deshmukh. It may be called 'feudalization from below' in contrast to the tendency of fief-holders (*mokāsāī* or *mokāsādār*) to become feudal lords, which may be called 'feudalization from above'. Fukazawa stressed the importance of 'feudalization from below' for it was this historical process that helped in the formation and development of Maratha power.

As Fukazawa saw it, the process of feudalization which took place in the medieval Deccan can be observed in other regions of India as well. However, it must be born in mind that the feudalization process in the Indian context had certain peculiar features which were not to be found in European medieval history. In this regard, several issues should be considered.

The Deshmukh was the head of the local society, corresponding in extent to the *pargaṇā*. He was also the local hereditary officer of the state. Both these functions of the Deshmukh, however, were so closely interwoven that it is difficult to separate one from the other. Within the local society, many disputes arose concerning various issues such as hereditary rights, known as *vatan* or *mirās* (for example, the *Deśmukhī vatan*, and the *Pāṭīlkī vatan* which was the hereditary rights of the village headman), or on the question of boundaries between villages, or relationships between various caste communities. In such cases, the Deshmukh, as the head of the local society, would summon and preside over a meeting of the local society. But it often happened that the complainant in a particular dispute would not bring his case to the Deshmukh straightaway. He would first go to the goverment (Hozur) or the district office (such as the *ṭhāṇa*). The government or district officer would then refer the case to the Deshmukh of the *pargaṇā* where the dispute originated, to be settled by the meeting of the local society. In this way, the Deshmukh functioned both as the head of the local society and as the hereditary district officer.

The Deshmukh's position as an intermediary between the state and the local society was very clearly seen at the time of tax settlement. He helped the village headman (Patil) to negotiate and settle with the government officer the amount of tax to be paid by the village as a whole. In times of calamity, as for example during a period of drought, blight or war, the Deshmukh, as the representative of the local society, would ask the government to reduce the tax payable by the village for that particular year.

In his capacity as mediator, the Deshmukh received emoluments from both parties. From the government he received *inām* in the form of tax-free land, and from the local society he received certain privileges and perquisites which were originally given in kind but which, later, became money payments. And, over the course of time, as the Deshmukh gradually usurped the rights and powers of the government and of the local society, his role was transformed from that of the representative of the local society to that of the local ruler. Thus a new class relationship emerged between the Deshmukh and the members of the local society. Although the Deshmukh did not cease being the head of the local society, he now acquired the character of a local ruler as well. This new class relationship might be called 'feudal'.

Relation between State and Society

In the three articles which comprise the second part of this anthology, Fukazawa looks at various aspects of the relationship between the state and society. He examines the caste system as well as the system of slavery and forced labour as carried out by the state. He makes a critical analysis of the traditional image of the medieval Indian state in which the relation between ruler and ruled was seen principally in terms of the appropriation of a substantial portion of the products of the ruled as tax payment in kind or in money. Apart from this, both parties (ruler and ruled) lived completely isolated from each other. Fukazawa attempts to show that the role of the state in the Deccan during the seventeenth and eighteenth centuries was to maintain public order by means of state control over the caste system and the system of slavery; but no less important were the financial considerations of the state as was indicated by its system of forced labour (*veṭha, begār*). This is an important point in light of the European-derived theory of the so-called 'Asiatic state' or 'Asiatic despotism', the relevance of which Fukazawa examines.

The state has always been the instrument of the ruling classes for the exploitation of the ruled (the direct producers). At the same time, there has been no state in history that has not performed public functions through which the ruled would have derived some benefits. That the medieval states in India were no exception to this rule was the point Fukazawa sought to make.

In this regard, the caste system as the system for defining status within medieval Indian society is of considerable interest. As Fukazawa demonstrates, the caste system served not only as the non-official, autonomous social order among the people but also as public order controlled and maintained by state power. Herein lies the peculiarity of the caste system as a status system. Status systems in history were generally elaborated and maintained by state power, the state seeking to do this by means of laws, judicial organizations, police and military power. Every society throughout its history has its own system of social ranks and social norms which have been made use of by the state as the basis of the status system. In other words, as the general character of status systems in history, the status system is the state apparatus and is imposed on the ruled by the state. The caste system, however, deviated from this in certain aspects.

Fukazawa shows that the state in the medieval Deccan did not assume sole responsibility, through its judicial organs, for punishing even criminal offenses such as murder. Those accused of such offenses were usually ordered to appear before a meeting of their caste communities (*jāti sabhā*) and, if proven guilty, were excommunicated. This means that the state depended on the caste system (originally an indigenous social order of the society) for the maintenance of public order, and the state itself imposed as punishment caste norms like excommunication on criminals. Further, if any dispute regarding caste ranking arose, the state intervened and regulated such ranking among the disputing caste communities. Since it depended on the caste system for the maintenance of public order, the state could not afford to leave unresolved any dispute on caste ranking, for it would have endangered public order. This reciprocal relationship between the state and society (the caste system) is one of the most important points which Fukazawa discusses in this anthology.

Another interesting question which Fukazawa addresses (in the fourth article) is the phenomenon of 'Sanskritization', although he himself does not use this term. The concept of Sanskritization, put forward by M.N. Srinivas, needs to be more thoroughly researched. Fukazawa shows that the Prabhus continually tried to imitate the social habits of the Brahmans to the extent of performing rituals that only Brahmans were allowed to practise. The state, however, intervened and prohibited the Prabhus from doing this and from adopting the professions of the Brahmans. Fukazawa goes on to suggest that, under colonial rule, the caste system, which was now deprived of state support, underwent certain changes and the Prabhus began to be free to engage in many of the social customs of the Brahmans. This view should encourage further research into the concept of Sanskritization and the change in the caste system under British rule.

Village Community and Peasant Land Right

The Indian village community has been the subject of much discussion. Many British observers viewed this community as a small 'republic', a self-sufficient cooperative body which had little connection with the outside world. Political power changed hands frequently but the village community remained unchanged. This image of the village community in India has been repeated in many books written by European thinkers, including Marx and Weber. Whether or not this is an authentic picture, however, remains to be seen through the study of historical documents left by the people themselves.

Fukazawa sought to examine this question by looking at Marathi documents of the eighteenth century. He presented two principal findings. First, there were two types of cultivators in the village community: the *mirāsdār* (*vatandār* or *thalkarī*, *thalvāika*), who had fairly well-established proprietary rights over the land he cultivated, and the *upārī* (outsider), a tenant who rented land for cultivation either from the state, the *ināmdārs* or the village body, mostly on the basis of *baṭaī* (a fifty-fifty sharing of the produce). Second, in the village there were various types of artisans and servants commonly called *bārā balute* (twelve sorts of *balute* servants). Within these *bārā balute* were included the Sutar (carpenters), Lohar (blacksmiths), Kumbhar (potters), Nhavi (barbers), and the like. They were supported by the village as a whole, either through payment in kind and/or cash or by the village providing tax-free land. Each of these servants had his own *vatan* or *mirās*, as for example, *Sutārkī vatan* in the case of the Sutar. His *vatan* was a well-established hereditary right (patrimony) of which he could not be deprived. Artisans or servants who happened to stay in a village and perform such jobs as carpentry were called *upārī* Sutar. *Upārī* artisans and servants were also supported by the village as a whole but they did not have any *vatan* rights.

From Fukazawa's work we get a fairly clear picture of the village community of the eighteenth-century Deccan. However, as the main aim of his study was to reconstruct the social structure of the village community, his approach was somewhat structuralistic. As a result, it is to be feared that his studies might be used to support the idea of the Indian village community as having a static or stagnant character. Although this question was not sufficiently discussed by Fukazawa, he did mention the term *bārā alute*, which may not be found in eighteenth-century documents but which was assumed to indicate commodity producers or sellers like the Teli (oilmen), Tamboli (*pāna* dealers) and Mali (vegetable and flower-sellers) who settled in the village. If Fukazawa had had more time to study these particular members of the village, he might have been able to give a clearer picture of the dynamics at work within the village community, namely the historical changes taking place as reflected in the development of commodity economy. This development was closely related with the feudalization process mentioned earlier. The relationship between these two processes needs to be examined more thoroughly if one is to arrive at a better understanding of Indian history.

The question of landed property was also a subject of much debate. It was necessary for the British to know who the proprietor of land was since he would be made responsible for paying land tax according to the tax theory of the political economy. Many 'theories', such as state landownership, joint tenure by the village or private ownership of landed property by peasants, were put forward. None of them was sufficiently supported by historical sources. Fukazawa, however, as mentioned earlier, showed that the *mirāsdār* (*vatandār*) Kunbi had a well-established proprietary right over the land he cultivated. This was a very significant finding.

In support of this position, Fukazawa quoted a very important document (*vatan patra*), according to which a plot of land was sold by a *mirāsdār* Kunbi to an *upārī*. This document adequately proves the existence of peasant land-proprietorship in the medieval Deccan. It also reveals some other equally interesting facts. First, the land sold was indicated by two different types of denominations, namely 7 *bighā* land and 3 *rukā* land. A *bighā* is a unit of land area (square measure). What then was a *rukā*? Fukazawa interpreted a *rukā* as being another unit of land area but it cannot be so. In my article 'The Vatan System in the Seventeenth-Eighteenth Century Deccan' (Chapter 1 of this volume), I indicate that a *rukā* means the proportion of village taxes (taxes were levied on the village as a whole) for which each peasant was held responsible. We can thus get a picture of the communal structure of the medieval Deccan village through an analysis of the term *rukā*. Second, this *vatan patra* seems to be the only document in print which shows the sale of land by a peasant (*mirāsdār* Kunbi). There may be other documents (not in print) of the same nature, but it seems that the sale of land by a peasant was not very common in the medieval Deccan though the sale of village land by a village community was not uncommon (see Chapter 2). The peasant had a right to sell his land, as shown by Fukazawa, but actually he seldom did so. This is an important point which should be closely examined for it seems to reflect a peculiar feature of the relationship between man and the land in the medieval Deccan.

(*Oxford University Press*, Delhi, 1991)

Bibliography

Classics and Periodicals (Sanskrit, Marathi, Persian, English)

Manusmṛti: *Manusmṛti with the Manubhāṣya of Medhātithi*, Ganganatha Jha, ed., 2 vols., Delhi, 1992.

Dñanodaya: Christian periodical published from Ahmadnagar and then Bombay since 1842.

Śivacaritra Pradīp: D.V. Apte and S.M. Divekar, eds., Bhārat Itihās Saṃśodhak Maṇḍal, Pune, Śake 1847.

Śivadigvijaya: P.R. Nandurbarkar and L.K. Dandekar, eds., Poona, 1895.

Futūḥāt-i Fīrūz Shāhī: edited with introduction, translation and notes by A. Alavi, Delhi, 1996.

Oriental Christian Spectator: Christian periodical published from Bombay.

Young India: edited by M.K. Gandhi and published from Ahmadabad.

Marathi

Jambhekar, G.G., ed., 1950: *Bāl Gangādhar Śāstrī Jāmbhekar yāṃceṃ Jīvanvṛtt va Lekhsaṃgrah*, Khand I-III, Pune.

Karhadkar, K.S. 1979: *Bābā Padmanjī, Kāl va Kartṛtva*, Mumbai.

Madganvkar, G.N. 1961: *Mumbaīceṃ Varṇan*, 2nd edn., Mumbai (original edn., Mumbai, 1863).

Mate, S.M. 1933: *Aspṛṣṭāṃcā Praśna*, Pune.

Padmanji, Baba 1879: *Aruṇodaya* (The autobiography of Baba Padmanji, 1831-1906), Mumbai.

Priyolkar, A.K. 1966: *Paramhaṃsa Sabhā va tice Adhyakṣa Rāmcandra Bālkṛṣṇa*, Mumbai.

Rajvade, V.K. Śake 1838: 'Hindū śabdācyā itihās', Bhārat Itihās Saṃśodhak Maṇḍal, ed., *Catūrth Sammelan Vṛtt*, Pune.

Valimbe, R.S. 1962: *Ekoṇisāvyā Śatakāntīl Mahārāṣṭrācī Sāmājik Punarghaṭnā*, Pune.

Official Publications in English

Decisions of the Sudder Dewanny Adawlut (of Calcutta), recorded in English, in conformity to Act XII of 1843, Vol. VI, 1850.

Official Correspondence on the System of Revenue Survey and Assessment best adapted and more or less completely carried into effect in the Collectrates of Poona, Sholapoor, Ahmednuggur, Belgaon, and Dharwar, in the Bombay Presidency with an Appendix, Bombay, 1850.

Papers Relating to the Settlement of the Hereditary District Officers' Watans in the Deccan and Gujarat, Selections from Bombay Government Records No. CLXXIV, Bombay, 1865.

The Reports from Committees of the House of Commons 1715-1801, 15 vols., microfilm, Chadwyek Healy Ltd., London, 1973.

English

Aiyar, C.S. Ramakrishna, ed., 1918: *The Hindu Law Journal* 1, Madras, March 1918 to June 1919.

Amin, Shahid 1995: *Event, Metaphor and Memory: Chauri Chaura 1922-1992*, Delhi.

Ballhatchet, K. 1957: *Social Policy and Social Change in Western India 1817-1830*, London.

Bühler, G. 1886: *The Laws of Manu* (English translation of *Manusmṛti*), The Sacred Books of the East XXV, Oxford University Press.

Carman, J.B. and Marglin, F.A., eds., 1985: *Purity and Auspiciousness in Indian Society*, Leiden.

Carroll, Lucy 1975: 'Swami Shivagan Chand, Kayastha Conference Organizer', *The Indian Economic and Social History Review* 17-3.

——— 1978: 'Colonial Perceptions of Indian Society and the Emergence of Caste(s) Association', *Journal of Asian Studies* 32-2.

Clarke, R. 1848: *The Regulations of Fort St. George in Force at the End of 1847 to which are added, the Acts of the Government of India in Force in That Presidency*, London.

——— 1851: *The Regulations of the Government of Bombay in Force at the End of 1850 to which are added, the Acts of the Government of India in Force at That Presidency*, London.

——— 1854: *The Regulations of the Government of Fort Williams in Bengal in Force at the End of 1853 to which are added, the Acts of the Government of India*, 3 vols., London.

Colebrooke, T.E. 1884: *Life of the Honourable Mountstuart Elphinstone*, 2 vols., London.

Commander, Simon 1983: 'The Jajmani System in North India; An Examination of its Logic and Status across Two Centuries', *Modern Asian Studies* 17-2.

Derrett, Duncan M. 1977: *Essays in Classical and Modern Hindu Law*, III, Leiden.

Dirks, N.B. 1987: *The Hollow Crown: Ethnohistory of an Indian Kingdom*, Cambridge University Press.

Divekar, V.D., ed., 1991: *Social Reform Movements in India*, Bombay.

Douglas, Mary 1984: *Purity and Danger: An Analysis of the Concepts of Pollution and Taboo*, ARK edn., London and New York (original edn., 1966).

Dumont, Louis 1980: *Homo Hierarchics: The Caste System and Its Implications*, complete revised English edn., Delhi (original edn., 1966).

Elphinstone, Mountstuart 1872: *Report on the Territories Conquered from the Paishwa*, 2nd edn., Bombay (originally printed in 1819).

Enthoven, R.E. 1990: *The Tribes and Castes of Bombay*, 3 vols., AES reprint, New Delhi and Madras (original edn., Bombay, 1920-21).

Frykenberg, R.E. 1997: 'The Emergence of Modern "Hinduism" as a Concept and as an Institution: A Reappraisal with Special Reference to South India', Sontheimer and Kulke, eds., 1997.

Fukazawa, Hiroshi 1976: 'Debtors and Creditors in the Deccan Riot 1875', *Ajia Keizai* (in Japanese) 17-4, Institute of Developing Economy, Tokyo.

——— 1991: *The Medieval Deccan: Peasants, Social Systems and States, Sixteenth to Eighteenth Centuries*, Delhi.

Galanter, Marc 1989: *Law and Society in Modern India*, Delhi.

Gleig, Rev. G.R. 1841: *Memoirs of the Life of the Rt. Hon. Warren Hastings*, I, London.

Gore, M.S. 1989: *Non-Brahman Movement in Maharashtra*, New Delhi.

Guha, Sumit 1987: 'The Land Market in Upland Maharashtra c. 1820-1960 (I)', *The Indian Economic and Social History Review* 24-2.

Gune, V.T. 1953: *The Judicial System of the Marathas*, Poona.

Habib, Irfan 1963: *Agrarian System of the Mughal India 1556-1707*, Bombay.

Hatekar, Neeraj 1996: 'Information and Incentives: Pringle's Ricardian Experiment in the Nineteenth-century Deccan Countryside', *The Indian Economic and Social History Review* 33- 4.

Hutton, J.H. 1961: *Caste in India*, 3rd edn., Oxford University Press (original edn. 1946).

Inden, R. 1985: 'Kings and Omens', Carman and Marglin, eds., 1985.

Israel, Milton and Wagle, N.K., eds., 1987: *Religion and Society in Maharashtra*, Toronto.

Jha, D.N., ed., 1987: *Feudal Social Formation in Early India*, Delhi.

———ed., 1996: *Society and Ideology in India: Essays in Honour of Professor R.S. Sharma*, Delhi.

———ed., 2000: *The Feudal Order*, Delhi.

Kane, P.V. 1968-77: *History of Dharmaśāstra*, 2nd edn., 5 vols., Bhandarkar Oriental Research Institute, Poona.

Karashima, N., ed., 1999: *Kingship in Indian History*, Delhi.

Kavlekar, Kashinath 1979: *Non-Brahmin Movement in Southern India*, Shivaji University Press.

Khandekar, D.G. 1938: *The Manual of Bombay Acts & Regulations*, 2 vols., Poona.

Kikani, L.T. 1912: *Caste in Courts or Rights and Powers of Castes in Social and Religious Matters as Recognized by Indian Courts*, Rajkot.

King, R. 1999: *Orientalism and Religion: Postcolonial Theory, India and 'Mystic East'*, London and New York.

Kotani, Hiroyuki 1979: *Marx and Asia: A Critical Examination of the Concept of the Asiatic Mode of Production* (in Japanese), Tokyo.

———1985: 'The Vatan-system in the Sixteenth-Eighteenth Century Deccan', *Acta Asiatica* 48, Toho Gakkai, Tokyo. Reproduced in Jha, ed., 1996. Revised in this volume as Chapter 1.

———1991: 'Introduction' to Fukazawa 1991. Reprinted in this volume with slight revision as Appendix.

———ed., 1997a: *Caste System, Untouchability and the Depressed*, Delhi.

———1997b: 'Ati-Śūdra Castes in the Medieval Deccan', Kotani, ed., 1997a. Slightly revised in this volume as Chapter 6.

———1997c: 'Conflict and Controversy over the Mahar Vatan in the Nineteenth-Twentieth Century Bombay Presidency', Kotani, ed., 1997a. Slightly revised in this volume as Chapter 7.

———1999a: 'Kinsgship, State and Local Society in the Seventeenth-to-Nineteenth Century Deccan with Special Reference to Ritual Functions', Karashima, ed., 1999. Reproduced with slight revision in this volume as Chapter 9.

———1999b: 'Land Relations in Pre-British Maharashtra and the

British Concept of Landed Property', Kulkarni and Wagle, eds., 1999. Extensively revised in this volume as Chapter 2.

——— 1999c: '*Doṣa* (sin)-*Prāyaścitta* (penance): The Predominating Ideology in the Medieval Deccan'. Paper read at the International Workshop, '*The State in India: Past and Present*', held at Kyoto University, 1-5 December 1999. Reproduced in this volume as Chapter 10.

——— 1999d: 'The Passage from Hinduism to Christianity: The Case of Baba Padmanji', Wagle, ed., 1999a.

——— 2000a: 'Historical Formation of Hindu Identity in Relation to British Colonial Rule'. Paper read at the International Conference, '*Fussing Modernity: Appropriation of History and Political Mobilization in South Asia*', organized by the Japan Center for Area Studies (JCAS), National Museum of Ethnology, Osaka, Japan, 17-19 January 1999 and printed in *JCAS Symposium Series* 11, 2000. Extensively revised as Chapter 11 of this volume.

——— 2000b: 'Rural and Urban Caste Structure in Eighteenth-Nineteenth Century India: The Deccan and Gujarat', Panikkar, Byres and Patnaik, eds., 2000. Reproduced in this volume with some revision as Chapter 4.

——— 2000c: 'The Transformation of People's Self-Identity under British Colonial Rule with Special Reference to Western India'. Paper read at the XXXVIth International Congress of Asian and North African Studies held in Montreal, Canada from 27 August to 1 September 2000. Reproduced with slight modification as Chapter 12 in this volume.

Kulkarni, A.R. 1969: *Maharashtra in the Age of Shivaji*, Poona.

——— 1996: *Medieval Maharashtra*, Delhi.

Kulkarni, A.R. and Wagle, N.K., eds., 1999: *Region, Nationality and Religion*, Mumbai.

Kulke, Hermann ed., 1995: *The State in India 1000-1700*, Delhi.

Kumar, Rabinder 1968: *Western India in the Nineteenth Century*, University of Toronto Press.

Masselos, J. 1982: 'Change and Custom in the Format of the Bombay Mohurrum during the Nineteenth and Twentieth Centuries', *South Asia* 5-2.

Mayer, Peter 1993: 'Inventing Village Tradition: The late 19th Century Origins of the North Indian "Jajmani System"', *Modern Asian Studies* 27- 2.

Mitchell, J. Murray 1858: *Memoir of the Rev. Robert Nesbit*, London.

Mukhia, Harbans 1979: 'Was there Feudalism in Indian History?', Presidential Address, Medieval Section, Indian History Congress, 40th Session, Waltair. Reprinted in Kulke, ed., 1995.

——— ed., 1999: *The Feudalism Debate*, Delhi.

Mulla, Dinshah Fardunji 1901: *Jurisdiction of Courts in Matters relating to the Rights and Powers of Castes*, Bombay.

Navalkar, G.R. 1893: *The Rev. Narayana Sheshadri*, D.D., Bombay.

Neill, Stephen 1985: *A History of Christianity in India 1707-1858*, Cambridge University Press.

O'Hanlon, Rosalind 1985: *Caste, Conflict and Ideology: Mahatma Jotirao Phule and Low Caste Protest in Nineteenth-century Western India*, Cambridge University Press.

Omvedt, Gail 1976: *Cultural Revolt in a Colonial Society: The Non-Brahman Movement in Western India 1873 to 1930*, Bombay.

Orenstein, Henry 1965: *Gaon: Conflict and Cohesion in an Indian Village*, Princeton University Press.

Pandey, Gyan 1986: 'Rallying round the Cow: Sectarian Strife in the Bhojpur Region, c. 1888-1917', *Subaltern Studies* 2, Delhi.

Panikkar, K.N., Byres, T.J. and Patnaik, Utsa, eds., 2000: *The Making of History: Essays presented to Irfan Habib*, Delhi.

Perlin, Frank 1978: 'Of White Whale and Countrymen in the Eighteenth-century Maratha Deccan: Extended Class Relations, Rights, and the Problem of Rural Autonomy under the Old Regime', *The Journal of Peasant Studies* 5-2.

Phadke, Y.D. 1991: 'The Satyashodhak and the Non-Brahmin Movement', Divekar, ed., 1991.

Phadnis, N.H. 1936: *The Law of Saranjam and Inams*, Dharwar.

Quigley, D. 1993: *The Interpretation of Caste*, Oxford University Press.

Raheja, G.G. 1988a: *The Poison in the Gift: Ritual, Prestation and the Dominant Caste in a North Indian Village*, University of Chicago Press.

——— 1988b: 'India: Caste, Kingship, and Dominance Reconsidered', *Annual Review of Anthropology* 17.

Ranade, M. G. 1961: *Rise of the Maratha Power*, Classics of Indian History and Economics Series, Ministry of Information and Broadcasting, Delhi (original edn., 1900).

Robb, Peter 1986: 'The Challenge of Gau Mata: British Policy and Religious Change in India, 1880-1916', *Modern Asian Studies* 20-2.

Sardesai, G.S. 1946-48: *New History of the Marathas*, 3 vols., Bombay.

Savarkar, V.D. 1989: *Hindutva, Who is a Hindu?*, 6th edn., Bombay (original edn., 1923).

Sharma, R.S. 1983: 'How feudal was Indian Feudalism?', *Social Scientist* 129. Reprinted in Mukhia, ed., 1999.

Smith, G. 1878: *The Life of John Wilson, D.D. F.R.S.*, London.

Sontheimer, G. and Kulke, H., eds., 1997: *Hinduism Reconsidered*, rev. edn., Delhi (original edn., 1989).

Srinivas, M.N. 1962: *Caste in Modern India and Other Essays*, Bombay.

——— 1966: *Social Change in Modern India*, University of California Press.

Steele, A 1827: *Summary of the Law and Custom of Hindoo Castes within the Dekhun Provinces Subject to the Presidency of Bombay, Chiefly Affecting Civil Suits*, Bombay.

Stenzler, A.F. 1970: *Yājñavalkya's Gesetzbuch, Sanskrit und Deutsch*, Neudruck der Aufgabe 1849, Berlin.

Stokes, E.T. 1959: *The English Utilitarians and India*, London.

Tanabe, Akio 1999: 'Kingship, Community and Commerce in Late Precolonial Khurda', Karashima, ed., 1999.

Thapar, Romila 1997: 'Syndicated Hinduism', Sontheimer and Kulke, eds., 1997.

Trautmann, T.R. 1997: *Aryans and British India*, University of California Press.

Verelst, Harry 1772: *A View of the Rise, Progress, and Present State of the English Government in Bengal*, London.

Wagle, N.K., ed., 1980a: *Images of Maharashtra–A Regional Profile of India*, London.

——— 1980b: 'A Dispute between the Pancal Devajna Sonars and the Brahmans of Pune regarding Social Rank and Ritual Privilege', Wagle, ed., 1980a.

——— 1987: 'Ritual and Change in Early Nineteenth Century Society in Maharashtra: *Vedokta* Disputes in Baroda, Pune and Satara, 1824-1838, Israel and Wagle, eds., 1987.

——— ed., 1999a: *Writers, Editors and Reformers: Social and Political Tranformations of Maharashtra 1830-1930*, Delhi.

——— 1999b: 'Readmission of Sripat Sesadri, Dharmasastra vs. Public Consensus, Bombay 1843-45', Kulkarni and Wagle, eds., 1999.

Whitehead, H. 1916: *The Village Gods in South India*, Oxford University Press.

Wilson, John 1832: *An Exposure of the Hindu Religion in Reply to Mora*

Bhatta Dandekara to which is prefixed a Translation of the Bhatta's Tract, Bombay.

——— 1849: *Evangelisation of India*, Edinburgh.

Wilson, John and Narayan Sheshadri 1853: *The Darkness and the Dawn in India*, Edinburgh.

Wink, André 1986: *Land and Sovereignty in India: Agrarian Society and Politics under the Eighteenth-century Maratha Svarajya*, London.

Wiser, W.H. 1988: *The Hindu Jajmani System*, 3rd. edn., Delhi (original edn., Lucknow, 1936).

Yamazaki, G. 1997: 'Social Discrimination in Ancient India and its Transition to the Medieval Period', Kotani, ed., 1997a.

Yang, Anand A. 1980: 'Sacred Symbol and Sacred Space in Rural India: Community Mobilization in the "Anti-Cow Killing" Riot of 1893', *Comparative Studies in Society and History* 22.

Yule, H and Burnell, A.C. 1886: *Hobson-Jobson, A Glossary of Colloquial Anglo-Indian Words and Phrases*, London.

Index

The Index is confined to the text proper (Chapters 1-12)